D0929814

SOMERSET
LIBRARY
CANCELLED

Gracie Fields

Other titles by David Bret and published by Robson Books

The Piaf Legend
The Mistinguett Legend
Maurice Chevalier
Marlene, My Friend
Morrissey: Landscapes of the Mind

Gracie Fields
The Authorized Biography

DAVID BRET

SOMERSET
COUNTY LIBRARY

2333746

J M | 920
FIE

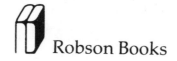

Robson Books

First published in Great Britain in 1995 by Robson Books Ltd, Bolsover House, 5-6 Clipstone Street, London W1P 8LE

Copyright © 1995 David Bret

The right of David Bret to be identified as author of this work has been asserted by him in accordance with the Copyright, Designs and Patents Act 1988

British Library Cataloguing in Publication Data
A catalogue record for this title is available from the British Library

ISBN 0 86051 958 9

All rights reserved. No part of this publication may be reproduced, stored in a retrieval system, or transmitted in any form or by any means, electronic, mechanical, photocopying, recording or otherwise, without the prior permission in writing of the publishers.

Typeset in Sabon by The Harrington Consultancy
Printed and bound in Great Britain by Butler & Tanner Ltd, Frome and London

This book is for
Irene Bevan
John and Anne Taylor and
Les Enfants de Novembre

N'oublie pas…
La vie sans amies c'est comme
un jardin sans fleurs

Contents

Acknowledgements

I would like to express my grateful thanks to Her Majesty Queen Elizabeth the Queen Mother for her personal message of encouragement, and for her warm words of admiration for Gracie Fields.

Writing this book would not have been possible had it not been for the inspiration, criticisms and love of that select group of individuals whom I still regard as my true family and *autre coeur*: Barbara, René and Lucette Chevalier, Jacqueline Danno, Hélène Delavault, Marlene Dietrich, Roger Normand, Annick Roux, Monica Solash, Terry Sanderson, François and Madeleine Vals. God bless you all!

To Irene Bevan, John and Anne Taylor, Giorgio and Jenny Iacono, my heartfelt gratitude for making Gracie's life that much more meaningful and special, and for sticking to her through thick and thin. What would she – or I – have done without you? Thanks too to Mary Whipp and Debbie Walker of Rochdale and to Rochdale Museum Service for promoting the name Gracie Fields so inordinately well, and to Morris Aza for graciously allowing me to quote from his aunt's correspondence.

Very special thanks to my agent, David Bolt. Thanks too to Gracie's fans, friends and acquaintances for sharing some of their most precious memories with me – particularly Rochdalians Ken Hill for the beautiful poem which Gracie treasured, Norman Taylor, Robert, Alison, and the late Mildred Ashworth – also the late Kevin Daly, the late Sylvie Galthier, Ivor Newton, Tommy Keen, Beryl Down and Martin Green.

For their help and contribution to this book, I thank the following journalists/columnists, living and deceased: Kenneth Allsop, Nancy Banks-Smith, Denis Barker, George Black, Thelma Craig, Charlie Dawn, Scarth Flett, Stephen Fay, James Green, Marcel Idzkowski, Stanley Jackson, D A N Jones, John Lambert, Rita Marshall, Maud M Miller, Alan Moorehead, Ann Morrow, Rex North, Denis Pitts, Arthur Pollock, J B Priestley, Edwin Schallert, Ann Sharpeley, Gordon Sinclair, Hannen Swaffer, David Taylor, Henry Thody, Bob Thomas, Dan Whitehead, Elizabeth Wilson.

For allowing me access to invaluable interviews, features and rare archive material, I thank the following publications past and present:

GREAT BRITAIN: *Rochdale Observer, The Play Pictorial, Daily Express, Sunday Chronicle, Sunday People, Sunday Pictorial, Daily Mail, Daily Telegraph, Yorkshire Evening News, Sheffield Telegraph, Sunday Express, Daily Mirror, Picture Post, Illustrated, Lancashire Life, The Times, Radio Times,* the *Guardian, Punch, Birmingham Post.*

USA: *Liberty, Today's Cinema, Jamestown Post, Columbus Dispatch, Hollywood Reporter, Variety, Denver Rock, Box-Office Digest, Motion Picture Review, Modern Screen, Los Angeles Times, Daily Film Reporter, Kalamazoo Gazette.*

CANADA: *Montreal Daily Star, Montreal Gazette, The Albertan, The Ottawa Journal, Toronto Star, Toronto Globe, Quebec Soleil.*

NORTH AFRICA: *Crusader, World Press News.*

SOUTH AFRICA: *Kinematograph.*

FRANCE: *France Soir.*

AUSTRALASIA: *Evening News Chronicle, Hobart Mercury.*

Most important of all, I would like to express my undying love to you, Gracie, and to my wife Jeanne, still the keeper of my soul.

David Bret

Introduction

'Who *is* this Gracie Fields? Who is this Great Lady of Song who entertains Kings and Queens and Presidents ... who has been honoured with a Commander of the Order of the British Empire, who has received an honorary Master of Arts Degree, who is a Member of the Order of St John of Jerusalem, who has even had a ship named after her – a gallant vessel lost at Dunkirk?'

It is hoped that this biography will go a step further in providing the answer to the question posed by Gracie's manager and close friend, Bert Aza, in the introduction to his brief biography of the star, published almost half a century ago.

Bernard Delfont hailed her as 'The greatest British entertainer that ever lived.' The Queen herself kept her public waiting once when, newly returned from a tour of the Commonwealth, she refused to appear on the Buckingham Palace balcony until she had finished watching Gracie's show on the then live-only television.

Professionally, Gracie was unmatched. One of the highest-paid stars in the world, she cut hundreds of superb recordings, and appeared in a series of optimistically titled films reflecting the spirit of a troubled decade. Yet although she opted to enjoy the lotus-eating opulence of Capri for forty-six years, Gracie always clung steadfastly to her Rochdale roots and what she called her 'common touch'.

Sadly, Gracie's personal life was plagued by tragedy, controversy, media prejudice, and by unavoidable mistakes brought about by her extreme naivety. Each of her three marriages became more troubled than its predecessor: Archie Pitt, the impresario who launched her and nurtured her talent, only to be abandoned by her; Monty Banks, the chirpy little Italian film director who made her a star in

1

Hollywood and then died tragically as she was reaching her peak; Boris Alperovici, the 'stateless' mid-European with alleged dubious connections. Then there were the lovers – Gracie's handsome adagio dancers and painters, most notably John Flanagan, the Irishman who remained the great love of her life, a love which she killed with kindness.

Gracie's stepdaughter, Irene Bevan, says, 'There have been so many books where Gracie has been given wings, and now is the time to set the record straight. She was no angel. She was a difficult, complex woman and a very strong personality who overran everybody. If you were not prepared to be submerged by her, you didn't stay her friend. But in the end everybody, didn't matter who it was, did something or other that displeased her. Even so, you couldn't *help* loving and respecting her – and I absolutely *adored* her!'

What Bert Aza wrote about her, all those years ago, holds fast today: 'Each generation seems to produce one outstanding figure in the world of entertainment who, by a combination of talent and circumstance rises clear above his or her contemporaries. The twentieth century has given us Gracie Fields, whose voice and artistry are unrivalled in their field.'

This then is a reaching out for the truth about the woman who sang, shortly before her death in 1979, her own epitaph:

> In the evening of my life
> I shall look to the sunset ...
> And the questions that I ask:
> 'Was I brave and strong and true?
> Did I fill the world with love?'

1

The Clatter of the Clogs

Arguably the greatest British entertainer of this century was born on 9 January 1898, above a humble fish-and-chip shop set into a tawdry terraced block in Molesworth Street, Rochdale, and baptized Grace Stansfield three weeks later at St Chad's Church. The property, formerly a barber's salon, had been purchased for £15 some years before by her paternal grandmother, Sarah Leighton, known locally as Chip Sarah. This rough-and-ready individual had begun working life by going down the pit at the age of six – opening and closing the iron doors which had separated the coal-faces not just to let the pony-drawn trucks in and out, but to prevent the lethal patches of firedamp from spreading. Many years later Gracie said of her illegitimate father, 'He never knew his real father, nor needed to. Chip Sarah would have made a man out of anybody.'

Gracie's mother, Jenny (Sarah Jane Bamford) was just nineteen at the time of her first confinement, and the future Gracie Fields was the first of her four children – over the next few years there would be Betty, Edith and Tommy, in that order. Their father, Fred, was a qualified engineer at Robinsons factory, though just before meeting and marrying Jenny he had worked on a cargo ship which had sailed to California. During this trip he had bought a ten-gallon hat and a pair of pointed shoes which, mindless of the stares and comments from passersby, he had worn each day to and from work and when taking Jenny out to the local pub. He was, in effect, the original Rochdale Cowboy.

The Stansfields had never known anything but sheer hard work. Jenny, orphaned at the age of ten and sent to live with her aunt on the outskirts of Rochdale, had gone straight into the mill. In those days it was not uncommon for youngsters to be enrolled as 'half-timers' spending the mornings at the mill and the afternoons in class and vice-versa on alternating weeks – and there were few complaints: for most families it was either this arrangement or starvation. Jenny appears to have loved the noisy, dusty atmosphere of the mill, while the only education that appealed to her was that afforded by the music-hall. She often played truant in order to catch up on the latest productions at the Empire, the Prince of Wales and the Old Circus (later the Hippodrome), and she is said to have possessed a good singing voice. When at the age of fourteen she left school, she always said to get away from her over-religious aunt's strictness and nagging, she moved in with two workmates and continued dreaming of a career on the stage. By the time she married Fred, however, and began having a family, she found she had to focus her attentions on her children, swearing to herself that one if not all of them would some day make it on to the boards. There was no pressure, just gentle, loving persuasion.

Even so, the lure of the theatre was too strong to keep Jenny away and though working full-time at the mill, and spending two hours each evening cleaning the kitchens at some of the 'posh houses' of Rochdale, she visited the Hippodrome every Sunday afternoon to sweep and scrub the stage, always taking Gracie with her. The manager, Mr Grindrod, became a friend of the family. Jenny also took in the theatre's washing, a practice very much frowned upon by the proud working classes of Northern England, for it meant that one had sunk below the poverty respectability line. Jenny used to collect the dirty laundry late at night, washing it and hanging it to dry when there was no danger of one of the neighbours dropping in for a gossip, and always returning with the utmost discretion a bit at a time, wrapped in newspaper. And if the pay was poor, she and Gracie always managed to see the show at least twice a week from the wings, where they were permitted to mingle freely with the stagehands.

By this time the Stansfields were living in a small terraced house in Baron Street – each time Fred got a pay-rise the family packed their chattels onto the back of a cart and moved 'oop in the world', as Jenny put it, even if it was only to a same-sized house in the next street – and Gracie, aged ten, had her first job of her own ... cleaning the six lavatories in her backyard for a halfpenny each! Here, singing whilst she scrubbed away with her cloth and tin of Vim, she was discovered by Lily Turner, a Midlands-born singer who was appearing at the Hippodrome and lodging a few doors from the Stansfields.

It was Lily Turner who arranged for Gracie to enter a talent contest at the Hippodrome a few weeks later, wearing a frock that Jenny had commissioned from Polly Pickles, a dressmaker who lived in the same street. Although Gracie was a year younger than the recently declared legal performing age of eleven, she got away with a 'little white lie' on account of her being so tall and she came joint-first, winning 10s.6d. – almost half the average mill worker's weekly wage – with a forgotten ditty called 'What Makes Me Love You As I Do?' which she refused to sing in anything but her rich and sometimes incomprehensible Lancashire twang. This was her most most endearing quality in those days and a trait which, though she eventually lost it to an American intonation, could always be picked up again later in her life – particularly if someone 'posh' was trying to drag her down by reminding her of her roots. Neither did she change the gender of the song, in an age when such things were not considered obligatory.

> What makes me love you as I do?
> There's other girls as nice as you!
> What makes me think you're so divine?
> What makes me long to call you mine?

Initially, Lily Turner positioned Gracie in the gallery, from where, after Lily had sung each verse to the song, Gracie would stand up and deliver the chorus. This worked well until an irate theatregoer took her for a heckler and hit her with her umbrella. From then on she was invited to join Lily on the stage, and the pair played successfully until Lily gave up her career to get married.

Whilst Gracie was working as Lily Turner's stooge, if it meant having time off school because they were playing away from Rochdale, Jenny had Fred write her sick-notes. Several times the family were reprimanded by the truant officer. Fifty years later, during a visit to her old school, Gracie was shown the register and was amused to see the number of crosses which had been entered against her name. During the reunion she also rebuked her former headmaster, Mr Brown, for banning her from singing in assembly – because he had considered her voice too raucous!

Over the next few years, Gracie worked with several juvenile troupes travelling around the county. The first was Clara Coverdale's Boys and Girls, whose average age was fifteen. Considerable favouritism was shown to the manager's two daughters, who each afternoon were given dancing lessons by their father. When Gracie asked if she could join in, however, she was refused, and because at twelve she was younger than everyone else, she was picked on and made to do acrobatics rather than concentrate on singing. During a rehearsal she tore ligaments in both legs, and was sent home without so much as setting foot on a stage.

Fred Stansfield was all for his daughter giving up her career and taking a job at the mill, but Jenny would not hear of this. She encouraged Gracie to join Haley's Garden of Girls, a troupe whose average age was a more mature seventeen. This was a very unhappy time for the youngster. Not only was she compelled to enrol at a new school each time the company moved on, but she was used by the older girls as their rubbing-rag by being made to run errands and skivvy for them. She also had her first sexual experience, in the most horrendous manner. One of her duties was to deliver jugs of hot water to the bedrooms, and one evening she caught a girl in bed with the landlady's son. With lightning speed, four hands grabbed her and held her down whilst the young man raped her on the floor. Gracie kicked and screamed, sinking her teeth into his neck and her fingernails where it hurt the most, and as she finally broke free she doused him with the jug of water. Running back to her room, she barricaded herself in with a heavy chest of drawers.

Gracie was still in a terrified state the next morning, so much so that a neighbour had to break the door down. She was taken in a state of severe nervous shock to a doctor, who diagnosed St Vitus's Dance, and she spent the next six weeks in the children's convalescent home at St Anne's on Sea. Some of her closest friends have maintained that this episode had a long-lasting effect on her in that for many years she was frightened of having any form of physical contact with a man, even one who loved her.

When she recovered, Gracie returned to Rochdale, where for once she was content to take her father's advice and take a job as cotton-winder at a local mill. She had to be out of bed every morning at five, but this did not bother her. 'The quietness of the cobbled streets is a wonderful memory of my childhood,' she wrote in *Sing As We Go*, her autobiography, which was published in 1960, and remembered Old Amy, who was paid twopence by each of the families in the street to tap on the windows every morning with her pole to ensure that no one missed a shift and thus a day's pay. She continued, 'I love Rochdale and I've never seen it as anything but a beautiful place. Though people have described it as a huddled, damp and hard little town, it was never like that to me. It was home, and I belonged there.' This of course was a contrived statement, as will later be seen, one of many that she made – quite unnecessarily – because in her later years when she had become a sophisticated woman of the world, she relied largely upon such announcements, hoping they would prove that she still retained what she called her 'common touch'.

Gracie would reflect on this period of hardworking contentment in one of her most important early songs, 'The Clatter of the Clogs', which transports the listener to a bygone age where, for almost everyone in the town, life depended on getting through those huge factory gates before they clanged shut, where the foreman was the friendly, but forceful dictator.

> See that throng!
> A thousand-strong toddle to work each morning,
> Lasses wearing shawls,
> Hefty chaps in caps and overalls.
> Working till their fingers ache,
> Earning all that they can make,
> They're saving up for next year's Wake,
> Everybody's gooin'!

Gracie was no enthusiastic millworker. Because she could not stop singing, and because her workmates were utterly enraptured by her sweet, almost flawless voice – when she as not mimicking Gertie Gitana and George Formby Snr, two of the big names of the day – they did most of her work for her, and would have continued to do so had she not been caught by the Foreman Jim of the song, and given the sack.

For a while, Gracie worked in a papermill. Then she became an errand-girl for a bread shop. Finally, thanks to a neighbour – the man referred to in her memoirs as Old Fred who moved in with the Stansfields when he became too frail to look after himself – she was introduced to the agent of Jessie Merrilees, in those days a popular star in Lancashire, but virtually forgotten today, who had been forced to cancel a week's stint at the Rochdale Hippodrome because of illness. Gracie attended an audition, and was booked as stand-in. She told her first biographer, Maud Miller, at the end of 1935, 'For once in my life I took the bit between my teeth. I demanded five pounds a week, and a silk frock!' The demand – at the time a veritable fortune for a child – was met, and Gracie proved so popular with the locals that her stay was extended by another week.

The attraction, initially, was that of a young girl performing 'sob-songs', though it did not stop there. One evening Gracie was halfway through a scorching ballad when a group of noisy latecomers shuffled into the theatre. On the spur of the moment she let out a whooping yell, before burlesquing the number in a piercing falsetto which halted them in their tracks, raising a few laughs from the rest of the audience. A new Lancashire comic in the very best Formby Snr tradition had arrived.

When Jenny saw the playbills, emblazoned with the words: YOUNG GRACE STANSFIELD, ROCHDALE'S OWN GIRL VOCALIST, and the cheap publicity photograph of her daughter wearing her Polly Pickles gown with its silver spangles she knew that a new star had been born. One, however, who might need a hefty push in the right direction – particularly as Gracie had a habit of listening to her father, whose answer to everything was, 'I reckon tha ought to get back to th'mill, Grace!' Jenny was said to be a domineering woman, though perhaps no more so than any other mother of her time and class. Her only ambition in life was to try and make sure that her offspring be given a better life than her own parents and aunt had been able to give her.

Though the relationship between mother and daughter was a great deal closer than most people later imagined, certain restrictions were of course inevitable. True Northerners are traditionally not supposed to be sloppy in their affections. Mary Whipp, Gracie's lifelong friend who was also born in Rochdale and attended the same school, remembered:

I believe that her autobiography gives by far the best insight into Gracie, the private woman. She did hide behind her image, and if you read between the lines this becomes apparent. For instance, towards the beginning she has a sudden urge to put her arms around her mother, but desisted because she thought her Mum would say, 'Get off, don't be daft!' I understand that feeling from my own childhood. She also always bemoaned her lack of education, though Gracie was educated by *life*, and she could put over her thoughts in a terse and to-the-point way. With her there was always the personal *and* the common touch.

Of course, as 'chief cook and bottle-washer', Jenny had the last say. *Gracie* would look after the house and family between music-hall engagements, and *she* would take the job her daughter had just been offered at the mill.

In 1912, when she as fourteen, Gracie was offered just over four shillings a week to join Charburn's Young Stars, then based in Blackpool. The fee just about covered her train fare to get to the resort, and she tried to borrow money from her family, but they of course were themselves counting the pennies and unable to help. Old Fred came up with a solution. He had read in a local newspaper of a talent contest being held at Middleton, not far from Rochdale, the prize being five shillings in cash. The only snag was that the contest was for 'locals' only. Gracie borrowed the bus fare from a friend, and decided to take the risk.

Not unexpectedly, Gracie won the prize, but this brought loud complaints from the audience, who accused the judge of cheating by selecting a 'foreigner'. She was demoted to second, then third place, and finally disqualified. Unknown to everyone else, on her way out of the concert hall the kindly judge slipped her the five shillings out of his own pocket because, he believed, she had been the best act of the evening.

Soon afterwards her mother urged her to change her name, having been told by a theatre manager that 'Grace Stansfield' did not roll readily off the tongue, and that in any case once she became a big star, entitled to have her name in large letters, it would never fit onto the playbills. Several pseudonyms were considered – including Stana Fields, the name which she would adopt many years later as a songwriter – but the one which everyone agreed upon was Gracie Fields.

Gracie stayed with Charburn's Young Stars for almost two years, appearing in innumerable song-and-dance routines. Her wages were quickly doubled to eight shillings a week, most of which she sent back to her family, wrapped up in newspaper clippings of her reviews, which were mostly very favourable. Her only 'luxury' was a wicker travelling basket on wheels, which took her months to save up for. She had it inscribed with the initials GF, and was once delighted when it was misplaced at the railway station in Leeds and the lost-luggage department there assumed that it must have belonged to George Formby Snr, in town for a show. Gracie got to meet her idol during the mix-up, and deemed this a lucky omen for the future. Jenny, fashioning herself as her daughter's manager, had a number of business cards printed, inscribed GRACIE FIELDS – VERSATILE COMEDIAN. These ended up at the back of the fire when a theatre manager handed her a scrap of paper upon which he had written '*Comédienne* – how long has she been a man?'

Upon leaving the troupe, Gracie, on her mother's advice, turned solo. The work was much better paid, though there were fewer engagements, which necessitated her taking on extra jobs such as running errands for local shops. Most important of all, she was independent. One of Gracie's friends at this time, whom she never forgot and was still inviting to tea fifty years on, was fourteen-year-old Mildred Ashworth, whose grandparents lived near the Stansfields. This last surviving link from Gracie's childhood was dining out on anecdotes when she was well into her nineties, but sadly died at the beginning of 1994 whilst this book was being prepared. She left a memoir with members of her family, part of which reads:

> She would call and sing for Grandma, as she called her, and then ask me to give her a middle C, adding, 'I don't want to get *too* high on this one!' I also helped with the impromptu concerts Gracie organized with the neighbourhood children – these took place in my grandfather's hen-pen and garden, with boxes given by Mr Reynolds, the local fruit merchant, for seats. I wasn't allowed to take part, however – I'd been given the job of looking after Gracie's brother, Tommy.

Gracie's very first major booking as a solo act was a week's slot at the Oldham Palace, which ended disastrously. For her last show, Gracie learned a new song, but in her enthusiasm forgot to hand the music to the bandleader. There followed a fierce battle for supremacy between the band and the singer when she attempted to sing her song to the tune they were playing. The manager of the theatre, Ernest Dotteridge, did not see the funny side when Gracie hit a series of high notes and completely drowned the din behind her, and brought the curtain down. When she made him feel guilty by causing a rumpus in her dressing-room after the show, however, Dotteridge made amends, when there was absolutely no reason for him to do so, by securing her a season with Cousin Freddy's Pierrot Concert Party, at St Anne's on Sea.

Now earning the majestic sum of three pounds a week, Gracie was given her own song, 'Coax Me' which her sister Betty recorded a few years later. Elsewhere in the revue, Gracie acted as Fred Hutchins's (Cousin Freddy) stooge – he would execute a fake magic act tapping her with his wand whereupon she would turn into stone. Gracie clowned around so much, getting so many laughs, that Fred abandoned his routine and the pair of them stopped the show each night just by ad-libbing. She threw a fit, however, the first time the audience chuckled whilst she was doing her song – it was one thing, she declared, to laugh *with* the act if the occasion called for it, but to laugh *at* it was the supreme insult.

After leaving Fred Hutchins's early in 1915, Gracie played the part of the Princess of Morocco in *Dick Whittington*, her one and only pantomime, which she liked at first, but soon grew to hate intensely. Her popularity, and her inadvertent knack of stealing every scene she was in, found her few favours with the rest of the cast, particularly when she introduced a song called 'There's Someone Who Wants You'. This was the height of the Great War, and the song – which the young Gracie sang with the dramatic enthusiasm of a much older artiste – was aimed at soldiers home on leave. Gracie put up with the hostility because she needed the money to send home to Jenny. Her father had recently been hospitalized following a serious accident at work, and for the first time in her life she was unable to spend Christmas at home. Her misery was eased a little when her sister Betty joined her. Speaking of this period some years later, Gracie remembered her 'grapefruit' episode. 'Having hardly any money, the sight of what I thought were some thumping big oranges at a penny each in a shop window was too much for me. I bought one, bit into it with gusto and ... well, you know what grapefruit tastes like without sugar, and the skin is ten times sourer than that!' Henceforth, whenever anyone mentioned the word grapefruit to Gracie, she would pull a face and think back to those unhappy days.

Gracie was happy again when the pantomime closed, even though it meant she was out of work. But sadly no sooner had she settled in at Whatmough Street – the Stansfields had moved 'oop' again during her absence – than Old Fred contracted pneumonia and died.

The old man's death was Gracie's first major tragedy, yet some good came from the heartbreak when Jenny was bequeathed all the money from his insurance ... just over a hundred pounds. Once the funeral expenses had been paid and the Stansfields' few debts settled, there was enough money left for Gracie to be enrolled at the Corlette Dance Studio in Manchester. For an exorbitant half-crown for thirty minutes, she learned the basics of tap. This paid off when Percy Hall, an eminent but not entirely reputable local impresario, signed her for a six-week tour which would guarantee her a minimum five pounds a week – if and when her fee exceeded his amount, Hall declared, then the difference would be split fifty-fifty. Hall knew that he was onto a good thing, and for Gracie this was invaluable experience. She was also playing a small but active role in the war effort by visiting local refugee houses and hospitals for wounded soldiers. At the cinema in West Houghton, near Bolton, she appeared on the same bill as a thirteen-year-old comic named Sandy Powell – some years later they duetted on two songs, 'Gracie and Sandy's Party' and 'Gracie and Sandy at the Coronation'.

Such as it was, Gracie's new-found 'wealth' came as a godsend when, for no apparent reason, Fred Stansfield left Jenny and the family to fend for themselves. Irene Bevan, Gracie's stepdaughter and only surviving relative from her younger days, told me, 'He was a very uncouth man. He went off one morning and said, "Ta-ta. I'll see you in a few weeks" and he was seven years in America, even though he had no job to go to. Then he came back, walked into the front room and announced, "Hello. What's for tea?" That's the type of family they were.'

Like most teenagers, Gracie was very much the soppy romantic, telling the journalist Gwen Robyns in the late 1940s, 'As a kid I was always in love. Every week the top-of-the-bill was my new hero. I couldn't eat or sleep for thinking about him.' She also explained how she had developed a crush on the famous double act, Jewell and Warriss, adding, 'If either of them had looked at me, I'd have jumped into marriage. Recently I saw them again in New York, two old men with dyed hair.'

Early in 1915, after a show in Chesterfield, Gracie was offered a fair-sized part in the Manchester-based revue, *Yes, I Think So*, starring Mona Frewer and a thirty-five-year-old comedian named Archie Pitt who soon would become an integral part of her life.

Born Archibald Selinger, this affable but shrewd Londoner had worked as a shop assistant and travelling salesman before turning his talents to the music-hall stage. An aficionado of the Anglo-Belgian entertainer Harry Fragson, whose songs Gracie would later sing, Archie had cut his first recording in 1912, 'Does This Shop Stock Socks With Spots?' coupled with 'I'm Just Going to Clean Father's Boots', at a time when he had been touring the smoke-filled East-End pubs and hazardous working-men's clubs of Lancashire and Yorkshire.

Little is known of Archie Pitt's first wife, May Deitchman, as Irene Bevan explained.

> She had me when she was seventeen. She was put into this big house with my grandmother and Archie's mad sister, Hilda, and she couldn't take it. One day she left. I was eighteen months old and never saw her again for years. I was very fond of Hilda. She and Grandmother brought me up. I even used to think Grandmother was my mother, until it was explained to me.

That Archie at once recognized Gracie's natural comic genius, and that he alone was responsible for the quite rapid progression of her career cannot now be disputed. Irene Bevan told me during our first interview,

> I could have told you all sorts of fairy-tales, many of which have been reported in other books. It's always been 'Our Gracie With Wings'. The balance has always been so ridiculous. You asked for the truth, and that's what you're getting. I don't hold any grief either way. I didn't always get on with my father. His life was Grace, his creation was Grace, and if I got in the way in the slightest, it was me who suffered. He had an awful balancing act to play, and psychologically he didn't always play it very well. Everybody talks about what a dreadful man my father was, but nobody ever says what a so-and-so she could be. Archie wasn't the ogre that he's been made out to be, particularly by the things she said about him. She created this myth about him being a wide-boy Jew. It just wasn't true. Talent or no talent, if it hadn't been for him she could quite easily have gone back to the fish-and-chip shop. There are thousands of very talented people out there, and if they don't have somebody to turn to, they stay where they are.

When she first opened in *Yes, I Think So*, Gracie was staying in free lodgings at a boarding-house owned by a friend of Jenny's, three miles outside Manchester – free, that is, in exchange for her doing most of the housework. Even so, she was so strapped for cash that she walked all the way to the theatre and back in all weathers, to save on the tram fares. Archie offered to help by inviting her to stay in the guest-house where he was lodging, still free of charge but without the skivvying. Gracie gratefully accepted, though she made every effort to keep away from him when they were outside the theatre, claiming, 'I didn't want to see too much of Archie. He made me feel uneasy, and I'd decided not to like him at all.'

Yes, I Think So toured successfully all over Northern England for eighteen months, and on 5 July 1915 came to 'Old Mo', the famous Middlesex Music Hall (later the Winter Garden) in London's Drury Lane. Gracie's first encounter with the West End was not short of its amusing moments, though she often became lost, wandering the streets alone. One afternoon she stopped at a cart which was selling cockles and whelks, and after boasting to the vendor about 'good old Lancashire 'ot-pot', she was handed a plate of jellied eels. Gracie mistook them for live snakes, screamed and dropped them all over the pavement, and ran off!

Eighteen years later, Gracie remembered her first visit to the big city and lampooned it as only she could. Although she did not arrive in London 'in clogs and shawl with a piece of bread and dripping in me hand', she may have been sufficiently naive to have needed to ask a policeman to explain the fundamentals of a back-street brothel.

> 'You're a silly little fool!' he starts to yell,
> 'Don't you know what that red light means?'
> I said, 'Red's for danger, if you please, sir!
> But don't switch it on for me, sir!
> 'Cos heaven will protect an honest gal!'

On 9 January 1916, in the dressing-room after the show, Gracie celebrated her eighteenth birthday with her very first taste of champagne, courtesy of Archie. Fortunately for all concerned, the occasion was a good deal more respectable than the one she lampooned in the comic song, written by Arthur Wimperis, about the hitherto innocent village maid who has been craftily seduced by the lusty local marquess ...

> It's just an old story ... always the same!
> Like a poor moth she flew too near the flame,
> She opened her wings, and lost her good name,
> All through a glass of champagne!

Ridiculously, each time Gracie achieved too much applause with a song in *Yes, I Think So*, it was passed to someone else, and she was given a new one to break in. Again, she considered this valuable training, and in any case none of the other cast members could make the numbers work quite the way she did. When the tour ended, Percy Hall offered her a pay-rise to stay with his company, but then Archie offered to buy her out of her contract, providing she promised to work for him in his yet to be formed repertory group. The deal was clinched, not with a contract but with a handshake. Gracie quipped, 'It's a bargain!', and this gave Archie an idea. The new revue, which he would write and score himself, would be called *It's a Bargain!*.

The new show was augmented by the Three Aza Boys – Archie's brothers Pat, Edgar and Bert Selinger, who had adopted the pseudonym Aza after a firm of suit manufacturers of that name had supplied them with free stage-clothes in exchange for advertising its name. 'The Three Aza Boys were not distinguished comics, but they did have other talents,' Gracie later said. She was most fond of Bert, who soon afterwards left the ensemble to become her manager and right-hand man. Many years later, in his brief biography, *Gracie*, Bert – who never once mentions in his book that they were related by marriage – remembered these early years:

> I knew quite clearly, without the faintest doubt, that I was talking to a girl with the seed of Fame and possible Genius within her. For years, Gracie endured all the worst aspects of theatrical touring – shaky finances, audiences not big enough to fill a bus, death-trap theatres, insanitary dressing-rooms, fire buckets for wash-basins, scratch meals and dingy lodgings. She never fought for a star dressing-room, and mothered the chorus girls with all the warmth of her Lancashire heart. In fact, she did most of the household chores and shopping whilst they

lounged about, as though they were the leading lady. And in spite of the hardships, she never once complained.

Mona Frewer, who was Bert's girlfriend at the time, again played Archie's leading lady, but Gracie, as second lead, was clearly his favourite and there was a backstage cat-fight when Mona's part was cut to accommodate a sketch in which his protégée was to imitate Charlie Chaplin in his famous 'Little Tramp' guise. Gracie stunned Archie by telling him she did not know who Chaplin was – adding that as an aficionado of the music-hall, she had hardly ever been to the pictures. However, after watching one of Chaplin's features twice, she walked out of the cinema as Chaplinesque as the little man himself.

Three weeks into its run, *It's a Bargain!* began running short of money. When it had first gone onto the road, Bert Aza had travelled ahead to plead with the theatres for an advance on everyone's salary so that they would have sufficient funds to move on to the next engagement. When the company got into a real fix, an anonymous benefactor – referred to at the time only as 'a young professional who had enjoyed the show' offered Archie an unsecured, interest-free loan of £40, and Mona Frewer pawned her jewels. Subsequently the revue ran successfully for over two years, touring the length and breadth of the country. Even when Gracie was offered £50 a week to appear in a rival revue, she would not leave Archie – to do so would have been letting not just him down, but also the rest of the company, which of course would not have survived for very long without her. 'After those first revues, my father said he could see something in her,' Irene Bevan reminisced. 'I don't think in those early days he even saw *what* she was going to be, but he certainly knew that she was going to be something. And gradually her personality developed, much to the detriment of his own because he used to give her what they called an unselfish feed, so that for her every possibility was exploited.'

A large portion of Gracie's success was as a result of her unpredictability. Although there was a script to be adhered to, she hardly ever stuck to it and sometimes never knew what she herself was going to do next whilst playing a scene, which infuriated the other cast members and caused many fights behind the scenes. One evening, she went on dressed as a cucumber and had the audience in stitches. In Bedford, when she was supposed to walk on as the parlourmaid and lay the table, she cycled on and rode around the table, throwing everything expertly into place! This caused such hysteria in the theatre that it was left in the revue.

Gracie's dissension with Mona Frewer came to a head when the revue reached the Bedford Theatre, in London's Camden Town. Her Chaplin sketch was a big hit and Frewer, aware that her own popularity had not only been challenged but surpassed, told Gracie, 'Any monkey can do imitations!' From that day Gracie never did any more impressions on the stage. A short time later Mona Frewer was forced to leave the company through ill health, and Gracie became Archie's leading lady. Her sisters, Betty and Edith, were then given parts in the chorus, along with a strange-looking but not unattractive young woman named Annie Lipman, who soon afterwards became Gracie's and Archie's musical director. Although Gracie formed a close friendship with Annie, within a few years she would prove a particularly painful thorn in Gracie's side.

Archie's next revue, the most successful he ever produced and wrote, was *Mr Tower of London* which was premièred on 28 October 1918 at Nottingham's Long Eaton Coliseum. Gracie played the part of Sally – the first of many – and over the next seven years there would be 5,824 performances, grossing in excess of £400,000 at the box office in what was essentially a Pitt-Fields family venture. Both Gracie's sisters had parts, and Tommy Fields joined when he was thirteen. Initially, he sold penny photographs of Gracie whilst everyone was on stage, but later he joined the finale for a comedy routine. Bert Aza took over the company's financial affairs. As well as taking the lead, Gracie supervised and trained the dancers, assisted by Annie Lipman. During morning rehearsals she would be tough and demanding, but when the weather was fine she would give the girls a treat, hiring a charabanc and driving them into the country for picnics.

Irene Bevan's memories of Annie Lipman were always recalled with great humour, in fact her humour made our meetings that much more delightful.

She had an enormous beak of a nose, and straight black hair which she wore in a fringe. A few years later, when everybody was into grey squirrel coats, she had a full-length one which almost reached to her ankles. I can see her now, running down the platform at Crewe or somewhere to catch a train. Why she didn't cluck, I don't know. She looked just like a pantomime chicken.

Twice nightly, Gracie clowned around on the stage, always able to get the best laughs by ad-libbing, particularly in an hilarious Madame Tussaud's sketch. Immediately afterwards, she would sing a sentimental song which, in the aftermath of the war, had the audiences reaching for their handkerchiefs. There were matinées most afternoons and if there were too many 'House Full' signs, Gracie or Archie arranged impromptu performances. One such took place in Llanelli, South Wales, at nine in the morning for a contingency of coalminers coming off the night-shift – when Gracie observed their blackened faces, she shouted to Archie, standing in the wings: 'How did you manage to get all these chimney sweeps at this hour of the morning?'

When she was not on the stage, Gracie passed the time playing cards with the cast. Something of a card sharp, she hardly ever lost, but at the end of each session she always threw her winnings on to the table for the others to share amongst themselves. She and her sisters also made most of the costumes for the show.

Mr Tower of London was scheduled to open for one week at its biggest venue so far – the Queen's Theatre, in London's Poplar – in 1919 when the country was suddenly crippled by the national rail strike. Not to be outdone, the company travelled in the back of the props wagon, rerouting several times in a dense fog. Gracie told Maud Miller of *The Play Pictorial*, 'The engine went asthmatic on us, the driver took us fifty miles out of our road, we nearly froze to death on account of the cold, and we accumulated bruises like small boys accumulate cigarette cards. Eeh, it was a journey!'

The company arrived in London with mere hours to spare, and to Archie's horror, a replacement troupe had been booked. Neither he nor Gracie would accept this. They kept the manager busy by arguing with him, whilst the others carried the props on to the stage. They then refused to budge until the other troupe had been sent packing!

Gracie's act won the admiration of another Archie, this one the brother of impresario Val Parnell, who offered her £200 a week to work for him – leaving Archie Pitt. The offer may have been tempting. She was only grossing around £30 a week with her revue. Politely, she refused Parnell's offer, though she agreed to a recording session with him at the HMV studios, cutting two sides – 'Tweedle-eedle-dum' from the show, and a French chanson, 'Romany Love'. For reasons of copyright, these were not released and some years later, when Columbia wanted to put them out, it was discovered that a clumsy employee had sat on the acetates. Gracie found this amusing, though many of her fans have since lamented what happened.

For many years, the relationship between Gracie and Archie Pitt has been shrouded in mystery. She never missed an opportunity to give him a bad press, though in her toned-down, ghosted memoirs she restricted herself to saying, 'He was not Svengali, but he was a passable imitation.' In her early years she was also fond of recounting her prejudiced feelings to songwriters, only to lampoon the lyrics once they had been set to music, as a means of camouflaging her obvious bitterness. One example was

> I followed you like a guiding star,
> Our hearts were beating in tune ...
> I was only too glad to give all I had,
> You made me believe the world was mine!

Like everyone else in the troupe, Gracie addressed Archie as 'The Guv'nor', and it has been suggested that he only asked her to marry him because he believed that having her as his wife would bind her to working for him, and keep the money coming in. Her sister Betty had fallen in love with Roy Parry, Archie's set designer, and their wedding had been a joyous occasion. With Gracie and Archie, things appear to have been different.

Whilst making her first film, a few years after she and Archie were married, Gracie told the actress Florence Desmond that she had only said yes, after turning him down several times, because she had been terrified of Archie firing her. This cannot have been true – she was constantly being urged to work elsewhere, and for comparatively huge fees.

Irene Bevan was very young at the time but has a clear recollection of that time:

> I remember being in a taxi with him one day and he said to me, 'I'm thinking of marrying again. Who would you like it to be?' I said, 'Auntie Grace, of course!' I can remember the conversa-

tion as if it was yesterday. They never started off as lovers, though from his point of view I think that in the early days he was genuinely fond of her. He'd seen something that he could create, and he *did* create her – nobody else did. But she was a very naive person, and I find it so sad that afterwards she did so many things to alienate him.

Whatever the reason, the couple were married on 21 April 1923, at Clapham Register Office. It was such a played-down affair that Gracie told her mother that she saw little point in wasting good money on a wedding dress when she had only recently bought a new black cocktail dress which would suffice! The honeymoon, in Paris, was a disaster. Gracie said later, 'We couldn't understand a word anybody said, and we couldn't get a decent cuppa for love or money. So we came home.'

In fact, the Pitts did not yet have a home of their own. When they were not in lodgings with the other cast members, they stayed with Gracie's parents. Archie had taken out a lease on a small maisonette above a confectioner's shop in Islington, north London, but instead of moving into it with his wife he handed it to the Stansfields and kept paying their bills, even after Fred had found a job. On top of this, he paid every penny of their relocation expenses from Rochdale.

Shortly after Gracie's and Archie's marriage, the unstoppable Bert Aza approached Sir Oswald Stoll, the head of one of the most important theatrical organizations in Britain, and asked him if there was any chance of bringing his revue to London's West End. He was put on to Stoll's assistant, an individual named Gillespie who considered the whole concept of a 'Northern turn' on a London stage nothing short of offensive. Hoping to dissuade Archie, and in an attempt to make Gracie a laughing-stock, he offered one week at Liverpool's Olympic Theatre, renowned as a show-business graveyard, and notoriously difficult to fill. So many people turned up at the venue that the box office started turning people away – one evening they became so angry that they rioted and had to be quelled by police with batons.

Gracie's proudest moment in *Mr Tower of London* occurred when Gillespie stood down, forcing Stoll to acknowledge her potential though she did try to laugh off the importance of the show being booked for the prestigious Alhambra, in London's Leicester Square, by remarking, 'We've done it in Huddersfield, so we'll do it in London!' Thinking the company's costumes too unrefined for London audiences, Gracie worked around the clock teaching her girls how to run up new ones, though she later confessed that her knowledge of needlecraft until then had never extended beyond the art of pricking her finger! She also perfected an awkward, formal bow – though on the opening night she forgot to do this and gave them her soon to be customary errand-boy whistle, a Gracie Fields trademark which was even delivered before royalty.

On the eve of the première, Gracie received a telegram from the doyenne of the British musical-comedy stage, Evelyn Laye, wishing her luck. She was so struck with stagefright that she almost cancelled the show – such was her awe of this woman that even when she had surpassed her in popularity, when they were reasonably good friends, she always addressed her as 'Miss Laye'.

After the first night show there was an amusing episode outside the stage door as Gracie was leaving to get into the car which Archie had hired to take some of the cast members for a night on the town. Gracie let out a piercing scream when two 'pansy boys', as she called them, ran up to her with autograph books – she later said that she had assumed them to be thugs, about to abduct her, and remembered what happened next: 'I was so nervous that I splashed ink everywhere. Through the windows of the Daimler I could see Betty, Edie and the lot of them falling about with laughter. I finished my signing, tripped over the step of the Daimler – then fell in head first!' Gracie would re-create his amusing scenario some years later in one of her films.

2

Dancing with Tears in My Eyes

Mr Tower of London did so well at the Alhambra that its run was extended and Gracie was inundated with offers of work from all quarters. She was by now on friendly terms with Sir Oswald Stoll, and when he offered her £100 a week 'to nip across the road' to do three songs during the interval, she jumped at the chance. Though Archie was not happy with the idea – he had a responsibility to her to ensure that she did not overtire herself – she opposed him further by signing a contract for a season of late-night cabaret shows at the Café Royal ... the fee was a staggering £300 a week. On her first night she was photographed with Noël Coward and Beatrice Lillie. A few evenings later her sister Betty introduced her to the painter Augustus John – a meeting which inadvertently sparked off a series of events which very soon turned her life upside down.

Augustus John had recently completed one of his most beautiful works – a portrait of the outrageous American actress, Tallulah Bankhead, at that time the toast of London's flapper set. Gracie met Tallulah one afternoon at John's studio, and though they never became close friends, they had a tremendous admiration for one another. Just as Gracie – with her old-fashioned values as yet intact, and still retaining her Northern accent – astonished Tallulah with her naivety, so the latter shocked her with her endless swearing, cocaine snorting, and her lectures to all and sundry, royalty included on drugs, religion, lesbian sex and not wearing underclothes – among many other controversial topics. And when the girl from Alabama promised to get Gracie 'fixed up' with Sir Gerald du Maurier, in whose play *The Dancers* Bankhead had made her London début, Gracie was over the moon.

Gracie and du Maurier first met after one of her afternoon matinées. Suave and sophisticated, Britain's greatest actor-manager of his day was also an insufferable snob – a trait which Gracie could not stand, and which rapidly effected a love-hate relationship between them. Du Maurier asked Gracie to play Lady Weir in his straight play, *SOS*, scheduled to open at St James's Theatre. He had even discussed the project with his friend, King George V, after fellow sophisticate Gladys Cooper had turned the part down. The king told him, 'This play is a tragedy, but it takes a great comedienne to play tragedy – and Gracie Fields is exactly that.'

This was the beginning of 1928, long before the era of the one-woman show, and Gracie knew that appearing in four different productions in one evening would not overtax her strength, even though her husband insisted otherwise. She was more concerned about 'botching up' her posh character, though the part of Lady Weir was confined to the first act only, which brought the wry comment, 'Lucky for me I died near the beginning, so the strain of being a lady wasn't too much!'

Gladys Cooper and Tallulah Bankhead invited themselves to sit in on rehearsals – on the stage itself. When the latter bantered, 'Gerald doesn't look a day over thirty, does he, darling?' Gracie piped, honestly, 'No, *darling*. He looks twenty *years* over thirty!' Du Maurier was hard put to discern whether or not she was joking, and there was worse to come. Very much a ladies' man – some said a philanderer – du Maurier had failed to seduce the man-hungry Tallulah, and he got no further with Gracie, who shocked him by turning up at his house a few days later – not in the dinner-gown which he had requested, but in a tartan kilt and purple blouse.

Well into his fifties, but still thought of as a matinée idol – especially by himself – du Maurier kissed Gracie one night, only to be told, 'Behave yourself, lad. Tha's older than me dad!' Du Maurier's further attempt to woo her also backfired. Buying a fake diamond ring from Woolworths, he placed it in a Hatton Garden box and dropped it on the dinner table one evening, suggesting that they get to know each other a little better and quipping that the ring had been a 'mere snip' at just £700. Gracie slapped him across the face. When du Maurier repeated what had happened to Tallulah, she kissed his cheek better – then promptly slapped him across the other one!

Archie was now managing several touring companies, including one headed by Betty Fields and Roy Parry, another by Edith and her husband Duggie Wakefield, and a third, a few years later, by Tommy. To begin with, Archie rented a theatre in New Brighton, West Sussex – this was used for rehearsals and first nights – but as his empire grew more and more successful, he took over London's Alexandra Palace. Here, all the scenery for his revues was made and painted. Some of his back-up musicians later became famous. Nat Gonella formed his own ensemble. Some time later, after a spell as Gracie's musical director, the violinist Lou Ross – who married Archie's daughter, Irene – worked with Josephine Baker.

In spite of the money and the success, however, the Pitts were not experiencing a happy marriage, and when she was not working hard on the stage, Gracie was battling to cope with the problems she was creating in her personal life. Irene Bevan was attending a school in Brighton, where she lived with her grandmother, but each weekend when she returned to London, she witnessed first-hand what was happening.

My father was a great stylist. Grace didn't have a clue, and she resented not having a clue. She would let him down in public by showing him up, or worse still by showing herself up. Archie wasn't a snob, or terribly well-educated. He was a retiring sort of man. He could never go along with all that fish-and-chip shop rubbish, and her behaviour used to make him cringe. One day there was a Sunday concert, and Grace came out of the dressing-room. The Duke of Kent was standing there, the one who was killed. He shook hands with her, and she turned around and bawled, 'Isn't he like our Tom?' Her abrasiveness, of course, was nothing more than self-protection. She was awfully conscious of not belonging amongst these people. I don't know where it came from, but Archie like all his brothers had this innate, fantastic sense of quality especially with clothing. He had all his shirts made at Salka's, and his shoes were always hand-made. Grace was very careless with her clothes. Naturally, my father hated that. That's one of the reasons why there were so many rows. They were so unalike and so ambitious for different things that it was friction all the time.

With his flair for style, Archie forked out exactly £12,000 to have a red-bricked palatial residence built on Bishop's Avenue, in London's Hampstead. Set in two acres of landscaped gardens, Tower – 'And it is *Tower*, not "The Tower" or "Towers"!' he told the press, adding that it had been so named after the revue – had eleven bedrooms, several reception rooms, a huge ballroom with a variable-tension sprung floor, five bathrooms designed by Froys who had worked on some of the fittings at Buckingham Palace, a vast servants' kitchen, and a garage equipped to accommodate four cars. The lift, which Gracie was terrified of using in case it got stuck, was trimmed with gold leaf and her and Archie's bedroom was filled with antique Chinese furniture and a bed on a dais.

All the leading society magazines of the day did features and photo-spreads on Tower, and Gracie was always the most diligent hostess whilst showing journalists around – posing for shots on expensive sofas and chairs, pointing at the paintings, or acting the fool with Archie's pet monkey which she said always had its own place at the dinner table. Seven dogs and a parrot also had free run of the house, she added, as did Annie Lipman, referred to politely but caustically as 'Archie's Number One'. According to his daughter, however, Archie had good reason to lean on this extraordinary woman.

Tower had a beautiful dining-room, and in that dining-room he liked to have his meals served properly. In those days, in a decent-sized house you had three or four servants. It wasn't the rarity that it is today, and they all did very well because their cost of living never altered – somebody else always paid their bills. Grace couldn't stand having a parlourmaid and a chef, and she would get up halfway through a meal and start clearing away. Eventually we got rid of the chef and she brought in Auntie Margaret [Margaret Fielding, Jenny Stansfield's cousin], which meant that we got plenty of hot-pot. As for Archie, he suffered from every ailment under the sun. He was a terrible hypochondriac, always changing his diet. For instance, he wouldn't eat new bread. All his bread had to be three days old. He also liked sardines and apples. Annie was prepared to go around after him with bags of stale bread or whatever else he wanted, and Grace was only too pleased to push him on to her because not only she wouldn't do it, she couldn't do it. All this business about their love affair – it was bits of stale bread more than anything else. Nobody knows what my father saw in Annie Lipman. I suppose in the end he felt that she was the only one who was loyal to him. She also used to humour him. He used to tell her, 'All the women in the family wear black, including Irene. Put on something coloured.' So she would wear bright scarlet or orange, just to keep him happy. Annie adored him, and Grace didn't. And if you get enough flattery from somebody, you fall for them. Grace always wanted to be off and away. She was never interested in my father. In the early days, yes, because he got her out of a fish-and-chip shop. But Annie and Archie never had a bedroom at Tower. Her room was next to mine. They never shared a room whilst Grace was in that house – not that she would have bothered if he had slept with her or with any of the half-dozen chorus girls he did sleep with. Just as Annie stuck with him through thick and thin, Grace couldn't have cared less.

Gracie hated the house – which went on to the market in 1993 at a staggering £24 *million* – and all that it stood for. She could not get used to the maid following her around and tidying up after her and Gerald, the butler, terrified her. She told journalists that she was happiest whilst relaxing alone in her 'Rochdale-type' sitting-room, drinking tea with the staff in their quarters, or playing with the animals. Her statement to the press of how she used to skip dinner by telling the butler that she was not hungry, then sneaking out into the night to the local take-away, was hotly denied by Archie's daughter.

This is such tripe! I defy you to find a fish-and-chip shop in Hampstead at that particular time. There was no such thing! You would have to walk four miles to find them. It is true about the animals. They were both dog-mad. One night a woman came to the theatre with four Pekingese pups. She told him a long story of how their pedigree had been destroyed in a fire. No trouble at all, we got four pups, and they were no more Pekingese than I am. We also had two Airedales that had produced five pups, and he kept them all. Sadly, the monkey died when the chauffeur shut it in the central-heating cupboard, so he bought another one which used to take the flowers out of the vases, then pee in them. In those days neither Archie nor

Gracie could resist any animal.

On 1 March 1928, Gracie appeared at the London Coliseum in the first of her ten Royal Variety Shows – sharing top billing with her were the comic Will Hay, and the dancer Anton Dolin. King George V had seen Gracie in *SOS*, and – in those days the royals actually had a say in who they wanted in the line-up – he had asked du Maurier 'to move heaven and earth' to get her. In her excitement, Gracie forgot which side of the theatre the royal box was on and curtsied in the wrong direction! She received a standing ovation for Irving Berlin's 'Because I Love You', a serious but already dated song which she performed faking sobs and frequently crossing her eyes like Josephine Baker, who had just performed it in Paris. One person who did not like the song was Queen Mary, who said to her afterwards, 'I prefer you singing songs like "Come Into the Garden, Maud" to the comic ones.'

'Because I Love You' was the first of the eighteen numbers she recorded that year in a new, lucrative contract with HMV – but if the public thought Gracie was merely clowning around, she later claimed that she had aimed the song at Archie.

> What should I care if you've broken your vow?
> Why do I wonder who's kissing you now?
> I often wish we'd never met ...
> Oh, mother! Was it worth it?

One evening at the Café Royal, Augustus John introduced Gracie to two young intellectual friends of his. Henry Savage was an up-and-coming writer with a high-pitched voice and an overt fondness for the ladies who immediately made her laugh with his witty, far-fetched stories. His companion, John Flanagan, was a softly-spoken Irish painter who, though nowhere near as well-known as Augustus John, had nevertheless held several important exhibitions in London, including one at the Royal Academy. Gracie described him as 'a handsome lad, but the saddest I ever saw, with big brown eyes that looked as though they were going to flood with tears'. Very much to everyone's surprise, she promptly fell head-over-heels in love with him.

At that time Flanagan was renting a property from Augustus John – a small studio in St John's Wood, hidden behind a huge terraced block and approached by a long narrow passageway. Most of the time he lived alone, unless Henry Savage was in town, and until meeting Gracie is said to have been a confirmed bachelor. She changed all that. Initially, there began a friendly rivalry between Flanagan and Augustus John as to which of them should paint her portrait. She decided upon the younger man, ultimately, because he needed the money – also, because in him she found a good listener. During the few days she sat for him Gracie told Flanagan all about her tribulations with Archie, and even tried to convince him that the titles of some of her songs reflected her plight – 'They All Make Love But Me', 'What Archibald Says, Goes', ''Appy 'Ampsted', 'It Isn't Fair' and even 'I Hate You'. Had Flanagan taken the time to listen to these songs, however, he would have realized that they were comedy numbers actually arranged by Gracie and Archie.

Flanagan urged her to leave her husband without further ado and move into the studio. Initially, she was horrified. Women brought up in the North of England during the first half of the century rarely separated from their husbands, no matter how severe their domestic traumas – they were taught to hold their heads up high and suffer with dignity. It was also an age in which wives were traditionally not expected to support themselves and, despite her high earnings, Gracie was not contributing to the running of her household. She did not of course refrain from visiting the Irishman when she was feeling down, which was often. If she could not get a taxi, she would travel by bus, annoying Archie who liked her to be driven everywhere in the chauffeured Rolls. 'I hated that damned car. It was like riding in the back of a hearse,' she said scathingly. Gradually, she and Flanagan braved going out in public, though to curb the gossips Henry Savage usually tagged along. And as Irene Bevan disclosed, the change in her personality was remarkable.

She was a woman who for years had never had any kind of freedom. First of all she had her mother who was pushing her into showbusiness, then there was Fred, who was permanently drunk. Grace suddenly became great fun to be with, mad as a hatter. We used to do all sorts of silly things, which in those days were quite outrageous – like walking along the promenade in our bare feet. That was something that my grandmother would have whacked me for. I absolutely worshipped her – not as an act but as a person because as a youngster I had been so constrained. John Flanagan taught her the fine arts, the difference between kitsch and the real thing. I sat for him several times and we all got on wonderfully. I liked all the Flanagan-Savage gang. Henry too was a scream. On Sundays we would trundle off to his cottage on the beach at Winchelsea. He had to live in the back because the front rooms were full of pebbles. I was there once with Grace when his girlfriend came out of the bedroom, stark naked, and put the kettle on. Henry told her, seriously, 'How many times have I told you to put your boots on? You'll catch cold.' Grace wouldn't have seen that sort of thing in Rochdale!

Unwilling to live with John Flanagan but eager to get away from Tower, Gracie began looking for a place of her own. Some years before, during a trip to Plymouth, she had discovered and fallen in love with a tiny cottage which had been for sale in Cawsand Bay. Archie had checked it out and bought it, since which time it had lain empty and crumbling. Just how Gracie would have coped with living so far from London, given that her professional life was now centred there, is hard to imagine, though she is said to have seriously contemplated turning the place into a love-nest for herself and Flanagan – providing, of course, she could entice him into relocating with her. In fact, before she could proposition him she learned that Archie had had the cottage demolished – not out of spite, as she said in her memoirs, but because he planned building a new house on the site. For Gracie, this was almost the last straw.

During a charabanc outing to Brighton with her parents, sisters and their families, Gracie noticed a house on Dorothy Avenue, in nearby Peacehaven, which was on the market. According to the story one of her party saw it and said to her father, 'This would be a nice place for thee to breed chickens, Fred!' Returning to London, Gracie consulted Archie and he (not she, as she later said) bought the place for her parents. A few months later, however, when Fred complained that the house was too far from the pub, and Jenny said that it was not convenient for the shops in Brighton, Gracie bought them another at nearby Telscombe, keeping the first house on until such time as she decided what to do with it – though legally of course it was not hers to do anything with.

Over the next few years the Stansfields, vastly out of their depth, effected a virtual non-stop 'restoration' programme at Telscombe.

Rooms and wings were added for grandchildren as they came along. A hole, dug to accommodate a goldfish pond, grew and grew until contractors were brought in to turn it into a swimming pool. It had been in use but a week when Fred rolled home drunk one evening and fell in head first. According to Gracie, she dived in and pulled him out, and the next day gave instructions for the pool area to be made safer. Irene Bevan was a frequent visitor to both houses.

Why she chose Peacehaven, I'll never know. There were no roads. I can remember in the depth of winter plodding through the mud to get to Dorothy Avenue. Telscombe was better because it was much nearer to the road, and they were able to get about a bit. Jenny joined the local amateur dramatics society – she had a wonderful voice, and she was in *Iolanthe*. Fred began breeding chickens and greyhounds. The greyhounds all got rickets, but they did most of their exercise in the public bar at the Peacehaven Hotel. As for the pool, the family were more concerned about the children falling into it than him. Some of them probably would have been pleased if he had. There were never any rails around it, though. First of all they built little bridges over it, so when you swam the crawl you caught your hands on them. The house had a square parapet on the top, which made it look like a ship, and they installed lifebelts right up there. If you did happen to be drowning, someone had to climb up on to the roof and throw them down into the water!

The final addition to the property – Jenny's particular idea of going 'oop' in the world, an aspect of her character which Gracie used as a basis for her 1935 hit, 'We've Got to Keep Up With the Joneses – was the tennis court, where Fred kept his chickens. Yet if the Stansfields were experiencing luxury for the first time in their lives, old habits died hard. One newspaper reported how Jenny, wary of her 'newfangled' electric stove, sill preferred frying sausages on the sitting-room fire! Maud Miller called on them one day and wrote: 'The Fields' home near Peacehaven doesn't sound either peaceful, or a haven. They are *too* hospitable, and they like lots of noise!'

Whilst Gracie was rehearsing Archie Pitt's latest revue, *The Show's the Thing*, early in 1929, she was asked to stand in for Rosetta, one of the Duncan Sisters, in *Topsy and Eva*, a hugely popular musical version of *Uncle Tom's Cabin* which was playing at the Gaiety

Theatre. Gracie learned the part in under twenty-four hours – using the 'well-tried Northern old wives' remedy' of wrapping a vinegar bandage around her head to enhance concentration – and she blacked her face every evening for two weeks until Rosetta Duncan was well enough to return to the production. She did not take one penny in salary – she later said that she was so relieved to be getting away from Archie for a while, it was worth giving the money to charity, which was perhaps being a little too hard on the man. After her first performance, she was cheered by two hundred people outside the stage-door and hoisted up on to the shoulders of two burly fans, who carried her triumphantly the entire length of the Strand.

Two weeks before *The Show's the Thing* was scheduled to open – not two days, as she said in her memoirs – Gracie and Archie had a blazing row, and she packed her bags. Taking a taxi to Victoria Station she caught the boat-train, and later that evening joined John Flanagan and Henry Savage, who were holidaying in Paris. The following day the trio visited the Louvre, then went for a boat trip on the Seine. They spent the evening at the Casino, where Harry Pilcer and Marie Dubas were appearing in the extravaganza, *Paris Qui Charme*. A vivacious, friendly Jewish woman, and quite phenomenally talented, Marie was Gracie's exact counterpart on the Continent, and she immediately became a trusted, valued friend. According to her lifelong companion, Sylvie Galthier, whenever Marie was in need of a shoulder to cry on in those days, Gracie would secretly visit Paris and the two stars would go out on the town, or simply chat over dinner in their favourite restaurant.

At the Casino Marie sang a song which had been introduced by Harry Fragson only months before his father had shot him dead during an argument over a chorus-girl.

> Reviens, veux-tu?
> Ton absence a brisé ma vie.
> Aucune femme, vois-tu
> N'a jamais prit ta place?
> My souffrance est infinie …
> (Come back, will you?
> Your absence has broken my life.
> Don't you see, no other woman
> Has ever taken your place?
> My suffering is endless.)

The gist of the chanson as explained to her by Marie Dubas – a man comes home to find that his wife has left him and wanders desolately through the rooms picking up his gifts to her, each carrying memories of happier times – apparently so struck her conscience – the absconding wife – that without further ado, she returned to London, where – she later told everyone – how she was shocked when the door to Tower was opened not by the butler, but by Annie Lipman. In fact, she could not possibly have been shocked at all – Annie had been living in the house as long as she had and this was common knowledge.

(Later that year, Gracie recorded 'Reviens, veux-tu?' phonetically in French. She performs the first three-quarters of the song beautifully, with virtually no trace of any accent then – promptly ruins the whole thing by interjecting in her broadest Lancashire, 'By gum, it took me a long time to learn that line!')

The Show's the Thing played a succession of West End theatres for more than a year, most successfully at the Lyceum, enabling Gracie to exploit her enormous comedy potential to the full. Her big hit in the revue was 'Laugh, Clown, Laugh!' In the opening sketch she played the madcap Lady With the Elastic Voice, while Archie played the Boxer. In another she played the dotty maid – skirt up at the front, down at the back, and stockings full of ladders – to a nouveau-riche family, and naturally she got to pour soup all over the guests. In another she played a bow-legged washerwoman. Then, when the audience was least expecting it she would deliver a spot-on aria from *Carmen* or *Rigoletto*, but substituting gobbledygook for the Italian or French phrases she could not remember. One evening, during the interval, she was in her dressing-room having just murdered *Turandot* – not simply getting all the high notes in the right places, but over-reaching them by half an octave, when someone told her that Luisa Tetrazzini was sitting out front. Not only this, the greatest diva of the day had sent her a note, requesting that she sing 'Addio Del Passato' from Verdi's *La Traviata*.

Gracie admitted in her autobiography that she was so nervous that she began the piece two tones too high – in effect, probably two tones higher than Tetrazzini would have been able to sing it herself. She also performed it as if it had been written into the revue – dressed as a charlady who, ending the aria with E above top C, unceremoniously flings her sopping wet dishrag into the audience!

On this occasion the cloth whizzed past Tetrazzini's ear, but the great lady was too moved by Gracie's extraordinary singing technique to notice. The pair met after the show – the diva was dressed in black, and Gracie addressed her constantly as 'ma'am' – posed for photographs, and later exchanged gramophone records. But when Tetrazzini begged Gracie to give up musical comedy and turn herself over to a career on the operatic stage – not the first time this had been suggested to her, and by no means the last – she replied, 'Thank you, ma'am. It's a very nice thought, but I'd sooner stick with the cod-opera I'm used to!'

Gracie's contract with the Lyceum stipulated that she should endorse several products she would not have used in a million years. As an old woman, she had a perfect peaches-and-cream complexion and claimed that this was because she had never put 'muck' on her face. It is therefore extremely doubtful that she would have used any thing as 'fancy' as Pond's Cold Cream. In all the years that she was with her, Irene Bevan gave her regular facial massages with cheap theatrical cream. 'She loved having her face pushed, slapped and pummelled,' Irene said. As for smoking – though she did not mind most of her entourage smoking in her presence, she abhorred the habit – she was photographed blindfolded and holding a Sarony, whilst the blurb declared that she had subjected herself to Test 65, trying five different brands between sips of coffee. Equally contrived was the caption, 'I'm hard to please over cigarettes. When I came across a cigarette during the Blindfold Test – which I really wanted to go on smoking – what else could I say but "This one is best!"?'

Working alongside Annie Lipman in *The Show's the Thing* more or less forced Gracie to contend with her misery. Her moments of true happiness, she maintained, occurred at Tower when she was alone reading the hundreds of fan letters she received each week – once Bert Aza had vetted those demanding money. He even hired a private detective, wisely perhaps, to ascertain which of these were genuine and which were cranks after Gracie sent a cheque to an old lady on the poverty-line who turned out to be a wealthy young man who raced sports cars!

There was another big row with Archie shortly after the revue closed. Gracie stormed out of the house and headed off across Hampstead Heath in a huff. Archie went after her – she took off her mink coat, and flung it at him. Understandably, he was concerned about his wife and her expensive coat, though she viewed things differently. Many years later she told journalist Denis Pitts of the *Sunday People*, 'It was when he picked it up and started brushing the mud off it that I knew exactly what sort of man he was.'

Inevitably, Gracie ended up in John Flanagan's arms, and this time when he asked her to move in with her she complied – taking Auntie Margaret with her to housekeep, though there was barely room in the studio for the two of them. Gracie's stepdaughter Irene was also with her most of the time, and remembered their weekly trips out to Caledonian Market – in order to secure the best bargains they would set off at five in the morning. Amongst the items they purchased for the studio was a huge, elaborately carved antique Dutch dresser. It cost just five pounds, and followed Gracie each time she moved house, creating any number of problems for removal men and interior designers.

A few weeks after moving in with Flanagan, Gracie travelled with him and Henry Savage to Cannes. Recently inducted by them into serious literature, she had just finished reading Norman Douglas's novel *South Wind*, set on the fictitious island of Nepenthe. When her lover pointed out that this was Douglas's name for Capri, the then unspoiled little jewel in the Bay of Naples, she announced that she wanted to go there at once. Neither man had much money, and they accompanied her, albeit reluctantly, when she insisted upon paying for everything. When they reached the Italian border, the ever-scatty Flanagan realized that his papers were not in order. Just as the customs officer was beginning to get stroppy, however, Gracie launched into a chorus of 'Santa Lucia', the only Italian song she could think of on the spur of the moment, instantly drawing a crowd. Money exchanged hands and the officer let them through.

For more than a week the friends explored virtually every inch of Capri, arriving at the Marina Piccola ('Little Seashore') on the very last day. Gracie's close friend and confidante John Taylor told me, 'When she came around that corner, she felt all the cares and worries had gone. I still get that feeling every time I visit.' Gracie herself wrote in her memoirs:

The horse clopped down a long, ever-winding hill. There were few houses. For a while all you could see were the green pine trees, the sprawling flowers and small vineyards. And then we rounded the final curve in the steep hillside and saw a blue bay with cloud-capped mountains towering above it, all the beauty of the island crowding to shelter and frame this one small cove in loveliness. Then I knew that if only one small blade of grass of this gentle, wonderful place could belong to me, I would be happy. This *was* the dream, come true.

Head-over-heels in love with the location, Gracie and Flanagan were invited to dine with the Patrizzis, one of the island's more illustrious families in its pre-society days, at their house, 'Il Fortino' … and they stayed for ten days. Before leaving, Gracie made their teenage son Ettore, the only member of the family with any knowledge of English, promise to contact her the moment a suitable property came up for sale.

In 1930 Gracie made her first trip to the United States, where she had been engaged for a two-week season at the Palace Theatre in New York. She was accompanied by Archie, Irene, Bert Aza and Annie Lipman. For the first three days Gracie felt uncomfortably out of place. On home ground, people were used to seeing her play the fool, but American society did not quite know what to make of her.

At the last moment, Archie had secured her a series of try-outs at Flushing Meadow, as a guest on *The Jack Haley Extravaganza* – the man later immortalized as the Tin Man in *The Wizard of Oz* knew a great deal about the British music-hall, and advised her which songs to choose for her programme. Many years later Gracie remembered the party at Flushing Meadow, thrown in her honour with George Gershwin acting as Master of Ceremonies.

There were lots of film stars there, and he was playing some of his own music on the piano. So I thought, 'I'll just show off and sing it with him!' I started to sing the song with him, and I suddenly got nervous in the middle and forgot every word. He was quite interested in me in the beginning, but when I forgot the words he looked at me with disgust. I felt proper daft!

Playbills for the Palace proclaimed: SEE GRACIE FIELDS – THE FUNNIEST WOMAN IN THE WORLD, and at a time when Fanny Brice was the virtual Queen of Broadway, she knew that she would have to work hard to live up to their expectations. The American promoter had already warned her that audiences might not be able to understand her Lancashire accent, and had even suggested elocution lessons. For Gracie, this was tantamount to sacrilege. 'They'll like me as I am, or lump me!' was her response.

In fact, the New Yorkers liked her very much indeed and thought it hilarious when she strode on to the stage and cut short their applause with her shrill, errand-boy's whistle before yelling, 'Now steady on folks. Wait till you see if I'm worth it before you start clapping!' The editor of *Billboard* was sitting in the front row and wrote:

She has a voice packed tight with soul appeal, the most gorgeous sense of comedy value, and a versatility in delineation rarely combined in one individual. These United States are going to hear plenty more of the Lancashire Lassie!

3

Looking on the Bright Side

When she returned to London, Gracie learned that her future had been decided without her say – or so she said. Archie and Bert Aza had elected for her to make a film. *Sally in Our Alley*, quickly completed in 1931 and co-starring Florence Desmond, was a comedy drama directed by Maurice Elvey and produced by the ubiquitous Basil Dean, a man positively renowned for his complete lack of sense of humour. 'He was a miserable bastard,' Irene Bevan said. 'There's absolutely no other way of describing him. He was thoroughly disliked in the business because he could be so nasty and spiteful. His wife was the ballerina, Victoria Hopper. She used to treat Grace as though she was something the cat had just brought in.'

Gracie hated every minute of this new enterprise – the drive to the Ealing Studios with Archie, always in total silence because there was nothing more to be said, the closed confines of the set, having to get up at six every morning – which reminded her of the days when she had worked at the mill – and not getting to bed until the early hours of the morning, and above all the lack of an audience's response. She told Maud Miller, 'I didn't know if I'd be a flop or not. It wasn't a question of the money. The film companies kept on making me big offers, and I didn't like the idea of them wasting a lot of dough, and then the picture might be a failure, so I agreed to try it and stand or fall by the box-office results.'

In particular Gracie would never forget her first day on the set, when for eight hours she did take after take of an insignificant scene where she had to say, 'Good morning, George!' to a cab driver. She told Basil Dean, point blank, that if he wanted her to continue with

37

the film he would henceforth have to make do with the first or
second take ... or get stuffed! Subsequently she became known in
the trade as 'One Take Joe', and the naturalness and spontaneity is
evident in every one of her films,

Halfway through shooting *Sally in Our Alley* Gracie took an
impromptu break, against Dean's wishes, and did a series of music-
hall appearances. One was at the Metropolitan Theatre in London's
Edgware Road, and it was here that Bill Haines, a composer friend
who owned the Cameo Music Publishing Company and who had
formerly worked as the London Consul for Haiti, offered her 'Mary,
Mary', a song he had written with pals Harry Leon and Leo Towers.
Its original title, 'Gypsy Sweetheart', had been frowned upon as too
kitsch by Haines, and Gracie was not too keen on its present version
either. Several months earlier she had recorded Haines's ''Fonso, My
Hot Spanish Knight', a hilarious number which had them rolling in
the aisles, and she considered Haines more suited to writing comedy
material. On top of this, the French star Mistinguett had a hit at the
time with a song called 'Mary-Marie' so Haines changed the title to
'Sally, Sally'. Though Gracie turned this down too, saying she was
not keen on singing a man's song, she changed her mind when
someone suggested that it would make a good title-track for the film.
The final touch was added one evening at Tower – ironically, it was
Annie Lipman who supplied the song with its last line.

Little did Gracie realize that for the rest of her life she would never
do one single professional engagement without this song being
played or sung – on average, she sang it once every day for another
forty-eight years!

> When skies are blue, you're beguiling,
> And when they're grey you're still smiling!
> Sally! Sally! Pride of our alley!
> You're more than the whole world to me!

Like Marlene Dietrich, who told me many times how much she
had hated her theme-song, 'Falling In Love Again', Gracie frequently
said that she disliked 'Sally' because of the film which had
introduced it. 'It made me millions, but I still want to bury it. Five
hundred songs in my repertoire, and they still ask me to sing the
bugger!' she would say. One of its first public airings was in May
1931 when she made her second appearance in a Royal Variety

Show. Sadly, it overshadowed the other songs in the film, particularly 'Lancashire Blues', which she composed under the pseudonym, Stana Fields. 'Give me some clogs and you can keep all yer shoes,' she trills working behind her counter, serving waffles and hot-pot. Over the years, 'Stana Fields' would come up with several memorable lyrics, including those to the English versions of 'The Song Of the Mountains' and 'Core 'Ngrato'. The film was of course a little gem, and is still considered by many of Gracie's fans to be the best she ever made.

Like many of the great *réaliste* entertainers on the Continent, Gracie was only content to play down-to-earth, honest working-class girls like herself. Sally is a singer-waitress in a rough navvies' café somewhere in a London slum who persistently turns down marriage proposals from her boss because she is waiting for her fiancé to return from the Great War. When he does come home, lamed, he is ensnared by a local slut (Florence Desmond), whose mind is 'warped by her father's cruelty'. She forces Sally into breaking off their engagement by enticing the young man to visit the smoky dive with her, whilst Sally is on stage. The smoke effect, in the days before dry ice, was achieved by setting a pile of brown paper alight, then sprinkling it with water so that it would smoulder. The stench and fumes from this made everyone on the set cough and splutter so much that there had to be over twenty takes of the song. This was why she disliked it so.

Gracie also condemned Florence Desmond for being such a snob, though they later became on-the-surface friends. Their antagonism began one day during a break in filming, when the studio provided everyone with afternoon tea which they ate on their laps. Irene Bevan remembered, 'Florence asked them to take the bread and butter back, saying she only ate brown bread. That stuck in Grace's gullet. It was something quite silly, but it gives a good insight into her weird outlook on life, and the way she had been brought up. "Stuck up so-and-so. White bread's not good enough for *her*. Who does she think she is?"'

It was at around this time that Gracie took her stepdaughter on a trip to sample some of the more 'cultured' delights of Paris, the first of many trips to the city she loved, certainly in those days, more than any other. Here, the young woman discovered yet another of Grace's 'talents'.

Grace had a smuggling complex. We used to go to a very posh shop on the Champs-Elysées where they made the most beautiful hand-laced satin underwear. She would buy a dozen sets for each of us, then we would put them on and sneak through customs. Similarly, whenever we went to Southern Ireland, she would buy Tussor silk for 1s.6d. a yard – a whole roll of this 'stuff' as she called it, then wrap half of it around me, the other half around herself. Then we would put our Scotch kilts on top, and smuggle it out. Both of us could quite easily have declared it and paid the duty, but she found it much more fun that way. I always ended up shaking like a leaf, but I did it, for sheer devilment!

It was also at this time that Gracie met Harry Parr-Davies, who was to become her exceptional young accompanist – exceptional in that in spite of her infuriating habit of suddenly changing key in the middle of the trickiest arrangement just to put her pianist off, he never once failed to keep up with her.

Born in Neath, Swansea in 1914, this temperamental individual – who had an utter lack of subtlety and manners when, according to Gracie, he was feeling 'that road out', which seemed to be most of the time – had learned to play the piano at six. Now, eleven years later he barged past the doorman at the Blackpool Opera House, stormed into Gracie's dressing-room without knocking, and announced that he wanted to play for her. She was so taken aback by his arrogance, not to mention his pasty, spotty complexion and thick-lensed spectacles, that she invited him to sit at her piano and play several of her songs. Harry's talent amazed her, even more so when he played some of his own compositions – she employed him there and then, not just as her accompanist but as a songwriter. His greatest test came the next evening, when he took his place amongst the other musicians in the orchestra pit ... there were complaints from the audience, who wanted to see what this brilliant pianist looked like!

Some years later, Gracie admitted ruefully what she had said to the manager of the Opera House: 'I'll give the lad a break. I'll bring him up on the stage. Nobody that looks like him could be a rival to me!' The young man became so paralysed with stagefright that at first he was unable to play a note – before Gracie had finished her opening number he was back in the orchestra pit, though he did eventually emerge to accompany her on the stage, brilliantly, for another ten years. He supplied her with some of her most celebrated songs, including 'Sing As We Go', 'Pedro the Fisherman', 'My Love For You' and 'The Sweetest Song in the World'.

The last revue Gracie ever did, *Walk This Way*, was written and produced by Archie Pitt, and opened at the Winter Garden on 17 December 1931. Her co-stars included Morris Harvey and her brother Tommy, and Duggie Wakefield and Irene, who sang a duet, 'Round About the Middle of June'. Irene recalled that,

> Duggie and I had a terrible row, though we soon made up. During that scene I had to smack his face, but I could never get used to my hand doing one thing and the noise coming from somewhere else, so I kept sloshing him for real until he complained to my father that I was hurting him. There was also the suspicion that Grace was having an affair with Morris Harvey, who was a great many years older than her, though we never got to know the truth about that one.

Some critics, seeing Gracie dressed as a Pearly Queen for the 'Way Down East' sketch, compared her not with the more obvious Marie Lloyd, but with the great French turn-of-the century singer Yvette Guilbert. The photographs do reveal a curious resemblance. The main feature, cleverly devised and choreographed by Archie was 'The Doll and Golliwog Ballet', with Irene playing Doll, and Gracie looking very attractive as Pierrot. The chorus girls came on in white oilcloth dresses, each one accompanied by an artist with a palette. Whilst Gracie was executing a nifty clog-dance and singing 'The Clatter of the Clogs, the painters turned their backs to the audience and covered the girls' dresses in flowers, which were of course washed off after the show. Later, Gracie sang 'Home, Sweet Home' to Tommy Fields, who played her son. The anonymous reviewer from *The Play Pictorial* was enthusiastic:

> ... She is the cynosure of all eyes, when her every movement is watched with rapt attention, when every inflexion of her inflexible voice pierces the auditorium with irresistible effect, and when her meaning, be it broad or subtle, is as patent as stars in frosty weather. In her characterization she is as variable as the chameleon and as rapid as the swallow, and her

portraiture has the accuracy of the camera. No wonder she has captured the British public of all class, from Mayfair to Mile End.

Sally in Our Alley, meanwhile, was a tremendous hit with the box office – catapulting Gracie to the position of Britain's top film actress. The primary reason for its success was that its star was playing an extension of herself, which made up for the feeble storyline. She later said that she was disappointed with her triumph because it meant that there would have to be another film. There was: Basil Dean's *Looking on the Bright Side* was made in 1932, under conditions much more harrowing for her than its predecessor.

In it Gracie played a manicurist who is in love with an impoverished songwriter. One evening they overhear a couple arguing, and when the girl says, 'I'm not giving you a second chance. After tonight, we say goodbye!', Gracie tells the songwriter this would make a good title for a song; the ensuing number earns him a fortune – and he dumps her to go off in search of the social whirl. Not to be outdone, Gracie the manicurist begins a new career – as a bungling policewoman! There is reality towards the end of the film, however, when she declares – almost proclaiming what might have been her own epitaph: 'Look at me. I've got what I wanted – success. I can have beautiful clothes, lots of money, everything I wish for. So what do I care about love? I'm … perfectly happy!'

For the film, Basil Dean commissioned the largest film set that had ever been seen in a British studio – a tenement block called Parker's Peace – and Gracie complained of getting corns by being made to climb its precipitous exterior stairs every morning, several times, for two months. She later commented that the first time she saw the finished film, at its Dublin première, her knees gave way as she rose from her seat after watching herself climb all those steep steps again!

Looking on the Bright Side was given a sublimely optimistic theme song by Howard Flynn. After several years of serious illness and deafness, including a twenty-month stay in hospital after a brush with death, Flynn wrote the words when he was hospitalized again and awaiting a delicate operation to restore his hearing.

> I'm waiting for the right tide,
> And if luck comes to my aid,
> Giving me a break,

I shall be awake,
Looking on the bright side of life!

Like Gracie's first film, this one was a mighty hit, for in a Britain crippled by recession and unemployment, she was exactly the tonic any doctor would have prescribed to cheer everyone up, though she herself had felt down in the dumps whilst making the film. She then announced that she was going to cheer herself up by leaving her husband for good – a big risk to take as far as her career was concerned, but ultimately necessary, for they had long since reached the end of their particular road.

After completing the film, Gracie and Flanagan travelled to Dublin. She had recently bought a 16mm movie camera, but after bungling an attempt to film her sister Edith's baby son, Douglas, she had given the apparatus up as a bad job and passed it on to Flanagan. He was not much more adept with it than she had been, though using it did lead to perhaps the most rewarding project of his career.

From Dublin, the couple moved West to Donegal Bay, where they rented a cottage near the sea – originally for one week, though they were so enchanted by the beautiful, unspoilt romantic location that they stayed on for another month, and would have stayed longer had it not been for Gracie's contractual obligations back home. Later that year Gracie and Flanagan returned to Donegal, accompanied by Henry Savage and a professional film crew to shoot *Riders to the Sea*, Flanagan's much-praised documentary, produced by him, directed by Savage, and financed by Gracie. One of the twenty-five locals who appeared in the film was Maire O'Neill, who a few years later played Gracie's landlady in *Sing As We Go*.

Back in London, Gracie fooled the press into believing that she was not living with John Flanagan by informing them that he had moved out and the studio in St John's Wood now belonged to her. And, with Auntie Margaret serving tea and sandwiches, she gave reporters the impression that she was leading a life of quaint respectability. All evidence of Flanagan had been moved into the bedrooms, but he was forever leaving tell-tale effects in the studio, so photographs were forbidden, in case something showed up on them, such as her lover's favourite mug or book. 'It looked like a good storage place for potatoes,' she reminisced. 'It had a stone floor, and a little alcove where there was a bath and a cooker. When you didn't need the bath, you covered it with boards and used it for a table.' However, when the press criticized her for wanting to live in such humble surroundings when, not even taking into account her earnings from her films and a hefty share in their profit, she was netting over £600 a week, she had the place carpeted, bought an expensive piano, and replaced all her cheap prints with authentic paintings. All these changes are said to have displeased Flanagan – it was, after all, an artist's studio and *his* place of work.

It was at this time that Gracie purchased her first car. Irene Bevan told me, with a shudder, 'She bought this enormous white Ford Coupé which she learned to drive with me sitting beside her. Going round and around Regent's Park with her, I've never been so frightened in all my life!' Gracie often repeated the story of how she was driving back to St John's Wood one afternoon when the car ran out of petrol. Leaving the car at the side of the road, she flagged down the first bus that came along – one which was not going to her part of town. The driver recognized her and insisted upon dropping her off near her door; the other passengers were so intrigued that they stayed put until the end of the journey, when Gracie invited everyone into the studio for a sandwich and 'a sup', and the obligatory singalong! 'She would invite anybody home,' Irene said. 'We went to dinner once at a Russian restaurant in Regent's Street, and she brought the entire orchestra home with her – eight or nine Cossacks. She loved impromptu arrangements!'

Soon after acquiring her car, Gracie received a letter from Ettore Patrizzi in Capri, informing her that the family's house, the very one she had stayed in with John Flanagan, had been put on the market. The asking price, which she could not afford, was £15,000. Even so, she sent out an architect to look things over, and when he saw the condition of the ramshackle buildings he persuaded the vendors to drop the price to £11,000. A subsequent Italian lawyer's report, however, suggested that it was not even worth this amount.

Confident that she was doing the right thing, Gracie left for a tour of Northern England which culminated in one of her 'Rochdale Weeks'. These were annual events during the thirties, usually taking place in March, which raised many thousands of pounds for local charities. There were twice-nightly concerts at the Hippodrome, visits to all the local hospitals and children's homes, and the week ended with the Mayor's Ball. The most important things in the world, Gracie often said, were God, the King and Queen and the

Mayor of Rochdale – in that order. She also donated large, though unspecified, amounts of money to the town's poor and unemployed. This particular visit was filmed by J J Thomas, a local chemist. When Gracie made her appearance on the Town Hall balcony, someone yelled up from the 30,000-strong crowd – referring to a scene from *Looking on the Bright Side* – 'Where's yer yo-yo, Gracie?' She bawled back, 'I've had it stuffed!'

Whilst in Rochdale, where she was staying at the house of a friend called Bertha Schofield, Gracie received a telegram informing her that Il Fortino, along with its land and stretch of beach, were hers – bought on her behalf in an auction, no one having matched her anonymous bid. The deal left her with just £25 in the bank. Typically, Gracie was terrified of telegrams and went into the kitchen to brew a pot of tea leaving Bertha to open it. Jenny Stansfield knew nothing of the bid, and Bertha's reaction was, 'Tha's better be careful how that tells thee mother, or she'll gi' thee a reet good clout round t'ear-hole!' Immediately, Gracie began fretting that she had done the wrong thing. Supposing her career folded suddenly? Or worse still, what if her voice packed up? Though she could never vouch for the former continuing at its current pace, according to the legend she let out a lengthy top C in Bertha Schofield's kitchen which rattled the window-frames and convinced her – and the entire street – that she could still sing!

Irene Bevan spoke of the tremendous prejudice encountered by Gracie from her family and friends at this time.

When Grace said she was going to live in Italy, they told her she needed certifying. It was pure xenophobia. They just could not understand why anyone should want to live amongst foreigners. And they *never* got used to her living there. Their attitude towards her had been the same as hers had been towards Florence Desmond and the brown bread. 'Who does she think she is? Isn't England good enough?' You must remember you're talking about a time when going to Italy was comparable to going to Polynesia, today. People didn't read books, not the sort of people she came from. They didn't know what the Isle of Capri was, or *South Wind* [the novel]. They were *horrified*! And Bertha Schofield was a dreadful woman, the very worst type of Lancashire – loud-mouthed, very crude. She always rubbed me up the wrong way because I was well-educated. I was regarded as posh, and this used to annoy them to death. The Jewish side they also disliked, and the fact that I was the daughter of a divorced man. It's what I call mother's-milk anti-Semitism, and it was bred into them. Then to top it all, Grace told them that she was very seriously thinking of becoming a Catholic, on account of John Flanagan and her affinity with things Irish. She liked the religion, she said, because it was colourful and emotional. Her family went mad!

When Gracie returned to London, Bert Aza told her that Archie had successfully negotiated a contract worth £72,000 for six films to be made over a six-year period. The snag was that she would be working for her husband again and, in her eyes, being manipulated by him, after she had fought so hard for her independence.

Gracie's problem was inadvertently solved by John Flanagan. When she rushed home bursting with her good news, she found him in the company of Henry Savage, and he gave her his good news. That afternoon the friends had been to a local market bargain-hunting, and they had acquired a tiny figurine for just four shillings – it now sat proudly on the Dutch dresser. Reflecting how her happiest moment had been when she had signed the cheque for her 'shack' in Capri, Gracie said, 'A few shillings could buy happiness for them, but seventy-two thousand pounds was going to buy me nothing but misery.' Thus, whilst admitting that she must be mad to do so, she rejected Archie's offer and asked Bert Aza to find her a more suitable alternative. Archie's daughter remembered the parting of the ways.

John Flanagan and Henry Savage urged her to break away from my father completely – they'd both left Tower by this time, and he was having a new house built in Frognal. Grace met him in the street and told him, 'I want nothing more to do with you. No more contracts.' He didn't know what had hit him. I think Bert Aza advised him to make some other arrangement with her, but he was too obstinate to do such a thing. He also thought that I should have walked out on her, and I didn't. I was very fond of her and my husband was working for her, so my being with her after they'd separated caused more bad blood. There wasn't any violent animosity between them. He was more upset and destroyed than annoyed. He had made her the star she was, and this was her way of thanking him.

Several days later, RK0 Pictures offered Gracie £20,000 to star in *This Week of Grace*, directed by Julius Hagen and with an appearance by Gracie's brother-in-law Duggie Wakefield. As with the previous films, she found it an ordeal, only made bearable, she said, because she was able to study her snapshot album of Capri between takes. As soon as the film was finished, she told Bert Aza quite categorically that she would never make another. This of course only increased her market value and had directors clamouring to work with her.

Shortly after completing *This Week of Grace*, Gracie and John Flanagan visited Marie Dubas in Paris. Here she was escorted to Chez Kornilof, a Russian-styled cabaret-restaurant which, though the 'in place' for émigré entertainers such as Marlene Dietrich and Josephine Baker, was not entirely respectable. One of the regulars – the ariste-in-residence at the gay-patronized Jockey Club, which Gracie visited several times – was the outrageous Kiki de Montparnasse, a phenomenally gifted chanteuse who quite possibly remains the most vulgar woman to have ever appeared on a music-hall stage.

Almost as controversial was the great Russian bass, Fyodor Chaliapin. Then in his sixties and coming towards the end of his mighty career, Chaliapin had a fondness for teenage boys, though when Gracie me him at Chez Kornilof he was with his common-law wife, Damia, one of the most important popular singers of her type in Europe before Piaf.

This was a significant but little-known meeting. Nine years older than Gracie, Marie-Louise Damien had begun her career at London's Savoy Hotel in 1909, dancing the apache with Max Dearly. Her singing career had taken off a few years later, but although the most popular star in France by the onset of the First World War, she had not cut her first record until 1926. With a deep, powerful and guttural voice – maintained, she claimed with a daily fix of cocaine and sixty Gauloises – Damia sang songs of such dramatic intensity that several of them, including her million-selling duet with Chaliapin, 'Gloomy Sunday', were banned in Britain and the United States. She performed several of Gracie's songs in French, including 'Because I Love You' and 'Crying for the Carolines', but never got around to recording them.

When Marie Dubas took Gracie to see Damia's recital at the Eldorado during the summer of 1933, Gracie fell in love with two of songs, 'Ne Dit Rien' and 'Chantez Pour Moi, Violons', and asked the singer's permission to sing them. No one else would have *dared* do such a thing, and Gracie was of course unaware of the unwritten laws of the French music-hall, otherwise she would never have asked. Although an extremely friendly woman, highly respected by her peers, Damia was so all-powerful that no one was allowed to sing her songs until six months after she had recorded them – and as she either recorded them several years after introducing them, or not at all, she managed to keep most of them exclusive. Nevertheless, she offered Gracie both songs. 'Ne Dit Rien' became 'Worryin'', which was sung but never recorded, and the other song became 'Play, Fiddle, Play'. The first time Damia heard it, she called Gracie and announced, 'That is the finest *English* song I have ever heard!'

> Now the gypsy band rest their caravan
> Where a hill conceals the sun,
> Dusky magic falls,
> Gypsy magic calls to lovers one by one,
> The campfires are gleaming as red as the sun,
> And my heart is dreaming, just dreaming,
> So softly play, fiddle play ...

During a subsequent visit to Paris – one which found her spending more time with Damia and Chaliapin – the Russian told Gracie how he had come to fall in love with the much younger chanteuse. He had visited Paris in 1917, at the time when she had been running her own cabaret in Montmartre, the Concert-Damia, and one day he had seen her photograph in a *bistrot* window, autographed simply, 'Alsace-Lorraine' (Damia had been born in the province, which still belonged to Germany – it was restored to France in 1918). For months, Chaliapin had carried the picture around in his pocket, lovesick and mindless of the young man who accompanied him everywhere, until someone had put a name to the face. Gracie found the story touching, and more than a little unusual, and she asked a songwriter friend to put Chaliapin's 'confession' to music. The result was one of her lesser-known but loveliest songs, within which she adopts the guise of the man who is expressing his joy to a friend.

Like a haunting refrain,
She found the key to my heart.
Her photograph, in a frame,
Is signed without any name,
It reads 'Alsace-Lorraine' ...

On her return to England, and content that she was 'back in business', Gracie put the Peacehaven house – the first one Archie had bought for her parents – on the market, then set about transferring the contents of John Flanagan's studio to Capri. She involved almost all her family in the move – Irene Bevan described this hilarious episode.

It cost £5,000 to move everything, which was then an awful lot of money. The family and the furniture, including that enormous dresser, all arrived at the same time. In those days there was no road, and everything had to be taken to the Piccola Marina by boat – you can imagine all this furniture sloshing around in the bottom of a boat, and Jenny Stansfield standing up there on top of those rocks, supervising the whole thing and screaming in broad Lancashire at the Italian removal men who were trying to get the piano up the side of the cliff!

Of course, when Gracie asked for everyone's opinion about her new abode, she got it. Her sisters, Edith and Betty, wanted to know why she could not have done like any 'normal' star and bought a nice little semi in Brighton. Jenny was worried about the island being too close to Mount Vesuvius, and she could not cope with spaghetti, garlic, and the fact that the Italians seemed to cook everything in olive oil. She 'triumphed' over the locals, however, when she taught several housewives how to cook Yorkshire pudding, dumplings and gravy! Fred complained that he could not get a decent pint of ale for love or money, called everyone 'Eye-Tie', and accused the workmen who were renovating the house of shirking, so much so that they downed tools, leaving Fred to finish most of the jobs himself. 'There wasn't any fresh water on Capri,' Irene explained, 'so rather than pay for it to be brought in, Fred mixed the cement with sea-water. A few months later it started to seep out of the walls, so the Italian workmen were brought back in.'

Meanwhile, back in Sussex, Gracie's house remained unsold, and now that she was no longer short of funds she joined forces with her friend Lottie Albert of the Theatrical Ladies' Guild (subsequently called the Variety Ladies' Guild), and turned the house into the Gracie Fields Home and Orphanage for the children of deceased or impoverished actors. The home's dictum was 'We aim to keep, clothe and educate the needy children of professional people until they reach an age where they are capable of looking after themselves – to give them a happier, sunnier outlook on life after they leave it to make room for other little ones.'

Gracie's entire family attended the opening ceremony, along with fellow music-hall stars Charles Coburn and Robb Wilton. Whenever she visited her parents' house, at Telscombe, Gracie was able to drop in on her many 'nephews and nieces' – eight, when the home opened in 1933, though soon there would be a regular number of twenty-five until 1967 when it closed – thankfully no longer a viable concern because of a shortage of patrons. 'It's the best investment I ever made,' she would say time and time again. 'Forget the cynics. Money really *can* buy you happiness!'

4

If I Should Fall in Love Again

A few months after the inauguration of her orphanage, Gracie returned to Capri. Il Fortino was still a mess because the renovations were taking longer than she had anticipated, and by the end of her first week on the island she had developed itchy feet. Irene Bevan was there with her husband Lou Ross.

> She was terribly, terribly restless. Suddenly, in the middle of the night she said, 'Let's go to San Remo!' We stayed there for twenty-four hours, if that, and she said, 'Let's go to Cannes!' After one night at the Carleton she said, 'I want to go back to England – we'll stop off in Paris!' By the time we got to England it was Derby Day, so she wanted to go to the Derby. John [Flanagan] hired a three-wheeled Morgan to drive us there. The rest of us were worn out by then, but she had this absolutely wild energy. Then when we finally got back to Capri she had me up at two in the morning, helping her to shift the piano!

Although Gracie had vowed never to make another film, even she could not sensibly turn down he £30,000 she was offered for her next two films. The first of these, *Sing As We Go*, was scripted by J B Priestley, who had dined with her and John Flanagan after one of her shows. Completely captivated, he wrote in his famous book, *English Journey*,

> Listen to her for a quarter of an hour and you will learn more about Lancashire women and Lancashire than you would from a dozen books on these subjects. All the qualities are there:

shrewdness, homely simplicity, irony, fierce independence and an impish delight in mocking whatever is thought to be affected and pretentious.

Many of Gracie's fans regard *Sing As We Go*, which co-starred the tall, dashing John Loder, as the funniest film she ever made. It was shot mostly on location in Blackpool, then as now Britain's most popular holiday resort, and the occasion justifiably forms part of the Golden Mile's history. Everything and everyone was placed at Gracie's disposal: amusement parks and funfairs, the Tower and town band, the Mayor and corporation, much of the police force. In anticipating that the pubs would stay empty during the lunchtime period when Gracie was around, the licencees successfully applied for an extension of drinking hours until midnight.

Blackpool had always been Gracie's favourite spot in England, as her stepdaughter remembered.

Whenever we were in Blackpool, there would always be a bandcall at the theatre every Monday morning. Then it would be off to the fairgound at South Shore. We would hire yama-yama suits to prevent us from getting dirty and splintered, and go on *everything*. Before she became really famous, Gracie's one desire was to travel, and even in 1934 she thought the only way she would ever get around the world would be as a dumb-act – so she fixed things for us to have acrobatic lessons! A well-known dumb-act in those days was the Bolton Brothers, and every day for weeks we watched them in rehearsal and tried to do back-flips, chucks and fly-overs. She was so agile, she could do almost anything. But can you imagine Gracie Fields as a dumb-act? She had absolutely no idea of her own value!

The journalist Hannen Swaffer, then recovering from a nervous breakdown, had been sent to Blackpool for a week's respite by his newspaper. Known as 'The Pope of Fleet Street', Swaffer was yet another snobbish individual who had been slapped publicly by Tallulah Bankhead, who had once warned Gracie to steer clear of him when he had wanted to interview her in London. A skeletal man who usually wore a flowing scarf and wide-brimmed hat, Swaffer was often very scathing when writing about the North of England, and Gracie in particular. When he discovered that he had been booked into the same hotel as her – the Metropole – he declared that this would prove suitably anodyne for any ailment, and over the next few weeks ignored his fatigue to become a Gracie 'groupie', chronicling her stay in Blackpool and the nearest he came to sniping at her was when he told his readers in the *Daily Express*: 'Gracie Fields is the quintessence of Lancashire. Behind all her crudity of utterance there is a great character and a surprisingly abundant humour.'

The irrepressible Swaffer was amongst the crowd of 30,000 who cheered her arrival at the railway station, and was one of those who rose at five one morning to watch her character, Gracie Platts, 'arrive'. In the film Gracie is employed at Rochdale's Grey Beck Mill, and lives with her drunken Uncle Murgatroyd and carping Aunt Alice in a house full of broken clocks. 'Even t'clocks are on strike,' she says when the mill closes and she sets off to look for work in Blackpool. To save money, she cycles all the way there. Wearing ridiculous shorts, a knapsack, and carrying an assortment of pots and pans she stops to ask the way from a policeman played by Stanley Holloway, and, referring to that actor's famous comic song, says to him, 'All right, Sam. Pick up yer musket', gets into a muddle and almost collides with a tram. So many people turned up to watch this one-minute scene that the police had to hold up the traffic, and the backlog took most of the day to clear. After the cameras stopped rolling, a kindly landlady invited Gracie into her house for tea – when told that the woman's eighty-five-year-old father was upstairs waiting to be introduced, Gracie cracked, 'You'd better be careful I don't run off with him!'

Gracie also refused to hand the bicycle back to the property department. 'I'm the one who's got blisters on my behind from riding the blessed thing. I'm keeping it!' she told Basil Dean. The following day she raffled it off and gave the £250 proceeds to a local children's home.

During the course of the film, Gracie's character bungles several jobs – lodging-house maid, fortune-teller, song demonstrator, magician's assistant, toffee-seller and human spider – sparking off a hilarious chase around the funfair which ends with her falling into the water-tank during the finale of the circus show at the Tower Circus. This scene had to be filmed on a Sunday, traditionally the day the establishment was closed to the public. A sign was hung on the door advertising for extras: COME AND BE FILMED WITH GRACIE!

The queues began forming at six o'clock in the morning and hundreds of people were still there twenty-two hours later. Five thousand fans were admitted to the Tower Ballroom itself, at a cost of one shilling each, and there was not one complaint that, unlike in America where extras got paid one actually had to pay to be in a film with Our Gracie ... and sat there watching twenty-four liberty horses, a pair of elephants dressed up with stick, hat and feathers to resemble Charlie Chaplin and Josephine Baker, and enjoying the spectacle of a dripping wet Gracie singing 'In My Little Bottom Drawer'.

> One bridal gown, one eiderdown,
> I've been saving 'em since eighteen-ninety-four!
> Got me ribbons and me bows,
> And me these and thems and those,
> All packed up in me little bottom drawer!

The film ended, typically, with Gracie losing her ex-boss and the man she has loved from afar (Loder) to her prettier friend, Phyllis (Dorothy Hyson), who has just won a beauty contest, but compensation comes when the mill re-opens and he promotes her to welfare officer – as the credits roll, Gracie leads her workmates through the factory gates whilst they belt out the title-song.

One day during filming, Gracie told the ever-bubbly John Loder that Basil Dean's morose expression during some of her funniest scenes was 'putting the pobs' on her. The actor suggested that she get to know the comic-actor-director Monty Banks, with whom he had worked on another film. She was interested, especially as her sister Betty had appeared in a Monty Banks comedy, but for the time being she put off meeting him because she and John Flanagan were by this time living in an almost empty studio, waiting to move into yet another new house.

Greentrees was an impressive building on London's Finchley Road whose staff comprised Auntie Margaret – who soon afterwards would return to Rochdale to wed her undertaker fiancé – an Irish gardener named Seamus and an Italian maid, Flo-Flo, and Gracie's companion helpmate, Mary Barratt. Mary was a Northern fan who for several years had been companion to an eccentric old lady. Her friendship with Gracie developed when she began writing to her, informing her of her charge's antics, and the pair had met in

An early publicity shot. (*John Taylor*)

With Sir Gerald du Maurier in *SOS*,
St James's Theatre, London, 1928.
(*Morris Aza*)

'Doing me bit'. In her early days, Gracie worked hard to make
ends meet, touring by night and 'skivvying' at her lodgings by day.
(*John Taylor*)

Gracie and Archie Pitt, looking rather glum during the tour of *Mr Tower of London*, 1922. (*Morris Aza*)

In *Walk This Way*, 1931. (*John Taylor*)

Gracie and Archie's wedding day, Clapham Register Office, 1923. (*Morris Aza*)

Gracie, Archie and Archie's daughter Irene, 1924. (*Jacqueline Swain*)

Gracie and John Flanagan en route for Capri, 1931. (*Morris Aza*)

Gracie's manager, Bert Aza (*left*), with John Flanagan in Capri circa 1935. (*Morris Aza*)

(*From left*) Bert Aza, Irene Bevan, Annie Lipman, Gracie and Archie on board the *Berengaria*, bound for Gracie's first season at the Palace Theatre in New York, 1930. (*Morris Aza*)

In her 'I'm Shy, Mary Ellen' pose.
(*John Taylor*)

Gracie's mother, Jenny Stansfield, at
Peacehaven in 1935. (*Morris Aza*)

Gracie with her parents, Fred and Jenny Stansfield, on the day in
February 1938 that Gracie was awarded the CBE. (*Morris Aza*)

The cast and crew of *Riders to the Sea*, filmed on location in Donegal in 1932. Gracie, wearing a checked scarf, stands to the right of Henry Savage, the director, while John Flanagan is seen seated far right with a stick. The star of the film, Maire O'Neill (in front of Gracie), later played the landlady in *Sing As We Go*. (*Morris Aza*)

Irene's wedding to Lou Ross in the early 1930s, with everyone strangely out of place. *Back row*: Hilda Finberg (Archie's sister), Bert Aza (Archie's brother), Lillian Aza and Douglas Wakefield (Edith's husband). *Front row*: Edith Fields, Gracie, Dorothy Fields (Tommy's wife), Lou Ross, Irene and Archie. (*Morris Aza*)

Gracie's Hollywood wedding to Monty Banks, April 1940. Douglas Fairbanks Jr is seen to the right of the bride. (*John Taylor*)

Tommy Fields, Gracie and Douglas Wakefield. (*John Taylor*)

A rare Hollywood publicity shot, 1936. (*John Taylor*)

With Victor McLaglen in 1937 during the filming of *We're Going To Be Rich*. (*John Taylor*)

Gracie among her many 'nephews and nieces', the children of deceased or impoverished actors to whom she gave a home at her orphanage at Peacehaven. (*John Taylor*)

Blackpool at the time of *Sing As We Go*, greeting each other like long-lost relatives, since which time the old lady had died and Mary had come to work for her idol.

Although she had loathed the expensive elegance of Tower, Gracie spent a great deal of money refurbishing Greentrees. Its most opulent feature was the drawing-room, which was turned into a 'Fatty-Do' room a Lancashire term referring to the grand meal usually served in the best-furnished room of a house after a wedding or funeral – with white furniture and fittings, a deep-pile yellow carpet, and a huge white grand piano. The pièce-de-resistance, which in those days was very unusual, was the huge tropical aquarium set into the wall, the first thing visitors saw upon entering the room. However, when she saw how nice the interior designers had made the room, Gracie put her foot down and refused to allow anyone inside it in case they got everything dirty! She bought a second piano for the dining-room because the workmen could not budge the first one, then bought a *third* one for the library because none of her guests ever bothered with books, and a *fourth* piano for her bedroom! By this time there was nowhere for people to eat, so she removed the original piano from the 'Fatty-Do' room and installed a billiard table and cocktail bar. Finally, she stocked the garden pond not with expensive Koi carp, as someone suggested, but with goldfish because she said they reminded her of the fairground she had visited as a child. In the garden she planted hundreds of her favourite tiger-lilies – though as Irene Bevan commented drily, 'They were only her favourite flowers after she'd seen how they turned out. In those early days she would have been hard-put to know the difference between a tiger-lily and a cabbage!'

From the point of view of her relationship with John Flanagan, Greentrees was a bad move for Gracie. No sooner had the dust-wraps been lifted than she was trying to tie him down, buying him costly presents he did not need, and generally treating him as if they were married. She also tried what on the face of it seemed like another scheme, though she was being desperately sincere. Irene Bevan says, 'Grace was always keen to have a child of her own – not with my father, but with John Flanagan. When nothing happened, I actually took her to see my Austrian doctor in Hampstead. After examining her he said there was no reason why she shouldn't have a baby. She was perfectly healthy.'

But Gracie took the news badly – henceforth her relationship with

Flanagan would disintegrate as quickly as it had begun. During one
of her trips to Paris, it is thought most likely at the Jockey Club, she
had met a young man named Philippe Vierchy, of whom almost
nothing is known save that he was an artist friend of Kiki de
Montparnasse, extremely good-looking and in the latter stages of
consumption.

Exactly where and when Gracie met Vierchy again is not known,
other than it was somewhere in London – this much she confided in
her stepdaughter – and without wasting any time he whisked her to
Paris, to live with him in his tiny apartment just behind Avenue
Rachel, in Pigalle. 'She rang home to say that they were going to live
for ever in a garret up by the Sacré-Coeur,' Irene said. 'Of course, I
knew that she would soon be back and that she wouldn't *really* give
up her career.'

For several weeks Gracie and her handsome lover were invited to
the most important artistes' meeting-places in Paris: Gerny's, where
Edith Piaf would make her début a few months later; Chez Kornilof;
Liberty's, run by the infamous drag-queen, Milady Patate, where
they shared a table with Maurice Chevalier and Mistinguett; and La
Vie Parisienne, the notorious nightclub on the rue St-Anne founded
by the great chanteuse Suzy Solidor, who fifteen years later would
disgust Gracie by having an affair with a high-ranking Nazi official.
Gracie's idyll, however, was tragically short-lived when Vierchy
suddenly contracted pneumonia. Within three days he was dead.
Gracie attended the funeral at the Cimetière Montmartre, then,
having realized what a fool she had been to wish to throw everything
away that she had worked for she returned to England, where she
promptly flung herself back into John Flanagan's arms as though
nothing had happened.

Gracie's next film, again opposite John Loder, was *Love, Life and
Laughter*, directed by Maurice Elvey. Loder played a prince in a
carnival procession who is smitten by Gracie's Nell Gwynn, when
she throws an orange at him. They fall in love, but she loses him to
a beautiful princess. Although the critics did not consider it one of
her best films, they unanimously applauded its closing scene, where
in the Nell Gwynn Children's Home she sang the title-song with a
group of children from her own orphanage.

In 1935, Archie Pitt arranged Gracie's first season at the London
Palladium – in spite of their split and her vow never to work with
him again, even she could not reject an offer from a theatre which,

then as now, was the most prestigious in England. The manager, George Black, had first seen her in Barrow-in-Furness when she had been touring with *The Show's the Thing*, and he wrote a long article in the *Sunday Chronicle* – trying but failing to explain what he called 'the secret of her charm and power'. Halfway through her act, whilst the audience were applauding, she suddenly turned her back on them and walked to the back of the stage. Maintaining this position, she began one of the most genuinely heartbreaking songs she ever sang. 'Three Green Bonnets' told the simple story of three sisters who, by end of the song, are devastated when one of them is stolen by the angels. Gracie had originally recorded the piece to a roistering organ accompaniment by Herbert Dawson, and listening to it even now, dated as it sounds, brings a lump to the throat. Little wonder then that George Black often said he had never been able to get over it. He later recalled the scene in his memoirs:

She turned her head, then her body, and began to walk slowly down the stage, singing. The house was hushed, breathless. As the last notes died away I heard a gasp. I, who had been a hardboiled showman since boyhood and thought I knew all the tricks of the trade, felt what the audience felt. This was blazing sincerity – a heart speaking to the hearts of the world.

Later in the show, Gracie appeared with the Crazy Gang, where she devised a sketch entitled 'Crazy Gang Display'. Each of the legendary troupe 'donated' an item of clothing . . . with Grace wearing Chesney Allen's shirt, Bud Flanagan's hat, Jimmy Nervo's boots, and Eddie Gray's jacket, they all crooned 'Little Man, You've Had a Busy Day'. She also raised a few eyebrows with 'What Can You Buy a Nudist For His Birthday?'

I have heard they play hockey,
So something I had got,
But I don't know for certain
If they wear shin-guards or not!
A shopgirl told me spats'd be all wrong,
She said, 'Good gracious, madam!
Just imagine spats on Adam!
And a watch-chain would look silly,
Draped across the front of Willie!'

Working with the Crazy Gang revived Gracie's flagging spirits. Avid practical jokers, with them around there was never a dull moment. 'They rigged up a hosepipe to the tap in their dressing-room, then hung it over the door,' Irene Bevan said. 'Every time anyone walked in, including my husband who was accompanying Grace [directing the orchestra], they got a soaking. They nailed a quick-change artiste's boots to the floor, and one evening even had the audacity to nail the Palladium curtain to the stage! We adored them!'

Towards the end of the Palladium run there was a blazing row with Archie which began in one car and ended in another – between which more than a few home truths were flung around on both sides. After the show, Gracie had emerged from the stage door to discover a spanking-new Rolls-Royce parked outside, surrounded by dozens of photographers. To tie in with his purchase of the car, and to celebrate Gracie's success at the Palladium – and show that from his point of view at least there were no ill feelings – Archie had arranged a publicity shoot. Gracie posed for the pictures, smiling mechanically while cursing under her breath, but as soon as the chauffeur drove off along Oxford Street with them sitting in the back, they began arguing again – so much so that Archie stopped the car at the junction with Regent Street and ordered her to get out and hail a cab. This much happened, though according to Gracie, there was more – a hundred yards up the road, she told the press, Archie's car had stopped for Annie Lipman to get in. Lillian Aza, who was on her side over most things, refused to believe this part of Gracie's tale, saying, 'I find it hard to believe that Archie would do such a thing. He wasn't a callous man.'

A few years later, Grace told Elizabeth Wilson of the American magazine, *Liberty*, a different story which has been dismissed by those closest to her as an out-and-out lie. 'I felt it was time to take on a little class,' she said. 'My in-laws and a fast-talking salesman persuaded me I owed it to myself. The car had a radio, a speaking-tube, a fur rug and a liveried chauffeur. You could see it in Calais on a clear day, and it weren't for the likes of me. So I ended up letting my relatives use it whilst I rattled on as usual in my second-hand old Ford.' 'My father had bought that car some time before,' Irene Bevan said. 'And she'd had that old car of hers for years. As for the relatives, they all had cars of their own and would never have been allowed near the Rolls. As for the incident with Annie Lipman in

Oxford Street, it would have been impossible for all the elements to fall into place like that. It sounds like something out of the Marx Brothers'.

Soon afterwards there was another incident involving Gracie's car when, as it was gathering speed after leaving Argyll Street, a middle-aged woman somehow managed to get onto the running-board and half climb through the rear window. When she yelled, 'I've been running all over England to meet you, Miss Fields!' Gracie retorted, 'You poor bugger yer feet must be sore!' – then pulled her into the car, and for the next half-hour gave her an impromptu guided tour of London!

Whilst she was appearing at the Palladium, Gracie received an unexpected visit from Monty Banks, who surprised her further by inviting her out to supper. The pair got on like a house on fire, laughed a lot at each other's jokes, and agreed there and then to make a film together. Money was not even discussed – only Gracie's conditions, to which Monty agreed wholeheartedly, that John Loder should be her co-star and that she should be allowed to sing Bill Haines's latest comedy number. 'One of the Little Orphans of the Storm', billed as 'The Woeful Tale of a Female Oliver Twist', was one of the wittiest songs she ever performed.

> I ain't got no motherly hand to guide me,
> Me father was sent to Dartmoor to reform,
> If there'd been a vacant cell,
> They'd have had me there as well ...
> I'm too proud to ever go in the workhouse,
> They'd never get me to wear the uniform,
> And I'd rather roam the street
> Than be forced to wash me feet ...
> I'll soon end it all with a dose of poison,
> Can anyone spare a glass of chloroform?
> But, if it's all the same to you,
> A glass of gin'll do,
> I'm one of the little orphans of the storm!

Short and stocky, with dark curly hair and a little moustache, Monty Banks had been born Mario Bianchi in Cesena, a small town in Northern Italy. He was the same age as Gracie, though he often maintained that he was two years younger, and his own upbringing had been similarly impoverished and harsh. Like Gracie, Monty was bubbling with energy, outspoken, cheeky, but above all capable of getting on with almost everyone. A gifted, natural comedian, he had appeared in several successful films with Fatty Arbuckle and the Keystone Kops before directing Laurel and Hardy in *Great Guns*, and he had scored a big hit as an actor in the 1925 film *Racing Luck*. Like Gracie, he had been embroiled in an unhappy marriage – to Gladys Frazin, a young silent-screen star with a history of mental illness. After numerous suicide attempts, Gladys finally succeeded in ending her life in March 1939 by flinging herself from her New York apartment window.

Monty took inordinate care to create a favourable impression the first time he met Gracie on 'home ground' – rather than risk him running into John Flanagan at Greentrees, she invited him for Sunday lunch at The Haven, her parents' house in Telscombe. Monty, unfortunately, had to make do with Gracie as he found her, as she explained in her autobiography, *Sing As We Go*:

> Sundays with the family were about the only times I ever got to myself. I wasn't going to smarten up just for him, so he found me in my old trousers, filthy from playing in the garden with the kids and dogs, and with my hair all screwed up because I'd just washed it. But then, on that first Sunday I had no idea that Monty was going to take over my life where Archie had left off.

Gracie was still contracted to make two more films with Basil Dean. *Look Up and Laugh* was again scripted by J B Priestley, and co-starred her brother Tommy and Robb Wilton. Returning to her hometown, Gracie's character discovers that the market where her father runs a stall is about to close, so she decides to do something about it. 'You seem to be one of those women who are always looking after other people,' she is told, a line which once more links the actress with her character. For a while, her plans are thwarted when her brother falls for the daughter of the man responsible for closing the market (a then virtually unknown Vivien Leigh), but after a few hilarious scrapes, several memorable songs and a superb example of Gracie's 'cod-opera', all ends well .

In *The Show Goes On*, Gracie played film star Sally Lee, and this time there were two love interests – a boy from her hometown (John Stuart), and a consumptive songwriter played by another heartthrob, Owen Nares. There were several beautiful songs – 'My Love for You' and 'A Song in My Heart' included – but without any doubt the most memorable scene is when, looking as radiant as any of her Hollywood contemporaries, Sally sings 'Smile When You Say Goodbye' from the deck of the *Queen Mary* to an adjacent shipload of sailors.

Neither of these films, Gracie declared, were anywhere near as interesting to make as Monty Banks's *Queen of Hearts*, which was released in 1936. On the first day of shooting, she arrived at the studio, where Monty greeted her and escorted her to her canvas chair. Seconds later she jumped up with a yell – he had set fire to a bundle of newspapers under her seat! She knew at once that they would get on, though she may not have been aware how very close they would soon become. She was also impressed by Monty's motto: 'Always arrive punctually late by twenty minutes, then spend the rest of the day catching up!' Hardly any of Monty Banks's films ran over budget, or over their allocated time-span, though this one did when one of the actors was taken ill during the last day of shooting.

There is no doubt that the funniest moment in any Gracie Fields film occurs in *Queen of Hearts* when she auditions for the part of a singer in a new revue – only to be shanghaied into dancing the *valse-chaloupée*, known to British audiences as the apache. She learned the basic movements for this potentially dangerous piece in Paris from her friend Damia, who had created it, and was so keen to do almost the whole of it on screen that she rejected the film's insurance company's demand to use a stunt double for some of the more perilous movements. The woman being flung around like a rag by the famous Carl Balliol, then swung up and around by her arms and feet before colliding with the property man who is carrying a dismembered shop-window dummy really *is* Gracie. And, as in many of his films, Monty 'did a Hitchcock', playing a passerby during an altercation with a policeman.

There was one further crisis when Monty walked into a piece of scenery and injured both his eyes. Knowing almost nothing about his personal life – least of all where he lived, or if he might have been 'involved' – Gracie took over. She rang a studio boss in the middle of the night, demanded Monty's address, then got in touch with Lottie Albert of the Ladies' Guild who arranged for Monty to be examined by Dr Rycroft, a specialist who had recently treated one of the boys at Gracie's orphanage. Rycroft later confirmed that

Gracie's quick thinking had saved Monty's sight.

Thus, literally hours after finishing *Queen of Hearts*, Gracie embarked on what she said was her biggest gamble this far in her career – a tour of South Africa. Accompanied by her brother Tommy and Harry Parr-Davies, she arrived in Cape Town wearing a green outfit – a colour avoided by all artistes, but obviously lucky so far as she was concerned – to the most rousing welcome the city had ever given an entertainer. Four thousand fans, who until now had been contented with only her films and recordings, cheered as her car slowly wound its way from the docks to her hotel and threw streamers, flowers and confetti.

Gracie's first show in South Africa, however, only brought out the worst in the critics, who complained that it was too short, though they did not attack her for giving them just thirty minutes, but her orchestra whom they claimed to be insufficiently rehearsed. Gracie managed to put things right, of course ... summoning a press-conference, she took *all* the blame, and gave a complimentary, full-length show which no one could complain about. And before she left Cape Town, just to show there were no hard feelings, the orchestra presented her with a silver platter inscribed 'Our Gracie' which was still displayed on her living-room wall forty years later.

The train journey between Cape Town and Johannesburg was a long one, with many stops. At the first station, a huge crowd clustered around the front of the rain, preventing it from pulling out. Gracie and Tommy, travelling in one of the rear carriages, leaned out of the window and asked what all the fuss was about. They were told that everyone was waiting for Gracie Fields! She then rushed to the front of the train, got off, and sang two songs unaccompanied. The news of this sped to the next station like wildfire, and of course the same thing happened each stop along the way – by the time the train reached its final destination, it was eight hours late.

Between singing engagements, Gracie visited hospitals, homes for orphaned children, and gold and diamond mines. She was photographed with ferocious-looking tribal chieftains who staged war-dances in her honour. Such was her popularity that the tour was extended by six weeks, and each evening she left her audiences in tears with her closing number, Harry Parr-Davies's beautiful theme from *The Show Goes On*.

Now you're going your way,
So smile for me from the start,
For that's the way I want to remember you!
You've go to smile when you say goodbye!

When Gracie returned to England, she made one last attempt to patch up her differences with John Flanagan. A moderately successful artist who could sell his paintings for upwards of £40 – quite enough to get him by, he told her – he had often stayed away from Greentrees during Gracie's lengthy absences, usually with Henry Savage in Winchelsea, where he had re-familiarized himself with his bohemian lifestyle. Gracie, without any doubt one of the least selfish entertainers of her generation, could never resist being generous to her friends and loved ones, even when she knew that her kindness was not appreciated. The crunch came when, during their last trip to Capri as a couple, she crossed the bay to Naples and bought Flanagan the most expensive crate of paints and brushes she could find, hardly knowing that one of the most rewarding pleasures of his work was purchasing such things for himself. Flanagan told her point-blank that he did not wish to be a kept man, and though they remained close friends until his death in 1976, what little was left of their love affair ended abruptly.

It is widely believed that Gracie only stayed on Capri because of her memories of John Flanagan. She confided in Denis Pitts, 'I told the world that I'd fallen in love with Capri. Well, even someone as daft as me doesn't fall in love with a piece of rock, no matter how beautiful!' Some years later, Gracie gave Flanagan a large sum of money which enabled him and Henry Savage to open a club-restaurant in Knightsbridge – it became a popular retreat for painters and actors.

In 1934 Gracie had recorded a beautiful song called 'The House Is Haunted', though she had never sung it on stage, thinking it somewhat over dramatic, after her split from Flanagan it became a regular feature of her repertoire – a reminder of the greatest love of her life which she had effectively killed by kindness.

I hate to be alone when evening falls,
I'm so afraid of all those empty halls ...
The house is haunted
By the echo of your last goodbye,
By the memories that refuse to die.

Over the next six months – her way, she said, of getting over Flanagan, Gracie flung herself into several brief but passionate relationships with men who could not have been more diverse in their make-up. Jack Daley was a young Irish comedian who had acted as a warm-up in one of her shows, and who sometimes worked stag-nights in some of the less respectable London pubs and clubs. Yet in spite of his outspokenness and cheeky charm, he was so terrified of asking Gracie out on a date that he got a stage-door Johnny pal to do it instead! Daley spent several weekends with Gracie at Greentrees and accompanied her on a trip to Paris where she introduced him to a few of her favourite haunts, then promptly returned to his wife. Sadly, like Philippe Vierchy he died suddenly, whilst still young. 'Oh, so gorgeous, it wasn't true!' was how Irene Bevan described him, though she was not so enthusiastic about the next man in Gracie's life. Carl Balliol was the adagio dancer who had executed the apache with Gracie in *Queen of Hearts*.

> He always used to wear leopard-skins. He was a great big, good-looking hunk of a bloke … but ignorant. They met clandestinely at first. Gracie said to me, 'I can't take this man anywhere because he speaks such bad English – he *wases* for his *weres*.' So she got me to sit in the dressing-room and try to get him to speak properly. I used to tell him, 'You don't say "He done it", you say "He did it"!' In all her sexual connections and relationships there was a certain reticence typical of a woman of her background and generation. The upshot of this one, however, was that she went off with him and signed the hotel register Gracie Fields. She didn't do this deliberately – again, it was her naivety.

Gracie's surviving friends have confirmed that her folly caused her a great deal of anguish for many years. As a result of this piece of indiscretion Balliol's wife Jessica Merton sent her threatening letters, which Gracie eventually dealt with. What she could not cope with were letters from other 'interested parties' – employees from the hotel who attempted to extort hush-money by threatening to tell all to the press. Gracie eventually called the police, and the matter ended there. Even so, she almost came unstuck again when she had what has been described as 'an embryo affair' with a famous comic who still cannot be named for legal reasons, and who is said to have called her every evening for several weeks – always reversing the charges. There were also alleged, but unproven, flings with both John Loder and Owen Nares.

On 8 April 1936, Gracie was in Southampton for the launching of the 390-ton paddle steamer, *Gracie Fields*, built by Sir John Thorneycroft at a cost of just over £35,000. Thousands of people sang along in a chorus of *Sing As We Go* as the ship slid into the water. Gracie was presented with a silver boat-christening cup, a huge bunch of Lancashire roses, an inscribed lifebelt and ornamental clog, and a flag-shaped brooch encrusted with jewels representing the ship's colours – sapphire, emerald, ruby and pearl. The *Gracie Fields*, during the tense days leading up to the Second World War was employed to convey passengers on the Southampton–Isle of Wight run, and Gracie was amongst the first to sail on her from Brighton to Beachy Head, accompanied by the children and staff from the orphanage, and most of her family.

In June 1937, Gracie went to Blackpool to open the Squire's Gate Holiday Camp. Five thousand people smashed through police barricades to get a closer look at her, and she was advised not leave the safety of the balcony – advice she promptly ignored when she saw a group of children holding up a card marked ROCHDALE. Rushing down to them, she ignored the rest of the crowd and the stupefied dignitaries and gave them a twenty-minute lesson in the art of 'gurning'! Later in the year she appeared at the Palladium in the Royal Variety Show – her first before the new King and Queen – alongside British stalwarts Norman Evans, Max Miller, Florence Desmond, George Formby and Cicely Courtneidge.

The year 1937 also saw the release of Gracie's second film with Monty Banks. By now, the pair were considerably more than just friends, though for the time being they decided to keep their romance very much under wraps. Gracie's co-stars for *We're Going to Be Rich*, an 1880s music-hall romp about the gold rush set in a wild and wet South Africa were Victor McLaglen and Brian Donlevy, who under the conditions of her contract were compelled to cross the Atlantic to appear in the film, Gracie having flatly refused to go to America. The action begins in Melbourne, where 'Lancashire Lark' Kitty Dobson is giving her farewell performance, singing 'The Sweetest Song in the World' and 'Walter, Walter', before returning to England. 'They have an arrangement,' someone says of Kitty and her wide-boy husband Dobby (McLaglen) – 'She earns it, he spends it.' And when Dobby tricks her into going to Johannesburg, where he has bought a half-interest in a defunct goldmine, she retorts: 'In Ceylon it was a tea plantation, in New Zealand a horse-racing syndicate, and in Australia you were going to make farm animals out of kangaroos!'

When Dobby starts a brawl and is temporarily jailed – his cellmate in a brief scene is Monty Banks – Kitty takes a job in a saloon owned by the irascible Yankee Gordon (Donlevy) and becomes an instant sensation. Gordon falls in love with her, to the chagrin of resident has-been songstress Pearl (Coral Browne) whose attempts at seducing Dobby end abruptly when he dumps her in the horse-trough ... though not before Kitty tells him they are through. Then, after a boxing match which the real-life fighter McLaglen loses, only to be bashed senseless by his wife wielding a tray, the ever-sympathetic Gordon turns matchmaker, and the film ends optimistically with the Dobsons becoming involved in a gold-rush, with Kitty singing 'The Trek Song' in Afrikaans and half the town joining in.

The film was an astonishing success.

In 1935, two years before, Gracie had been 'vetted' for Hollywood but MGM's London representative had dismissed her as being 'too national'. Now, however, Darryl F Zanuck, the head of Twentieth Century-Fox, thrilled with the film's reception, offered her £200,000 – at the time more than Mae West, the highest-paid actress in America, was earning – for a four-picture deal. Gracie was ever-cautious. She certainly needed the money, for she had received a huge tax demand – huge enough for her to want to put Greentrees on the market. A deal like this would give the the house a reprieve.

Making films in the United States, however, even with Monty Banks, was something that Gracie was not having at any price, and though she did sign Zanuck's contract, she added a clause of her own – like *We're Going to Be Rich*, all four films would have to be made in England.

5

Painting the Clouds with Sunshine

Towards the end of 1937, Gracie, Monty, Harry Parr-Davies and
Mary Barratt flew to New York where, within one hour of her
settling in at her hotel, Gracie's 'glamorization programme' began.
Gracie, of course, did not like it one bit, but when Monty told her
that this sort of thing was expected in America, she submitted. One
of the city's most exclusive hair stylists prepared her for her publicity
photographs – when she saw what he had done, she yelled that he
had made her head resemble a Japanese pagoda, and rushed off to
the ladies' room, 'to wash out the muck'. Thirty minutes after, her
hair still wet, she faced her first major American press-conference at
the Waldorf Astoria. She then moved on to a champagne party
hosted by Zanuck at the Trocadero, where she performed several
comedy songs, including a raucous 'I Never Cried So Much in all My
Life' which, observed one journalist, made all the glasses rattle on
his table. Another critic wrote, 'She's such a natural, just like a gust
of wind' – Gracie was not sure how to take this.

Over the next few weeks, Gracie attended numerous glitterati
receptions and parties, and was again made to feel out of place in an
environment where everyone was trying to outclass everyone else.
She did not mince words, however, when asked for an opinion about
a person or place. The actress Constance Bennett, with whom she
would one day really cross swords, was 'an out and out snotty
bitch', and Palm Springs was 'Capri, without the water'. Many of
these actresses and social darlings whom she dismissed to their faces
as 'mutton dressed as lamb', were horrified to hear her telling
journalists her age – and telling the truth. At one bash she made a
meal of her hostess, Mrs Vanderbilt, who announced her with: 'And

now I would like to present Miss Gracie Fields, an English music-hall artiste who is so working class that she even travels without a maid!' Gracie looked her straight in the eye and retorted for all to hear, 'Aye, love, and I also does all me own laundry even washes me own drawers!'

Though not a beautiful woman by any standard, when photographed with the likes of Paulette Goddard and Sonja Henie, Gracie came across as infinitely more attractive than any of her so-called peers because her looks were her own – she never even *thought* of putting on airs and graces, or having her face 'done'.

For the Hollywood moguls, of course, this was not good enough. Gracie had already had her teeth 'mucked up' during a visit to her old school dentist in Rochdale, Irene Bevan told me. 'She had a pain in one tooth, so the dentist told her that he would take that one out, and another from the other side to make sure that her face was evenly balanced! That's how naive she was. She was having two teeth out for the price of one!' Now, to perfect a 'Hollywood smile', she was made to have four teeth extracted and then four more. On the morning of her second visit to the dentist, Zanuck's publicity agent told her that a dinner date had been arranged for that evening at Charlie Chaplin's home (earlier in the week she and Monty had joined a coachload of trippers to Beverly Hills, where they had marvelled at the rich folks' houses, hardly aware that they would soon be seeing one from the inside). When the publicist asked Gracie if she had any particular likes or dislikes, she quipped, 'Better tell him to open a tin of soup, love!' This, the dentist informed her, would not be necessary – one hour later she was fitted with dentures, straight onto her bleeding gums.

Chaplin, always keen to make his guests feel at home, served a traditional English Sunday roast – cooked by his Japanese chef. Gracie remembered her ordeal many years later in her memoirs:

Don't tell me that Rochdale folk aren't tough! As I chewed I remembered the Old Folks' Treat. It's a dinner for the real old 'uns, hardly anybody under eighty, with scarcely a tooth between them, but they always insisted on finishing up with cheese and raw celery! I thought of them with every mouthful and it gave me courage.

Two years before, Gracie had performed the hilarious song 'Ring

Down the Curtain' at the London Palladium, and she sang it again
in America, unashamedly telling her audience that it reminded her of
her evening with Chaplin.

> Ring down the curtain, I can't sing tonight!
> Their money back you'll have to pay ...
> They've taken me false teeth away!
> I can't sing tonight with me tonsils in sight,
> I haven't a tooth in me head!
> The heroine swooned on a velvet settee,
> But jumped up again with an 'Ouch!'
> Which rapidly turned to a cry of delight,
> For there were her teeth on the couch!

And there was Gracie's disastrous evening with Eddie Cantor, who
had booked her for an appearance on his radio show. Cantor spent
the whole of the time they were together criticizing everything about
her – her accent, clothes, make-up, hair and gestures ... When he
began making comments about her voice and her songs, she put her
foot down and advised him, 'Mr Cantor, you should try talking out
of your mouth for a change.'

Although none of the films in her current contract were to be shot
in America, Monty convinced Gracie that, in view of her popularity
there, other work offers would be inevitable, and that in future she
would probably spend several months out of every year in
Hollywood. She decided therefore that it might be prudent to put
down a few roots – and in any case she had always hated staying in
hotels. After little searching she opted for a small but rambling white
stucco property, with lots of Spanish-style ironwork and the
obligatory swimming pool, on Santa Monica's Amalfi Drive. As
Irene Bevan said, Gracie had a mania for swimming.

And it *was* a mania! As a child, she swam in the local canal or
river, mindless of the danger. Many years later, after a matinée
in Norwich, we were walking along the river-bank when we
came across two girls in a boat. They leapt out and asked her
for her autograph – which she gave in exchange for a loan of
their swimsuits. It was like swimming in milk! Whenever we
stayed at the Adelphi Hotel in Liverpool, we spent every living
moment in the tiny pool in the basement. In Paris we always

went to the Lido for afternoon tea because afterwards they lowered the floor and it became a pool. Then my father got hold of this story that all the prostitutes swam there and that it was probably riddled with syphilis – that put the fear of God into both of us! And even as an old lady, when she could hardly get about, Grace loved to dive into her pool in Capri.

To furnish her new acquisition, Gracie visited every auction house in Santa Monica for several weeks, heckling the prices down so low that the auctioneers frequently found themselves out of pocket. She bought a grand piano for $150, and enough light-fittings to replace every socket in the house for $49. Each evening, instead of attending the by now-irksome Hollywood parties, she stayed at home making curtains and covers ... While she was thus domestically occupied, Monty was letting his hair down; always a heavy gambler, he spent most of his free time gambling away her earnings at the card tables – he once lost over $10,000 in a marathon four-day poker game! Gracie did not complain, however, and neither did she complain about his having a girlfriend in Santa Monica: whatever their relationship at the time, they were after all not married ... and Gracie herself had fallen for an auctioneer.

This time, the relationship was strictly platonic. Gracie had not worked much in America, but she was bound by the film-world's on-the-surface almost draconic code of morality and could not afford to have a scandal attached to her name – several so-called Hollywood sophisticates, who thought her vulgar and who were jealous of her success, were keeping tags on her every movement, waiting to pounce. She and her auctioneer – whose name she never revealed, and who probably never knew her true feelings – frequently lunched together, and one day this kindly middle-aged man asked her if she would sing for his son who, he said, was running for president. Gracie obliged, and was not in the least put off when she discovered that the son was a teenager, running for presidency of the students' union at his Los Angeles high school. Apologetically she said to the massive gathering of students, 'I know you were expecting Betty Grable in a bathing suit, and all you've got is an old gal in a frock, but I'll do my best!'

Only minutes later, Gracie had her audience eating out of her hand and yelling for more. One of the new songs in her portfolio was Bill Haines's 'The Biggest Aspidistra in the World', which she had rehearsed over the last month or so but had never sung in public. When, after her third song, she crossed to the piano and saw that her accompanist had taken the sheet music for this out of his folder by mistake, she almost told him to skip the song – it brimmed with North-England innuendo, which, she was convinced, the general American public would not begin to understand, let alone a hall full of students. Then, amused by the thought of the challenge, she decided to sing it ... to such a roar of approval that it had to be repeated four times:

> When Father's had a snootfull
> At his pub, the Bunch of Grapes
> He doesn't go all fighting mad
> And getting into scrapes.
> You'll find him in his bare skin
> Playing Tarzan of the Apes,
> Up the biggest aspidistra in the world!

(Later that year, Gracie recorded 'The Biggest Aspidistra in the World', and it became her best-selling comedy song, notching up a million sales worldwide within weeks of its release, outselling even 'Sally'.)

A few evenings later, Gracie bumped into the dreaded Eddie Cantor again, who this time attempted to tear a strip off her 'for giving away so much high-priced talent for free'. Infuriated, Gracie turned on him and snarled, 'And what do you expect to be paid for a charity show, Mr Cantor – the Hope Diamond?'

Gracie returned to England in January 1938, for what would be one of the most fulfiling years of her life. That month, she was asked to play the lead in *Me and My Girl* but turned the part down because, she said, a long run in the West End would only tie her down. During that month, too, the *Rochdale Observer* launched their 'One-Shilling Portrait Fund', so that they could have a lasting souvenir of the town's most famous daughter, hanging in its Art Gallery. In five weeks, the newspaper received over £750, enough to commission the artist James Gunn to paint her. Gracie would of course have much preferred something by John Flanagan or Augustus John, but she was satisfied with the result and when she unveiled the portrait she could not resist the quip, 'He's made me quite nice-looking, hasn't he?'

The second honour was the naming of the Gracie Fields hybrid tea-rose, which went on sale that spring for 2s.6d. a bush – not at all cheap, though thousands of bushes were quickly snapped up by fans. The fragrant, buttercup-yellow rose won its nurseries, Letts of Suffolk, that year's Gold Medal.

On 15 February 1938, Gracie was the very first variety artiste to be made a Commander of the Order of the British Empire. The award ceremony took place in the ballroom at Buckingham Palace, where King George VI presented her with the medal. She later confessed that she had been a bag of nerves, and that her hair had resembled 'a sackful of watch-springs'.

On 20 May, Gracie went to Clerkenwell Priory to receive the Order of St John of Jerusalem, for her tireless charity work for hospitals and the Red Cross. She was invested Officer Sister of the Order – again, the very first celebrity to be given the award. Within the confines of the Priory, away from the crowds, a kindly policeman had allowed an eighty-five-year-old fan to watch the proceedings from behind one of the arches. In the ensuing confusion surrounding Gracie's departure, the old lady missed seeing Gracie, but Gracie saw her. Stopping the car, she got out and held up the proceedings for almost half an hour, 'having a good old chin-wag and showing off me new brooch'.

For Gracie, however, the greatest accolade of all came when she was granted the Freedom of Rochdale, the highest honour the town could offer an ordinary citizen. The events of the day were relayed live to her admirers in Canada, Australasia and South Africa via Empire Transmitters. After a lengthy, occasionally tearful return speech, Gracie presented the Mayor – Alderman Crowder – an old friend of hers, with the Borough Arms emblazoned on a rug which she had commissioned from the Disabled Men's Handicrafts Group. Tens of thousands of people cheered Gracie as she waved from the Town Hall balcony, flanked by her parents. 'It will always remain the most important day of my life,' she reflected. 'But, more than anything I felt proud for Jenny and Fred, standing there, being fêted like royalty by the town where they'd fallen in love and struggled to bring up us kids.' Then, as with her stage shows when her moods alternated between sobriety and mirth, after the seriousness of the official luncheon came the hilarity of her town tour – perched on the back of a fire engine, wearing the company's full livery.

*

At the end of 1938, Gracie appeared in Twentieth Century-Fox's *Keep Smiling*, a fine film directed by Monty Banks. Her co-stars in what effectively was a burlesque were Roger Livesey, the Australian actress Mary Maguire ... and the famous terrier, Asta, which had appeared in the film *The Thin Man*. The story told of a stranded, has-been music-hall troupe who in an attempt to regain their popularity hire a renowned pianist. Gracie played the pianist, with hilarious results, of course. During the course of the film she milks a cow, is terrorized by hundreds of lost dogs, almost drowned in the Thames, tours in a charabanc with a concert party of down-and-outs, rescues several victims from a fun castle and, for once, marries! In a tender moment she sang what would become one of her most requested songs, 'The Holy City'. The film was a huge success, not just in Britain but throughout the Commonwealth. 'Following her brief Hollywood glamorization, Gracie Fields gets back to earth,' reported the *New Zealand Herald*.

Gracie and Monty were now living openly as lovers, and both were, deservedly happier than they had been for some time. Irene Bevan told me how the chirpy little Italian had swept her stepmother off her feet.

When Monty came along with his five telephones – 'Hold on Moscow whilst I speak to Paris!' – she fell for it hook, line and sinker. *And* he was a very attractive man. He made her laugh, which my, father never did. Archie was a very retiring man who would give the most wonderful parties, then hide behind the piano just to *watch* everybody having a good time. Monty was the opposite. He did crazy things which impressed her, such as ordering drinks if they were on a ship, then flinging the tray and glasses over his shoulder into the sea. That made Grace hoot with laughter. So they became friendly ... We were in Blackpool. She and I had a weird sort of rapport – one always instinctively knew what the other was thinking. One Monday night we got back to the theatre after the weekend break. I asked her, 'Did you?' She replied, 'Yes, I did!' That was how it began with Monty Banks.

Early in 1939, Gracie made *Shipyard Sally* another of the contracted American films, with Sydney Howard and Oliver Wakefield. Set in Clydeside during the Depression, it is said to have been her favourite film. Sally and her 'rich' uncle (Howard) are out-of-work variety stars who sympathize with the plight of local unemployed shipyard workers. When her uncle buys Sally a pub (with her own money!) she provides the unhappy men with beer, encouragement, and of course entertainment, though apart from their obvious devotion she gets little return, financially, for her efforts. Eventually she travels to London, where she pleads the workers' case with largely indifferent shipowners and politicians. Time and time again her efforts are botched by her bungling uncle, though she wins the men's case in the end. The film was highlighted by such songs as 'Wish Me Luck' and 'Danny Boy', which would stay in her repertoire for another forty years.

There was a private screening of the film, one month before it went on general release, at the Holloway Gaumont. The privileged audience were invited to fill in 'opinion' cards. The critic from *Today's Cinema* was asked to vet the replies and commented, 'After wading through the first fifty or so, the eulogies began to get monotonous – if you get my drift. How those fans worship the Lancashire Lass!'

Whilst waiting for the film to be released, although most of her financial problems had been resolved, Gracie decided once and for all to sell Greentrees. A deal was finalized at the end of May 1939, when the house was purchased for an unspecified amount by a contractor who wanted to turn it into a private bridge club. Gracie was pleased when the new owner promised to leave her bar intact and not to change the name, but she was not happy about deserting her garden and goldfish. Ten huge pantechnicons conveyed her furniture to Peacehaven – an exercise paid for, Gracie claimed, by the sale of just one of her crystal chandeliers. She then moved into a small flat at Queen's Gate, off Hyde Park – this would tide her over until she moved to Capri permanently, and it was from here a few days later that she asked Monty to drive her back to Greentrees, under cover of darkness, to retrieve her beloved tiger-lilies and goldfish.

All the way through shooting *Shipyard Sally*, Gracie had complained of feeling unwell, though ultimately she had attributed her fatigue to stress and overwork. Rita Holmes, the wife of her occasional pianist, Teddy Holmes, urged her to see a doctor. The doctor in turn referred her to Mr Searle, a young New Zealand gynaecologist at the Chelsea Hospital for Women who recommended exploratory surgery. Gracie said at the time that she was actually glad to be going into hospital for a few days because Lady Allendale had 'sprung' a charity garden-party on her, to take place at her parents' house in Telscombe ... to which she had invited several duchesses, and the Queen!

This minor operation, performed in early June, discovered advanced cancer of the cervix. The actual condition – in those days a subject which was hardly ever talked about – was not revealed to anyone outside Gracie's closest circle. The press were told that there would have to be an emergency operation, without which she would almost certainly be dead by the end of the year. Monty, intent on her having only the very best treatment, brought in Lord Dawson of Penn, King George VI's personal physician. Gracie would have nothing to do with him, insisting that as Mr Searle had done the first operation, he should also do 'the big one'. Even then, she put others before herself. She had arranged to do a radio appeal for a local hospital, and her brother Tommy had been booked as her stand-in. Gracie could not bear letting people down, and only minutes before the broadcast she arrived at the studio, leaning on her father's arm. Her appeal raised £21,000.

Although she knew that she might not survive the 'big' operation, which took place on 14 June 1939, Gracie never lost her sense of humour, touching her gown as she was being wheeled into the theatre and joking with the orderly, 'Don't *we* look smart in our new Ascot clothes?'

It took Gracie seventy-two hours to come to after her hysterectomy, and Mr Searle was given the task of informing her family that even now she only had a fifty-fifty chance of survival. This, and the fact that she would now never have children of her own, utterly devastated her. On the positive side, if indeed there was such a thing, her illness taught her how to re-evaluate her life.

Before I came out of hospital I was to come close to the meaning of death and heartbreak, the meaning of love and of God ... it was in that illness that I learned all those things which have carried me through my life ever since.

The devotion of Gracie's fans was quite extraordinary. So many of them kept a vigil outside the hospital that the porters spread straw on the pavement to deaden the noise. She was visited by her friend the Bishop of Blackburn, and in churches all over the country prayers were said for her recovery. She received no less than 600,000 cards and letters from wellwishers, including one from Queen Elizabeth, and there were so many flowers that they overflowed into the corridor outside her room. Strube, the *Daily Express* cartoonist, drew his famous sketch of the little man in the bowler hat with the umbrella and bunch of flowers, gazing up at the half-open hospital window. The caption, 'Our Gracie', of course said it all. When Strube sent her the original cartoon, she presented it to Mr Searle – 'It's for saving my life, love!' – and a few years later an anonymous admirer sent her a copy which he or she had executed in needle-point. It hung on the bedroom wall in Capri for the rest of her life.

Gracie recovered slowly but surely, attended by her parents and Auntie Margaret – she thought it hilarious that at fifty-one Auntie Margaret was getting married to an undertaker, and cracked that with a job like that the family would never starve, a joke which was not appreciated by her family, who had come so close to losing her. Mary Barratt and Monty Banks never left her side, unless to fetch food over for her from the Dorchester. 'Monty bought a meat-press,' Irene Bevan explained. 'He used to buy the very best quality steak, put it through the press, then make her drink the blood. Through him, she pulled through. She got over it rather quickly, though during her first concerts after the operation she would stand in the wings, bathed in sweat from head to toe.'

When she was feeling a little stronger, Gracie toured some of the other wards in her wheelchair, cheering up the patients and sharing her flowers amongst them. She left the hospital in the middle of July, having been there six weeks, to find several thousand people gathered outside waiting to cheer her – when they observed how ill she still looked, they fell silent. There then was an immensely moving moment when, almost on cue, every man in the crowd raised his hat. Every now and then, Gracie would have to return to the hospital for a check-up. Though the operation had been a complete success, she was not given the all-clear until the end of 1954.

Also in the middle of July 1939, the paddle steamer *Gracie Fields* was involved in an accident. As she was entering Southampton Water, her foremast was clipped by the starboard wing of a flying boat which had just taken off from Calshot. Though the ship was showered with chunks of broken metal, none of the passengers were hurt and Gracie's namesake was taken to the yard for repairs.

Gracie, however, can hardly have been concerned about this as at this time she learned the secret which her family had kept from her for some time – that her mother was slowly going blind. She immediately summoned Dr Rycroft, who had been treating Jenny for glaucoma. He suggested a warmer climate, and Gracie arranged for her parents to transfer to the house in Santa Monica.

On 22 July 1939, Gracie's divorce petition was heard. Clinging to the arm of her sister, Edith, and accompanied by a nurse, she arrived at the court twenty minutes before the proceedings began. It was raining heavily, and she looked pale and emaciated as she entered the building via a back entrance. She asked for a chair when summoned to the witness-box. Referred to constantly as Mrs Selinger, Gracie petitioned that unhappiness had compelled her to leave her husband in 1932, since which time she had had absolutely no communication with him – which was of course not true. It was then alleged that in October 1938, Archie had 'committed misconduct' in a Hastings hotel with his 'secretary' Annie Lipman – evidence of which was supplied by Gracie's private detective, George Watts, and a chambermaid from the hotel named Ada Skinner. 'These people were *paid* to come forward with the evidence,' Irene Bevan stressed. 'In those days you had to have all this nonsense about having to see the couple in bed. As a rule it was arranged with a prostitute, and she was paid. Sometimes a couple would stay up all night playing cards, then get into the bed just as a maid was about to come in with the morning coffee.' Whatever Archie's 'misconduct' within the hotel, nothing was mentioned of John Flanagan or the fact that Gracie was conducting a very open relationship with Monty Banks, and Mr Justice Bucknill, the presiding judge, granted a decree nisi with costs in her favour.

Speaking to Denis Pitts thirty years later, Gracie called her first marriage 'a registered-company situation' and 'a star-spangled humiliation'. Her ex-husband, she added, was the brains and she the asset, continuing bitterly, 'All the way to the register office Archie was reading balance sheets. Everything, and that means bed too, was a board meeting.' She concluded that he had worked her so hard that her feet had ended up a mass of blisters, and that her throat had become so sore that it had felt raw. 'Absolute rubbish!' declared her stepdaughter. 'All Archie did was drag her up by her bootstraps, and make her the big star she was!'

Even so, the divorce must genuinely have been an ordeal, coming as it did so soon after her illness. Both her personal doctor and Mr Searle prescribed complete rest for two years – a promise which Gracie made with her fingers crossed behind her back, for whilst agreeing to return to Capri with Monty and Mary Barratt she also arranged with the BBC to broadcast her gratitude to the nation. Gracie wrote out the script herself, and the event was of such importance that Sir Samuel Hoare made an afternoon announcement in the House of Commons: 'Gracie Fields is on the air tonight. It is obvious that the debate must end at an early hour.'

The broadcast was taped and issued on a recording backed with 'I Love the Moon', a beautiful song written during the First World War by Paul Rubens, when he had been dying from consumption. More than anything she had done in the past, the work expressed Gracie's pure, unadulterated love for her public, and many of the 600,000 admirers who had written her letters of encouragement are said to have wept when the song was first aired. An old Rochdale friend of Gracie's, Mary Whipp, told me, 'Tommy Fields was to deputize, but Gracie felt she owed it to her public, and weak as she was she sang her thanks, conveying superbly her emotion and ours. I remember we were having a meal, and instinctively I rushed from the table and knelt in front of the radio cabinet. Tears ran down my face ...'

> I love the moon, I love the sun,
> I love the forests, the flowers, the fun ...
> I love the wild birds, the dawn, the dew,
> But best of all, I love you!

What no one has ever bothered to chronicle – unfairly, because in the break-up of every relationship there are always two sides to the story – is Archie Pitt's ordeal after his divorce. Already a sick man with his empire almost in ruins, he went back on the stage and at the end of 1939 married Annie Lipman. Tragically, they were married just eleven months before his death from cancer of the liver in November 1940. Archie's daughter, whose fondness for Gracie knew no bounds, nevertheless revealed her true feelings when speaking of her loss.

I firmly believe that her walking out on him was the cause of his death – some doctors actually believe that a severe shock can bring on that form of cancer, and he was dead within three weeks of being diagnosed. All his life he had been looking for health, and he had been unable to find it. When Grace left, he lost all his energy and will to live. Annie was left the house in Hampstead, but she went to stay with Pat Aza and his wife. When that didn't work out, she went back to Leeds to live with her sister. She died there some years later.

Gracie had made big plans for her property in Capri, and hoped to put most of these into action during her convalescence. She told Monty that she wanted an avenue of olives to be planted to form a windbreak for her orange grove – unaware that the location could not cater for this – and a small restaurant and pool overlooking the sea. The house, which had been totally renovated, would become a haven where she would welcome friends and family alike. Monty hired a team of workmen, which to the distress of the neighbourhood began blasting away some of the big rocks where their pool was going to be. He also played a practical joke on Gracie which, she said, almost gave her heart-failure. One morning as she was setting off to the town of Anacapri he asked her if she would collect a box of provisions that had come for him. Gracie duly obliged, and on her return down the steep road she stopped for a rest and peered inside the container – it was full of cardboard tubes marked DYNAMITE! Later, of course, she realized that the tubes had only been filled with sand – but not before she had delivered a few 'choice Lancashire expletives' to the hapless Monty.

The couple's tranquil sojourn was to be short-lived. They had been in Capri just six weeks when it became certain that war would be declared imminently, and Gracie at once decided to return to England so that she could 'do her bit' for the war effort by singing in concerts organized by ENSA to entertain the troops. She was still recovering from her operation, but would not listen to reason, and Monty quickly realized that he would only be wasting his breath in trying to stop her. She also vowed never to take a penny for her services – even though 'ENSA wasn't the joyous thing that everyone made it out to be,' according to Irene Bevan. 'There was a lot of jealousy, which Gracie didn't like. Even so, she had to return to England. It was where she belonged.'

Getting across to the Italian mainland was the first hurdle that Gracie, Monty and Mary Barratt had to overcome. There was a blackout in the Bay of Naples, where the Italian fleet had been rapidly assembled, and there was an embargo on small craft. This did not put Gracie off. She contacted Ettore Patrizzi, the young man whose father's house she had bought, and he ferried the trio across to Naples. They were stopped by the port authorities, who took them for Italian VIPs, saluted them and waved them off in the direction of the railway station. An hour later they were speeding towards the French border. They arrived in England on 1 September, just two days before war was declared.

Gracie's first port of call was Telscombe where she made arrangements for her parents' house and the orphanage at Peacehaven to take in as many evacuated mothers and children as possible.

By the beginning of November she was en route for France, where she had been booked to top the bill in two ENSA galas in Douai and Arras. The journey was hampered by torrential rain, and they kept on having to dig the car out of the mud. Outside Lens it broke down altogether and the trio had to be rescued by the British Army. Still too weak to stand for lengthy periods of time, and framed against a backdrop of tanks and armoured trucks, Gracie expressed her gratitude the only way she knew how to – by leaning against the car's bonnet and singing 'The Lord's Prayer'. Both her concerts went ahead as planned, along with two more at Lille and Amiens with Arthur Askey, Richard Murdoch, and Sir Seymour Hicks who compered most of her shows. When she was not singing, on her good days she and Monty ran a mobile tea-van provided by the YMCA, or simply made sandwiches for the troops.

On 15 November, Gracie learned that a large regiment from Lancashire was stationed in the region, and she insisted upon seeing them, ignoring the pleas of her doctor and 'that old woman Hicks'. It was already dark when she set off, and on the way there a large number of German bombers flew past, perilously low, causing great consternation amongst her entourage. This was the beginning of the 'Phoney War', with the two sides on the Western Front firmly entrenched behind their defensive lines. When her concert promoter begged her to call off the show, she scoffed: 'Don't be soft. It's only a few planes!' When her legs started to give way, she refused to be carried and in the most superb triumph of mind over matter she leaned against the piano until well after midnight, performing thirty mostly comedy songs in Lancashire dialect. When Sir Seymour Hicks tried to talk her down from the makeshift stage, she yelled, 'Bugger off!' though by this time she was clearly on the verge of collapse. She explained to some of the soldiers who clamoured for autographs afterwards that from the hips up she felt perfectly normal, but that rheumatism had claimed the rest of her body.

During the tour, Gracie anxiously tried to contact Marie Dubas, having read the sensational reviews for her new show at the ABC in Paris. Her sources told her that Marie had fled to Marseilles and that she was now safely on her way to South America, on the *Florida*, with the American jazz-singer Lena Horne.

Gracie and her company spent the Christmas of 1939 in Rheims. To get there they had braved some of the most appalling weather conditions imaginable, so much so that there were fears that her concert at the huge Opéra de Rheims would have to be cancelled. Gracie would not hear of this. She also put her foot down when she learned that there were not enough tickets to go around – she would only entertain ordinary soldiers and maintenance men, not the 'snooty' officers who might not appreciate her 'common touch'. Even so, this left 100,000 men for just 3,000 tickets, resulting in heavy balloting and in-camp squabbles among her admirers.

Residents living close to the venue, upon hearing the deafening roar which erupted when Gracie walked onto the stage, could almost have been excused for thinking that a riot was taking place. And 3,000 red-blooded males wept unashamedly when she sang 'Home'.

> When shadows fall
> And trees whisper day is ending,
> My thoughts are ever wending home.
> When love-birds call,
> My heart is forever yearning
> To be returning home ...

The Rheims recital ended with a riproaring 'For She's a Jolly Good Fellow!', and was followed by a NAAFI variety concert, with Jack Payne and his Orchestra, which was broadcast across France, Belgium and Holland, and picked up by the BBC. Gracie made an emotional appeal for the King's Hospital Fund – in less than one week, the coffers of the organization's headquarters in London's Old Jewry had been boosted by more than £15,000. There followed a two-week respite on Capri, but Gracie could not possibly take things easy whilst she was in such demand and she flew to England, initially to sing for the Navy at Greenock. This led to a gruelling tour of army camps and factories which would have taxed the strength of the fittest individual. She then returned to Capri for a break, while it was relatively safe to do so.

This time Gracie found a letter waiting for her from her mother, a genuine *cri de coeur*. Jenny had lost the sight of one eye and wanted to see her daughter married whilst there was time for her to do so. The timing was perfect – Gracie's divorce from Archie Pitt had become absolute. So she and Monty decided to wed without delay. They would have liked the ceremony to take place at Peacehaven, but this was impractical as Gracie's parents and most of her family were in California. So the couple were married at Gracie's Santa Monica home on 19 March 1940 – Douglas Fairbanks Jr and Alfred Hitchcock were among the guests of honour. Gracie wore a simple blue two-piece and a matching pillbox hat. A church ceremony had been planned to take place later in England – this would require a dispensation from the Bishop of Chichester because both parties had been divorced, and because Monty was a Roman Catholic. Through sheer pressure of work, illness, and problems associated with the war, however, it never happened.

The couple's major problem, a very definite threat to both their future happiness and Gracie's career, was the fact that Monty was Italian, and a potential 'enemy alien', should his country opt to support Hitler during the conflict. As far back as 1922 he had taken out naturalization papers to become an American citizen, but he had failed to fill them in ... and although he had spent his entire adult life outside Italy, he still owned several farms there which were being managed by his sister. The Italian government had informed her, in no uncertain terms, that unless she signed a pact with the Fascist Party, she would be prevented from buying fodder for her cattle. This would spell ruin not just for the Bianchi clan, but for several small village communities.

For the time being, the newly-weds hoped that such a thing would never happen, and shortly after their wedding they flew to London, where on 30 April Gracie appeared with Maurice Chevalier in an Anglo-French Matinée at the Drury Lane Theatre, which aimed at raising funds for British services. Chevalier's slot was given a mixed reception because of his insistence that a no-smoking call be given out over the tannoy – only when Gracie, herself a non-smoker, supported him did the audience settle down. Several days later, the show was repeated at the Paris Opéra, and the pair received a raucous standing ovation when they embraced after a dozen curtain-calls.

After the show, Chevalier introduced Gracie to the songwriter Jean Saint-Granier, almost a Gallic equivalent of Noël Coward, who between the two world wars put on a series of scintillating revues in and around Paris. Saint-Granier engaged her for one of his *cantine-déjeuners* at the Bal Tabarin, an establishment renowned for its can-can floor shows and expensive gourmet cuisine. These events were similar to the Hollywood canteens, save that clients were not servicemen but out-of-work or retired music-hall stars and musicians.

In just three days, Gracie learned two songs in French – 'Mon Homme' and 'On Dit Ça' had both been introduced by Mistinguett. She sang these, along with 'Reviens, veux-tu?' and 'Chantez Pour Moi, Violons', in front of the cabaret's huge inclined mirror – a contraption which ensured those patrons sitting at the back of the auditorium a clear view of the stage. After her performance, she mucked in with established French stars such as Lucienne Boyer, Damia and Fernandel, waiting at the tables and doing the dishes. The shock of the afternoon was her meeting with the awesome Mistinguett herself. Sixty-three years of age, and still possessed of the loveliest legs in show-business, La Miss loathed being upstaged by anyone – her quite vociferous feuds with Damia and Josephine Baker were as famous as her meanness and bad temper – and though her singing voice sometimes left much to be desired, she hated it when other artistes covered her songs. Irene Bevan remembered, 'When we first went to Paris together in the thirties, the first artiste we went to see was Mistinguett. Grace always used to say that though the French accepted Mistinguett, if she ever got up and sang in England they'd throw bricks at her.'

Miss and Gracie squared up to one another in the Bal Tabarin's kitchen – a few days earlier, in a press interview, the French star had called Gracie 'that English washerwoman' – and for several anxious moments the other celebrity helpers watched with bated breath, wondering who would strike first – Miss with her mop, or Gracie with her dishcloth. Then the older woman flashed her notorious smile and pronounced in heavily accentuated English, 'You are the friend of Marie Dubas! Any friend of La Grande Marie may kiss La Miss!' The two women embraced, and this most extraordinary scene was reproduced in newspapers all over France.

That evening Gracie, Chevalier and Mistinguett dined together at Maxim's – a historical event in itself, for very soon each would step onto the pathway of their particularly thankless Calvary: Mistinguett and Gracie both working for their war effort, and the hapless Chevalier walking straight into danger and controversy. 'He was the gay, unconquerable soul of La Belle France,' Gracie reflected a few years later, when she learned of the ridiculous collaboration charges trumped up against him, from which he was of course exonerated.

One of Gracie's rare concerts for ENSA on home territory took place at the Drury Lane Theatre on 6 May 1940, when she sang for the Senior Service. She was introduced personally by Basil Dean who, though he disliked her only slightly less than she him, put anyone who might want to stir up trouble firmly in their place by announcing, 'As director of entertainments it is my privilege to make public acknowledgement of the debt that the Army, Navy and Air Force Institutes and ENSA owe to this great personality. The best propaganda for victory is not words, but a spirit of vigilant cheerfulness. And what better doctor of good cheer could there be than Our Gracie? And so we say to you, "The whole country thanks you!"'

Gracie walked onto the stage, and the applause was so noisy that she tried several times to begin her opening number, 'We're All Together Now'. From then on it was sheer magic, with the largely male audience singing along word-perfect with almost every song. Then halfway through 'Goodnight, Children, Everywhere' she proclaimed, 'Now, at this stage in the show I want all you daddies to sing to your kids.' The emotion was crippling for the hundreds of valiant young men who had little idea of what fate might have in store for them. Gracie, however, was their precognitive dream – the fact that all *will* turn out well in the end, if one so wishes.

The Drury Lane concert was followed by another brief tour of Belgium and France. This time there was less secrecy and Gracie stayed at a small hotel in Arras, and besides her usual recitals for the troops she made several appearances on the radio singing in English and French. One of her numbers – though she had vowed never to sing any 'regular' war songs ('I'll leave that sort of thing to Vera

Lynn and Anne Shelton') – was 'Nous Irons à Valparaiso', more a collection of vulgar statements and innuendo than an actual lyric, and unknown to Gracie at that time, the anthem of the uncloseted Parisian gay community. Many years later, when she was told what the lyrics meant, she said she wished she had never sung it. In 1940, however, each time she performed it, the radio station switchboards were jammed with callers asking to hear it again.

> Adieu misère, adieu bateau,
> Adieu Bordeaux!
> Hurrah pour Mexico!
> Nous irons à Valparaiso, all-away!
> Pour le salé, pour le couteau,
> Pour faire la paix
> Pour foutre les filles,
> Et les matelots!

There was another song which Gracie sang on the French radio at this time, and one which very nearly cost her her life. This was her own adaptation of 'The Biggest Aspidistra in the World' which the Germans, understandably, did not find amusing at all. The famous plant has now been transported across the Channel, where it is taking part in the Allied Advance ...

> Then Goering saw him from afar,
> And said to his old Frau,
> 'Young Joe has got his blood up,
> So the war's all over now!'
> 'Cos they're going to string old Hitler
> From the very highest bough
> Of the biggest aspidistra in the world!

Several months before Gracie recorded the song and released it on the flipside of 'He's Dead but He Won't Lie Down', Goebbels, Adolf Hitler's 'Minister of Popular Culture' – propaganda minister – heard it in a broadcast and began taking an active interest in Gracie's movements. Within a few months, groups of censors would be set up to enable the Germans to vet song lyrics in particular before allowing them to be performed. Gracie's lyrics, particularly those of her comedy songs, were virtually unvettable as few foreigners could understand their Lancastrian argot. And when Goebbels attacked her over the airwaves, dubbing her 'Little Miss Gracie-Wacie, England's Number One Beggar', she retorted with a curt 'Beggar off, Joe!'

Matters came to a head in the middle of May when a leading German magazine declared, 'Gracie Fields has earned for England the equivalent of a hundred new Spitfires. She is adjudged a war industry and should be therefore treated accordingly.' When Basil Dean read this, and in the wake of the Occupation, he recalled Gracie and his other ENSA entertainers from across the Channel. She left Arras quietly, under cover of darkness and without any luggage. Two days later, assuming she was still there, the hotel where she had stayed was bombed by the Germans. The room she had slept in was reduced to rubble and seven people were killed.

During her French broadcasts, Gracie had often dedicated a song to the crew of the *Gracie Fields*, which in September 1939 had been requisitioned for war service as a minesweeper with the Tenth Flotilla. On 27 May 1940, the ship served at Dunkirk, transferring troops to the HMS *Calcutta*. The next day, whilst lifting eight hundred men from the beach at La Panne, she was attacked and hit by a German dive-bomber. The soldiers on board were evacuated onto three other craft, including HMS *Pangbourne*, which began towing the crippled paddle-steamer into Margate. On 30 May, in the early hours of the morning, the *Gracie Fields* gave out a Mayday signal that she was sinking fast.

'She went down doing her duty,' Gracie said tearfully. 'That makes me feel very proud.'

6

If I Can Help Somebody

On 1 June 1940, Gracie was alone when she received a telephone tip-off from Monty's friend, Lord Castlerosse, the columnist from the *Sunday Express,* warning that news was expected any day of Italy's pact with Germany. To avoid certain internment, Monty was advised not to delay sailing for the Irish Republic or the United States. Gracie later told Stanley Jackson, a journalist friend who offered support during her subsequent crisis,

> That telephone call was the dividing point in my life. My husband or my country? The choice wasn't as simple as that. Had I stayed, I would have endangered Monty's freedom. Had he been sent away on the *Arandora Star*, he almost certainly would have lost his life when she sank. My friends pointed an easy way out. 'Divorce him and stay in this country,' they said. 'or why not go through a sham form of divorce, then remarry him when things quieten down?' They don't do that sort of thing where I come from. God knows my heart was with my folk and my country, but somehow I just couldn't leave Monty to face all those years of internment. I refused to quit just because the going got tough, and any decent wife would have done the same thing.

Sound advice came during a private meeting with Churchill, who told Gracie, 'Go out and earn American dollars, not English pounds, for all the folks back home who love you. That way these people will *see*, like I do, how sincere you are.'

Through Churchill, Gracie met Lord Lloyd, the head of the Navy

League, and it was agreed that she would travel to Canada for a series of thirty-two concerts which would raise money for British soldiers fighting at the front. She and Monty arrived at the Canadian port of Halifax on 9 June, en route for what should have been her first concert in Montreal. During the long crossing, leaving Monty to gamble to his heart's content, Gracie had formed a concert party with sixty-three refugee children, entertaining the other passengers with sea-shanties and folksongs. She accompanied herself on the piano – Harry Parr-Davies, having been called up, was now in the Irish Guards Orchestra.

Many of these children disembarked at Halifax, and Gracie's first dockside interview was held up as she patted each one on the head and offered words of encouragement as they stepped off the gangplank. She met a French reporter who told her that since the Nazi bombing of Arras, French planes had bombed munitions factories around Berlin, and chirped, 'Good! I'd like to have a squad of planes myself and bomb the hell out of the buggers!' She was thrilled when, before leaving the dockside, a British sailor rushed up and demanded her autograph – she had last seen him six months before, behind a shop counter in Middleton, near Rochdale! She was displeased, however, when she read reports of her arrival in the evening papers, for they all referred to her 'British husband and ultra-Cockney accent'.

Gracie changed her mind about going to Montreal straight away, and gave an impromptu recital to Canadian soldiers at the Valcartier military training camp near Quebec, where she walked on to the stage belting out 'Roll Out the Barrel'. Then, at the start of the next number when her stand-in accompanist played the wrong introduction, she stopped him with a loud 'I'll sock thee in t'jaw if tha argues with me, lad!' The young man did not quite know how to take this, though the audience roared its appreciation. The officers were sitting on benches at the front of the hall, partly obscuring the view of the men sitting on the floor behind them who began chanting that they could not see a thing. Gracie came down from the stage, shouted, 'Come on, shift yer bums!', and would have completed her show standing on one of the benches had it not suddenly collapsed. The offending benches were subsequently removed, and the officers were compelled to enjoy the show the same as everyone else – squatting on the floor.

Immediately after appearing at the Valcartier camp, Gracie and

Monty flew to Montreal where, in spite of her protests that she did not want any fuss, she had been booked into a suite at the plush Château Frontenac. It was here that the couple were told that Italy had entered the war on Germany's side – in effect, Monty Banks was now officially an 'enemy alien'.

The Mayor of Montreal, Monsieur Houde, had arranged to meet Gracie at the City Hall, where she was to sign the Golden Book, one of the province's greatest honours. She and Monty had actually reached the venue when the Mayor sent the message: 'I will not attend any function or ceremony which is no more than a cheap publicity stunt.' Gracie was hurt, but wisely decided that it would be useless to argue. She merely returned to her hotel and set about planning her programme for the next leg of her tour. The editor of the *Montreal Daily Star*, however, would not let the matter rest, and he defended Gracie by launching a ferocious attack on Mayor Houde. Accusing him firstly of jealousy because a woman had been awarded the CBE – Houde had received his award in 1935 – he concluded:

> Some may think that the lady was better entitled to it than the Mayor. 'Our Gracie' needs no publicity that a hundred Houdes could give her. She is on a tour, every cent of which will go to the soldiers' fund. His action was a graceless one. On behalf of the citizens of Montreal we apologize to Miss Fields for the treatment she has had to endure at the hands of a Mayor who evidently does not know the elementary rules of courtesy to a distinguished artiste from the Old Country who can also sing songs in French.

This was only the beginning. Monty's intention was to accompany Gracie on her Canadian Navy League tour, then travel to Hollywood where he was hoping to acquire American citizenship and possibly extricate himself from the whole sad mess. Instead he was apprehended by the Canadian police and threatened with internment. Gracie told Navy League officials, 'I'm his wife. You lock him up, and you'll have to lock me up with him!'

The Navy League, of course, knew only too well that if Gracie was allowed to take offence and drop out of the tour, they risked losing a potential fortune in the funds she was expected to raise. Monty was allowed to leave for Santa Monica, and to ensure that nothing happened to him on the way, Gracie travelled with him. The brief respite with her parents, in view of her health, was long overdue and whilst there she was pleasantly surprised by the arrival of Harry Parr-Davies, who told her that he had been 'excused' from the army to accompany her because the complaints about his replacement had reached the ears of his superiors!

At the end of July, Gracie returned to Canada for three concerts in British Columbia, and a gala in Vancouver. She had also been booked for the Fresh Air Fund Broadcast, hosted by the *Toronto Star*, and scheduled to go out from the Eaton Auditorium on 7 August. The event was to raise money for children who had been evacuated to camps in and around Ontario. Gracie was disappointed that none of these youngsters would be allowed into the concert hall, and she asked if she might be permitted to fit in a tour of the actual camps between her already tightly packed schedules. Speaking over the telephone from Santa Monica, she told the newspaper, 'If the lads and lasses want me to sing them to sleep, I will. I'll even tidy their faces and tuck 'em up in bed!' Not only was she told by the camp director that she would not be welcome in the camps, her application to the British government to bring some of the children from the Peacehaven orphanage to the safety of Canada (Noël Coward had been allowed to take sixty such children out of England) was rejected with a curt 'Not enough room on the boat. Send them somewhere else.'

Suddenly, all hell broke loose when several newspapers on each side of the Atlantic branded Gracie a traitor, accusing her of deserting England with an estimated £100,000 worth of jewellery and most of her personal fortune. Monty, spiritually much weaker than she was, aggravated the dilemma by publicly urging her to give up her career – something she would not have even considered. Journalists pursued her everywhere, and though she persisted that her only 'crime' was loving her husband, who just happened to be Italian and who in any case was not with her, they hounded her remorselessly.

Her ordeal reached its zenith in Toronto. To get to the venue from the West Coast meant a turbulent twelve-hour flight there and back for a single show. She and two famous film stars – Johnny Weissmuller and his 'Tarzan' girlfriend Maureen O'Sullivan – were met at the airport by the Mayor, who spent a great deal of time fussing over the film stars and completely ignored Gracie. Whilst this trio sped off to their joint official function – a hospital walkabout – in the Mayor's limousine, Gracie was left to make her own way there. She got her own back at the hospital by ignoring them and quietly going off to sing to the patients. Matters came to a head at the Town Hall when the arrogant Mayor was heckled off his podium by several hundred of Gracie's fans, who chanted for her to sing 'There'll Always Be an England'. She obliged, and this helped to renew her self-confidence, as she recalled in her memoirs.

> This, then, was the stuff their love was made of when half a million unknown people had sent it to me when I was dying. Here it was, real understanding, pouring out of me just when I needed it most. If they would give it to me in Canada, then surely I must still have it in England. This was the goodness of the everyday folk that I had known, believed in and belonged to ever since I was a child. They *knew* I wasn't running away, and that was all that mattered.

Gracie's fans would have done absolutely anything for her, but the belligerence and sheer bloody-mindedness of the Mayor and the press persisted. When photographs of the day's events appeared in the evening papers, there were none of Gracie. At the actual show – mindless of how long it had taken her to get there – she was told, 'Keep it down to fifteen minutes.' Ever-dignified, she complied, but as soon as she left the stage, the audience began yelling and stamping their feet and would not stop until she had gone back on. Silencing them with her 'errand-boy' whistle, she told them that she had arranged to return to Toronto for a full two-hour concert at the spacious Massey Hall ... not for the dignitaries, but for the ones who cared.

Back in Britain the Labour MP for Glasgow's Maryhill District, J J Davidson, petitioned the House of Commons and demanded an enquiry into why Gracie had been permitted to take £8,000 out of the country, and Monty in excess of £20,000. The regulation specified just £10, but Gracie had been given permission by the authorities, upon her doctor's recommendation that she was single-handedly supporting her parents and her sisters' children. On top of this, as she was working *against* medical advice, she had been obliged to take out a hefty life insurance in order to work overseas in the first place. And of course the sole purpose of this work was to give away everything she earned. Therefore it was again stressed that since arriving in Canada she had not so much as earned a single cent for herself. As for her jewellery, all she had were her wedding and eternity rings, the ship brooch, one bracelet and her 'lucky' diamond clip which she usually wore on stage – and in any case, she had left Britain before the motion which prohibited taking any such valuables overseas was passed by the government in July 1940.

Davidson's diatribe resulted in an investigation into Gracie's financial status, which of course revealed that she still had a large number of assets in England. She was defended by the Member of Parliament for Rochdale, H B W Morgan, who countered, 'Her patriotism and loyalty are unchallengeable.' Gracie herself hit out at her persecutors in a rare outburst of temper, declaring, 'There's always somebody making trouble, as if there isn't enough of it in the world. Perhaps if some folks worked as hard as others this war would end sooner.' Captain Crookshank, the Financial Secretary of the Treasury, issued a further statement confirming that Gracie had not taken unauthorized money out of the country. The newspapers, aware that this would hinder their smear campaign, did not print it.

Monty Banks launched a vitriolic attack against the press and accused them of bullying his wife, which was of course true. His warning, however, issued from his Santa Monica base: 'Leave my Gracie alone or I'll telephone her, order her to come home, and henceforth live the life of a normal person!' was a silly ploy which everyone ignored, and which got him an earbashing from the wife he was trying to protect. Gracie, still weak, merely plodded along with her tour.

In Calgary, where Gracie sang in front of 9,000 people, there was no mention whatsoever in the press about her 'problem'. The only criticism, if indeed it was one, came from *The Albertan*, which alerted the public to the fact that Gracie was so down-to-earth that she often appeared in public with a hole in one of her stockings! In several subsequent interviews, when Gracie thought a journalist was spending too much time looking at her legs, she would excuse herself, borrow a cigarette from someone, and purposely burn a hole in her nylons, 'To give 'em summat to look at!'

There was some light relief when Gracie went on a two-day trip to the picturesque Lake Louise, near Banff. Referring to one of the local beauty spots near her birthplace she crooned, to the tune of 'There's a Lovely Lake in London', 'There's a lovely lake near

Rochdale, and they call it Hollingworth!'

During her stay in Lake Louise, Gracie, a keen photographer, announced that she wanted to go out on her own and take a few pictures of some of the other tourist attractions – the wild bears. At her press-conference she announced that she had 'gone round the back of a muck-heap to investigate a lot of grunting', only to disturb a couple who were making love! She added slyly, 'They weren't *quite* the bears I'd expected to find, but I took a few photos in any case. Then when I got back to my room and looked out of the window, the lad and lass were on the lawn, and this bloody big bear came ambling up to them. The man didn't run but when I saw the girl running, I yelled through the window, "That's what I'd do, Lizzie!"'

From Calgary, Gracie returned to Toronto, where she had earlier promised to sing at the Massey Hall. So many people turned up to cheer her as she entered the theatre that the traffic was brought to a standstill. It was still so when she left. There was such a demand for tickets at this rather highbrow establishment that she played five concerts consecutively, breaking all box-office records. Each began with Harry Parr-Davies's 'The Sweetest Song in the World', followed by his latest composition, 'Smiling Along' and ending boisterously with his 'Wish Me Luck', now another of Gracie's signature tunes.

> Give me a smile I can keep all the while
> In my heart, while I'm away ...
> Till we meet once again, you and I,
> Wish me luck as you wave me goodbye!

The *Toronto Star* impressed with Harry's superb playing and arrangements, reported: 'Harry Davis is such an accomplished musician, he would have no trouble filling a concert hall on his own.' Gracie's temperamental accompanist took great exception to having his name misspelled, refused to give interviews, behaved rudely to everyone but Gracie, and *still* had a major and extremely complimentary feature written about him in the *Toronto Telegram*. 'It was Harry's constipation that always made him grumpy,' Irene Bevan said. 'That troubled him more than anything. He used to come down to breakfast on a morning and say, "The Chooser has been!" – we all knew then that he'd been to the lavatory and that he would be in a good mood!'

By the time Gracie reached Ottawa on 12 September, she was truly exhausted. Each night when speaking to Monty in Santa Monica, he had ended his call with the same three words, 'Please come home!' each time she answered, 'Just a couple more of these dos, and I will!' The Mayor of Ottawa, unlike some of his contemporaries, could not have treated Gracie more kindly. Presenting her with the keys to the city – the only other British person to receive this honour had been the Queen herself – and referring to the bombing incident in Arras, he put his arm round Gracie's shoulders and declared, 'This is one little gal that Hitler will *never* get!'

Gracie's decision to leave Canada came about after something her father had said a few weeks before: 'While you're out there with your tour, Grace, you'll be sure to bump into a couple of cousins. There'll be lots of cranks, but you'll recognize the ones who're genuine!' Gracie mentioned this in a radio interview, and by the time she reached Ottawa in the middle of September, a handful of 'relatives' were waiting to be reunited with her. 'One relation was a better actress than I was,' she said, explaining how this woman had gone on and on about an 'Uncle Tom' who did not exist, and Fred Stansfield's equally fictitious 'war-service' record. There were at least ten 'next-door neighbours', and even more artistes who claimed they had worked with her on the stage as far back as 1907. She *did*, however, meet a genuine cousin who had emigrated to the United States just before Fred's sudden departure from Rochdale some years before, and who now lived in Edmonton. Gracie said he was the spitting image of her father, and when she saw several photographs taken with the Stansfields, back home, she interpreted this as an omen and immediately began planning her return to England.

No sooner had she packed her trunks than Gracie was advised by British officials to stay on in America – as the wife of a listed 'enemy alien', she was no longer welcome in her own country. This must have come as a tremendous shock to her, particularly as those journalists who had openly accused her of 'copping out' were in no hurry to report in their columns that, carried out in the very poorest health, her war efforts thus far had raised $1\frac{1}{2}$ million – or that the Navy League had recently presented her with their most prestigious award, the Service Medal.

In an uncharacteristically vicious attack on the British press, Gracie declared that she had every right to perform on her native soil, and that if need be she would parachute into the country in the middle of the night! During her absence, Basil Dean had received anonymous threats from journalists detailing all too graphically how they would exact their revenge on Gracie should she ever set foot on any British stage – this ranged from throwing eggs to dousing her with paraffin. Dean took the threats seriously, but Gracie was not afraid. 'All these snooty buggers need to have their heads seen to,' she told one publication. 'Well, it looks like the public'll decide what's to be done with me!' Her tour of factories, army camps and shipyards was temporarily delayed, however, when, unable to fly directly to London, like many other stars she ended up in neutral Portugal. Her companions-in-exile in Lisbon included Anna Neagle and her husband Herbert Wilcox, and she was reunited with her French chum, Marie Dubas.

There were tremendous difficulties to be encountered securing air travel, and the friends spent much of their time at the Lys Hotel, playing cards or entertaining the other guests. Marie's companion, Sylvie Galthier, in an interview with me, remembered this anxious period.

Gracie had earned thousands of dollars for others, often less fortunate than herself, and now she was flat broke. Marie was able to help her and her young man with their hotel expenses. Sometimes they sang together, duetting in a couple of numbers in the first half of Marie's show at the Trinidad Theatre – traditional *fados* such as 'Don Solidon' and 'Primavera'. Gracie would execute a beautiful vocalise, and Marie would fit in the words in her stilted Portuguese. Both women had problems with their respective religions. Marie was Jewish, her name was forbidden over the airwaves, the Germans had taken over her house in Paris, and she wanted to marry the aviator Georges Bellair, the father of her small son, François. As civil ceremonies were not allowed in Portugal, it was necessary for her to convert to Catholicism. Gracie also spoke about converting, not just then but each time we met over the years, but she never did. When Marie and Georges married, she was guest of honour and in her speech Marie called her one of the gutsiest Englishwomen who ever drew breath – Lancashire's very own Jeanne d'Arc. Personally, I found it utterly loathsome that these two very wonderful women were hounded simply for falling in love.

To a certain extent, Gracie and Marie Dubas had been emulating

each other for years. Like her English counterpart, the great French
star was able to switch smoothly from an absurdly comic ditty to a
lyrical song such as the intensely emotional 'La Charlotte Prie Notre
Dame', which Gracie arranged to have transcribed into English but
subsequently dropped when told that its over-dramatic theme – a
desolate prayer to the Virgin Mary – would never have been
accepted by British admirers.

Marie Dubas, who always preferred public recitals to cutting
records, was one of the first artistes to travel around with a portable
taping machine which she used to monitor the audience's response
to certain songs. In this way she had been the first to record Edith
Piaf, when the teenage singer had called in at her dressing-room after
a show. According to Sylvie Galthier, Marie 'recorded' several songs
with Gracie, including the two *fados* and Francis Carco's touching,
'Le Doux Caboulot'.

> Le doux caboulot,
> Perdu sous les branches,
> Est tous les dimanches
> Plein de populo ...

Because of her generosity towards others, Marie herself soon ran
out of funds and she had to borrow money from the manager of
Trinidad Theatre to enable her to sail for the South of France. At the
same time Anna Neagle loaned Gracie the money for two air tickets
to England. Both reached their respective destinations on 8 July –
Marie to begin a hugely successful tour of the Free Zone, and Gracie
to kick off her tour with a visit to Rochdale.

The British press would have had a field-day had they known that
her companion, a young Dutchman she introduced to everyone only
as 'Ted, my ace', was considerably more than just a pilot friend
engaged by Basil Dean to fly her to and from venues. Almost a Carl
Balliol look-alike, and twenty-three years her junior, Ted had been
introduced to Gracie by his friend, Georges Bellair. 'We knew
nothing about him, other than the fact that he had been very, very
brave during the first week of the war, and that he had been shot
down over France,' said Sylvie Galthier. 'Gracie always considered
herself unattractive, and her ability to seduce an attractive, much
younger man gave an enormous boost to her then shattered
confidence in herself. They shared a hotel room all the time they

were in Lisbon, acted just like any normal couple, and a few months later they returned to their respective spouses a good deal happier, and with no regrets.'

In England, of course, Gracie and Ted slept in separate rooms. 'Mind you, we wore out the carpet on the landing!' she later joked with friends. The pair were met at the Rochdale borough border by the Mayor and several somewhat apprehensive local dignitaries, and when Gracie saw the hundreds of people lining the streets she assumed them to be there out of curiosity – or, worse still, to vent their anger. She soon realized that this was not to be so when the vast crowd congregated in the Town Hall square began cheering, and when all the factory whistles hooted a deafening salute in unison. On the Town Hall balcony, Gracie stroked one of the stone lions and said, 'I wish one of these buggers'd get hold of Hitler!'

In thirty-nine days, Gracie sang all over Britain: eighty-six full-length concerts, in and out of doors, which were seen by more than half a million fans. At Tunbridge Wells – at three o'clock in the morning – she was briefly reunited with her brother Tommy, who was appearing in a revue at a local theatre. After her show in Manchester, the *Guardian* applauded her 'immense vitality and rich theatrical exuberance'.

When Gracie sang at one Glasgow shipyard, an adjacent yard actually threatened industrial action if she did not sing for them! She repeatedly turned down radio broadcasts – an important decision, for in view of the recent press attacks she needed as many people as possible to *see* that she was sincere. Also, Basil Dean insisted that from now on she should always be the one to close the show, for if she did not, the audience simply got up and walked away as soon as she had finished because they were interested in no one else. Playing a clip of film from this tour, many years later on his *Fame* television series, Clive James called Gracie, 'A voice from downstairs that told the upstairs people that the British classes were all in the war together.'

Throughout the tour, Gracie never let Ted out of her sight. It was he who acted as Master of Ceremonies for her concert in the Orkneys, when she sang on a platform surrounded by dozens of tubs and pots of flowers, planted for the occasion by wounded servicemen. When one of these called out, 'What do you think to all the pansies, Gracie?', she could not resist retorting, 'Ee, they all seem like nice lads to me!'

During the flight back to the Scottish mainland on 28 July, Gracie was 'acting the goat' with Ted when he let go of the controls and was forced to make an emergency landing. She was flung forwards in her seat, and her face missed going through the shattered windscreen by a hair's breadth. Gracie laughed off the incident, though when Ted addressed her RAF audience later that afternoon, he was not joking when he said, 'Your Gracie has just been nearer to the angels than she realized.' After closing her recital with Ted Grouya's 'Safe In My Arms' and receiving a bouquet of roses from a young airman, she selected the largest bloom, pressed it to her lips and tossed it to her pilot sitting in the front row.

The next day, in Darlington, Gracie gave two women-only shows in local factories, and was presented with a cheque for several hundred pounds for her orphanage. The tour ended on 17 August, with a gala at the Royal Albert Hall in aid of the Red Cross and the St John's War Organization. It is a great pity, however, when one considers the recent malicious attacks on Gracie by her own media, that her tour was by and large reported only by regional newspapers who were instructed to keep coverage to a minimum. The best the broadsheets came up with was a tiny piece in *The Times*: 'The latest reports of Miss Gracie Fields' tour of Service units and munitions centres suggest that she has completely overcome any critical feelings due to her departure to the US, last year.'

When the Americans entered the war after the bombing of Pearl Harbor, Gracie announced that all the money she raised would now be divided equally between the two countries. Then, bidding her fighter-pilot adieu, she flew to New York to join Beatrice Lillie, George Burns and Gracie Allen in Carnival for Britain, a three-way radio broadcast (with New York, Hollywood and London, linked by land-line and submarine cable respectively) which raised funds for British air-raid victims, with down-the-line participation from Sir Cedric Hardwicke, Noël Coward and Robert Montgomery in Hollywood, and from London, Laurence Olivier and Vivien Leigh.

Gracie's American tour proved no less arduous than her Canadian one. A bonus was that Monty, albeit often hundreds of miles away, was at least in the same country. Her posters proclaimed:

YOU'LL LAUGH! YOU'LL CRY! YOU'LL LOVE GRACIE FIELDS! Before the war, Miss Gracie Fields was offered fabulous sums to appear in America. Too busy then, she comes now and takes no money! All the profits go to the British War Relief Society.

Eschewing the larger cities, Gracie hoped to work in smaller communities often overlooked by major show-business personalities – Duluth and St Paul, Fort Custer, and Kalamazoo – where a six-year-old dancer fan, Joan Biljum, presented her with a bouquet ... of celery! Most of the venues were high schools because, she said, she felt more comfortable working in a young people's environment. When she suddenly began demanding $6,000 a performance, no one balked. The money, once her expenses had been taken out, went straight into the British War Relief Fund.

On the eve of her 26 September concert in Jamestown, Dakota – famous for giving the world Peggy Lee – Gracie went down with flu, but refused to cancel. She closed with Kate Smith's stirring 'God Bless America', and had the entire auditorium in tears. The *Jamestown Post* wrote, 'Many geniuses have come up through the London "halls" – one thinks of Charlie Chaplin, Harry Lauder, and a few others of the elect, but no greater one than this Englishwoman from the North Country.'

This report made Gracie inconsolably homesick, though she knew that it would be some time before she saw England again. Neither was she too keen on staying for too long in America. As she had explained in an interview, 'I love America, but it's a bit too big for me. It would take a lifetime to know it, then you would find something just around the corner that you had missed.'

7

Red Sails in the Sunset

On 29 May 1942, Gracie opened in *Top Notchers* at the 44th Street Theatre, her first Broadway appearance in twelve years. Originally launched as *Keep 'Em Laughing!*, the revue had been flagging for some time and now the legendary Shubert Brothers stepped into the breach and asked the producer, Clifford Fischer (later the American manager of Edith Piaf) to revise it. Gracie was his first choice, and she was signed up at the same time as Argentinita and Frédéric Rey, at the time two of the most famous but volatile dancers in the world. The support acts included The Hartmans, and comedian Zero Mostel.

Gracie's contract, originally, was for four weeks, and to keep things above board she wisely told the press that, as she had not earned one penny for herself since the beginning of the war, she was doing this one to support her family. One newspaper, the *Columbus Dispatch*, even did a little 'investigating' of its own, announcing on 6 June, 'Miss Fields' personal appearances have earned a net total of $2,291,837 for the British War Relief Fund and the Navy League of Cañada, and right now, while she's taking "time out", she's preparing *another* cross-country tour!'

Gracie and Frédéric Rey had met several times in Paris and more recently had shared the bill in Brest – a port renowned for attracting only the rowdiest sailors. Born in Vienna, Frédé had been discovered by Mistinguett at the city's Ronach Theatre in 1933. He then became a sensation as the nude adagio star at the Folies-Bergère.

Although Gracie did not resist when the astonishingly handsome, virile Frédé made a play for her, there was another reason why she admired him so – he was actively working for the Résistance, and

100

had only left France to work temporarily in the United States because the Gestapo had become suspicious of his activities. Only weeks after leaving *Top Notchers*, along with Josephine, Piaf and Lucienne Boyer, he would constantly put his life on the line in the fight against Nazi oppression. Also, unlike the copiously vulgar Carl Balliol, this man radiated class. When Frédé donned a posing-pouch to dance around Gracie Fields while she was singing 'The Last Time I Saw Paris' a routine they had performed in Brest – there were no complaints from the audience.

Gracie aside, *Top Notchers* was not generally well-received by the critics, most of whom thought that it dragged on for too long. In fact, the reason for it doing so could have been attributed entirely to 'the Pied Piper of the English music-hall', as the *New York Times* called Gracie. She came on just before the first interval, and though her songs were ones she had been doing for years, because her repertoire was so unusually varied and large there was always something that she could pluck out of thin air. Halfway through 'Turn 'Erbert's Face to the Wall, Mother', she stopped the orchestra and yelled for the house-lights to be kept on. She told the audience, 'I want to see all your faces whilst you're singing – and if you *don't* sing, I'm off home!' They kept singing, Gracie fulfilled every request, and the interval arrived forty minutes late – by the time Frédéric Rey and Argentinita got on to the stage for their routine, at 11 p.m., most of the audience had left.

'I never know exactly what I'm going to do when I walk on,' Gracie told the leading theatre critic, Robert Coleman. 'It takes a couple of numbers to find out what an audience likes, then I gives it to 'em!' Coleman was a member of that dreaded clique of critics who, with a single column-inch, could make or break a career or show. He probably did not know what he was letting himself in for, however, when he wrote, 'We would like to hear her do more comedy, more popular songs, in place of this semi-highbrow material.' Gracie's response was, 'Get yourself another job, lad. You don't know what the hell you're talking about!'

Besides her twice-daily performances in *Top Notchers* – three on Sundays – Gracie made innumerable appearances in and around New York to raise money for British War Relief. It was as though she was *ashamed* of earning something for herself and her family. She bumped into Tallulah Bankhead, who took her along to one of the many Hollywood canteens which had now begun popping up all over America, and begged her to sing 'I'll Be Seeing You'. The Master of Ceremonies asked her not to sing anything too 'sentimental' declaring that such things only upset the soldiers, then introduced her as 'Britain's greatest comedienne'. Gracie walked on the stage and scoffed, 'Britain's greatest comedienne, indeed! Who does he think I am, the Queen? Now then, who wants to hear me do "Ave Maria"?'

At the beginning of September, Gracie made her American night-club début when Mike Fritzel and Joe Jacobson engaged her for a season at the Chez Paris, in Chicago. Unusually for her, she did not come on until the stroke of midnight, and she opened with a strange number, 'I Came Here to Talk to Joe'. 'Sally' had never caught on in the States as it had in Britain, and the Americans had their own Gracie theme-song, 'All For One and One For All', and she always sang this and much of her regular repertoire including the show-stopping 'The Thingummybob' her biggest hit in America, which was being played on juke-boxes all across the country.

> I'm the girl that makes the ring
> That holds the oil that oils the ring
> That takes the shank
> That moves the crank
> That work's the Thingummybob ...
> That's going to win the war!

At the end, Gracie always closed the show with her arrangement of 'The Yanks Are Coming' to resounding applause.

Before leaving Chicago, Gracie made several visits to the Hollywood canteen there, and in the middle of the month was included on the bill at the All Star Bond Show – for the purchase of a $25 bond, wealthy fans heard her sing 'Nighty-Night Little Sailor Boy' and 'Sleepy Lagoon' – some years later the theme to BBC radio's *Desert Island Discs*. The cabaret season brought Gracie another reward, too, when Tallulah Bankhead introduced her to the film producer, Sol Lesser, who offered her a part in his film *Stage Door Canteen*.

There was some dissent over the matter of what Gracie would sing in the film (in her role of Gracie Fields). The ebullient producer stipulated no sentiment, just a couple of comedy numbers. Gracie compromised inasmuch as she sang the semi-comic 'Machine-Gun

Song' – the story of a Yank who, remembering Pearl Harbor, had shot down two Japanese warplanes. Then she announced that she would be doing 'The Lord's Prayer' – and when Lesser told her that this would not be possible, many of her fellow stars, including Tallulah Bankhead and Ethel Merman, threatened to boycott the production. Gracie performed 'The Lord's Prayer'.

The scene was captured in just one take. Lesser had instructed the extras playing soldiers to remain seated during the two-minute performance – but as soon as she began they rose, to a man, and as she sang 'Amen', to a man their heads fell forwards, and many of them actually cried.

Gracie then presented the hapless Sol Lesser with a demand of her own – that 25 per cent of the British gross on the film be given to *her* war charities ... she had already promised her fee to Lottie Albert of the Ladies' Guild. When Lesser shunned her, Gracie protested to the film's director, Frank Borzage – and won her case.

The plot for *Stage Door Canteen* was publicized as 'The Love Story of a Soldier', with the main characters played by unknowns – Lon McCallister the all-American teenage soldier who has never been kissed, and Marjorie Riordan the girl who has the privilege of kissing him – so that they might be more identified with the average man and woman in the street, and with all the bit-parts going to a veritable host of international stars making appearances more or less as themselves. The reclusive stage actress, Katharine Cornell, who had never appeared on the screen before, was seen in a delicatessen reading an excerpt from *Romeo and Juliet* to a youth who had played Romeo in a school play. George Raft and Johnny Weissmuller were seen washing dishes, Gracie sang, Yehudi Menuhin played 'Ave Maria' – Merle Oberon, Tallulah Bankhead, Katharine Hepburn and Judith Anderson played hostesses. The film ran for almost two and a half hours, but there were complaints from neither public nor press. 'It is an *embarrassment* of talent!', proclaimed the *Hollywood Reporter*.

Immediately after *Stage Door Canteen*, Gracie took a big risk by appearing opposite Monty Woolley in Nunnally Johnson's screen adaptation of Arnold Bennett's Edwardian drama, *Holy Matrimony* – a risk in the sense that this was her first serious, middle-aged non-singing role. Woolley, a former college professor, had shot to fame in *The Man Who Came to Dinner*, and at the time was the long-term lover of Cole Porter – three years hence he would portray himself opposite Cary Grant's Porter in the largely fictionalized biopic, *Night and Day*. If Woolley's character in his film with Gracie comes across as staid and retiring, the actor himself was anything but, as he had a tendency to invite all manner of rough trade onto the set which, after her adventures in Europe, amused Gracie rather than disgusted her.

In *Holy Matrimony*, Monty Woolley played a famous English painter, Priam Farll, whose hatred of the limelight has compelled him to spend the last twenty-five years in a remote tropical land with his valet, Henry Leek, emerging only when informed that he is to be knighted. Fate proves advantageous when, on their first day in London, Leek dies and Farll assumes his identity. Unknown to him, however, the valet has written to a matrimonial agency and sent a photograph of his employer to comfortably-off widow, Alice Chalice (Gracie). She and Farll meet, fall in love, and she becomes Mrs Henry Leek, and all is well until Leek's wife (Una O'Connor) turns up with her sons and he is accused of bigamy! Even greater is the fiasco which ensues when Alice begins selling his paintings for a few pounds to a crafty art dealer who sells them for many thousands. Now rightfully calling himself Priam Farll, the still shy painter is taken to court but is too stubborn to really prove who he is by revealing the twin moles on his neck – only when Alice does this, and when it is realized that the real Henry Leek has been buried in Westminster Abbey, is the matter resolved. Priam and his wife then return to the tropics, where Alice pampers him and serves him his favourite lunch – kangaroo chops in crocodile sauce! Gracie handled her role extremely well, telling the press that if it had not been for the advent of fame she too would have ended up like Alice Chalice – serving chips in Rochdale – and the film took a then astonishing $2 million dollars at the American box office and fared almost as well in England.

After completing the film – looking and sounding bubbly as ever, but thoroughly exhausted, Gracie spent the next few months resting with her family in Santa Monica. On 8 August 1943 she was doing a radio show in Baltimore when a call came through from Basil Dean in London, inviting her to participate in a six-week fund-raising tour of Northern England, this time with several radio broadcasts. Four days later she flew to London, leaving several contracts uncompleted – a major film, a one-woman show on Broadway, and innumerable concert and charity engagements –

though when she told her 'bosses' in America that she would be back by the end of the year there were no protests. Little did she realize the problems this promise would cause.

Replacing the tetchy Harry Parr-Davies who was suffering from exhaustion was Ivor Newton, who had played for many of the big stars including Tetrazzini. Unlike his predecessor, however, Newton was not quite prepared for Gracie's unorthodox method of working with musicians. Harry Parr-Davies had never used sheet music because he had been too short-sighted to read it, and Gracie had loved getting him in a stew by suddenly changing key in the middle of a song. 'It kept him on his toes, and made him play more passionately,' she said. Newton met her at the Dorchester, where she asked him if he was able to transpose. His response was that he could, so long as she told him before the show if he should be transposing up or down. Gracie replied, 'Ee, I couldn't tell you that – you'll have to wait till I start singing, luv!'And if this did not unnerve him enough, the fact that she did not feel any particular need to rehearse made Newton's task of accompanying her that much more invidious. He included her quirky rebuff in his memoirs 'If anything goes wrong, I can always say, Ivor's promised to do better tomorrow!"'

For once, the tour did not kick off at Rochdale but at Ashton-under-Lyne, where the men of the REME presented her with a brass key inscribed 'For Our Darling Gracie So That She May Hold The Key Of Our Hearts'. The next morning she travelled with Basil Dean and Mary Barratt to Rochdale, where 10,000 people turned out to greet her. In a long but thoughtful speech the Mayor praised her '... for helping to foster a feeling of understanding between the peoples of this country and America, which must play a vital part in the shaping of the post-war world'. Earlier, Basil Dean had arranged for her show to take place at the Hippodrome, but Gracie insisted on changing the venue – to the mill where she had worked as a girl. Afterwards, she stood on the balcony of the Town Hall and sang 'You'll Never Know', breaking down at the end. Then, after a quick dab of her eyes she launched into 'Don't Be Angry With Me, Sergeant'.

One triumph followed another as Gracie zigzagged across the North of England, though the press were never far behind her. She made the mistake of allowing Rex North of the *Sunday Pictorial* to badger her into answering several contrived, awkward questions which, had she answered them truthfully in the first place, would have saved her a great deal of humiliation in the near future. 'I've sat next to her during some of these interviews,' Irene Bevan said. 'She would say one thing one minute, then go off and tell a completely different story immediately afterwards, with some real whoppers. Why she did this I'll never know.' Rex North's piece was published on 22 August 1943 under the heading, 'I Have Nothing To Hide – I Did Not Run Away!' and quoted Gracie on her fear for her sisters and their children when her house had, for two nights running, shaken with exploding mines ...

> I told them, 'For God's sake, go out and live with Mum and Dad in America, then I won't have to worry about you any more.' My sisters pleaded, 'Come with us!' And then a horrible thought struck me. What would I feel like if the boat went down? How would I ever be able to hold my head up if my sisters – and those children I love as if they were my own – went down and I was not with them? *That* decided me.

This was of course untrue. Gracie had sworn to stand by Monty no matter what happened. Sending her sisters and parents to the United States, the long way round via the Panama Canal, had been a totally unrelated exercise. She also changed her story about the money and 'few trinkets' she had taken with her, even though it had been *before* the embargo, and of no concern whatsoever to any third party:

> Monty took what he had – just a few thousand pounds which he had brought over here from America in the first place. And the jewellery? Of course I took a lot with me. I had made a lot of money in the past, and like any other woman had treated myself every now and then, though I only bought one ring specially for the trip. Do you blame me for taking my bits and pieces with me? Had I thought there would've been this much trouble over my jewels, I would've sooner given the whole lot to the country!

North then 'voiced public opinion', he said, by saying, 'They have said that charity was merely a sideline with you, that you were more concerned with making another personal fortune.' Her response was that she had only appeared in *Top Notchers* to put an end to a whispering campaign.

> Performers who had come back from Canada had spread the rumour that I was only good for charity work and no longer able to pack them in for myself. So I set out to make liars of these rumour-mongers. I earn a lot of money out there, and can keep on doing it for years!

So, had she given England up for good? Gracie was asked. Adding a few more little white lies for good measure, she ended the interview:

> I shall always come back and sing in England so long as I have a voice left to sing with – and I shall never charge anyone in this country a penny to hear me sing. But I am going back to America. I am a businesswoman with four years of a five-year contract left to run. And when that's over, there is Capri, gorgeous Capri. I can rest there with Monty. You won't believe this but I've persuaded him to take up farming!

The matter should have ended there, but as she had a little time on her hands – and because, though she disliked Basil Dean, Gracie could never say No to him – she consented to a 21-day tour of North Africa, Italy and Sicily with the Eighth Army. She was in good company: although not all working for the same organization Damia, Josephine Baker, Marlene Dietrich, Frédéric Rey and Alice Delysia were touring the same camp-circuit, and their paths frequently crossed

In Algiers, on 17 September, Gracie appeared in a benefit gala with Jack Benny and Al Jolson – included in her programme was the Mistinguett number she had performed in Paris. She was halfway through another show there – battling to keep in tune to a broken piano which had half its keys missing – when there was an unexpected windstorm. When all her sheet-music blew off into the desert she threw up her hands in desperation … then guided the 20,000-strong contingent through two hours of community singing. And *still* the press hounded her.

Contractually, she was bound to return to America by the end of September 1943 to begin a nationwide radio series sponsored by Pall

Mall cigarettes, and to make a film, her first on American soil, not counting her cameo in *Stage Door Canteen*. Basil Dean had known this before engaging her for the ENSA tour, and knowing her schedule was tight, arranged her transport from Algiers and urged her to return to the United States as soon as possible. Gracie, who could not have cared less that she had signed a contract with her sponsors, the American Tobacco Company, had already begged them to allow her another month in Europe, but her pleas had fallen on deaf ears. She now issued a statement which read 'I have this radio series to finish and a picture to make, and make no further commitments. The one thing I want most is to get back to the boys, and I hope it will be some time in January.'

According to the *Daily Mail*, Gracie left Algiers in tears. A few weeks later, on 23 October, the Eighth Army's weekly newspaper, *Crusader* – picking up on the headline which had appeared in *Reynold's News*, 'Gracie Gets the Bird From the Eighth Army' – printed the accusation, 'You and the rest of the top-liners of the theatrical profession have let down the fighting soldiers.' In an open letter to Gracie, singling her out as an 'example', and taking up most of the publication's front page, the editor D H Martin launched a blistering attack.

> You told the *Crusader* you thought the Eighth Army saved England. You said if you had your way you would follow us to the end, entertaining whenever conditions permitted. Your wish reached the case of Army Headquarters. They sent you a signal saying that all facilities would be given to you to stay with us for as long as you liked. But you did not stay. The Eighth Army was in the hell of desert battle when you were singing 'Don't Be Angry With Me, Sergeant' to enraptured American audiences. We know you are a great turn – along with Dan Leno and Marie Lloyd, you are one of the greatest artistes who ever trod the boards. But you would have been a greater trouper if you had forgotten your commitments and your contracts and stayed with us a little longer. Men whose lives you could brighten have had to break many more sacred contracts and commitments. We're keeping the Hun away from the shores of Britain, and his bombers away from the skies above Rochdale!

When an American reporter had asked Gracie why, unlike

Marlene Dietrich and Josephine Baker – both honorary lieutenants in the United States Army – she always eschewed khaki, on and off the stage, when visiting the troops, she had replied, 'Those soldiers appreciated changes in my costumes. Instead of saying, "I saw Gracie the night she sang such and such a song", they say, 'I saw Gracie the night she wore the white dress.'" This in mind, the *Crusader* concluded, attacking artistes in general:

> *All* of you should have been in khaki at the start of the war. Men and women whose job is entertaining should not be allowed to paint or wear pretty clothes unless they are on their *own* side of the footlights – entertaining an audience of Servicemen.

Gracie was back in America, working on her *Victory Show* radio series – broadcast for just five minutes each weekday evening, this had proved so popular that it had soon been upped to half an hour – and she actually received news of her *defence* before getting to know what she had been accused of! Tommy Trinder said of Sergeant Martin, 'It's only a sergeant's opinion, and after all, we're *all* fighting for our opinions.' Trinder had himself been criticized for leaving the front to appear on the London stage. He added, 'That's one for the tax-collector. And in any case, isn' t it just as important to entertain the troops and war-workers at home?' The comic then put one snooty reporter in his place by confessing his 'secret' – that he had been at Dunkirk, helping the evacuation with his motor-boat.

Al Jolson, writing in *Variety*, said, 'Out there, you have no idea whether you're going to play before two hundred boys, or twenty thousand. With no planned schedule, you can't get out to see them all, and the ones you don't see are hurt deeply. They'll call you all kinds of names, and deservedly.' Jack Benny added, 'Unless you can reach *all* the boys, there'll be more ill-feeling left behind than if you never made the tour.' The *World Press News*, branding the *Crusader* 'unfair and unchivalrous', issued its own open letter to Sergeant Martin beginning 'Since when has it become the practice of British journalists to urge the breaking of contracts?' – and ending 'You pillory and flay her in a letter which reaches the public press of two continents. *Shame on you!*' The *Daily Mail* launched an attack of its own against greedy agents and managers who, in the interests of their ten per cent failed to release their clients from lucrative West

End contracts which grossed them anything up to £300 a week, while the fixed rate for ENSA entertainers was only £10 a week. One of the most powerful impresarios in Britain, Charles B Cochran, added to this by with a letter published in the *Daily Telegraph* on 27 October, part of which read: 'With the exception of Alice Delysia, who stands alone in her war efforts, what lady of the theatre has done more, or as much as Gracie Fields? Before there *was* a war, Miss Fields was a great, and silent, worker for good causes. If artists *are* to be conscripted for entertainment, so let it be – I suggest other famous women stars (who have not been overseas at all) might be called upon to forgo commercial contracts and make a tour overseas.'

Gracie's biggest ally in this unfortunate mess was the Prime Minister, Winston Churchill, the man who had in the first place suggested that she work in America. Convinced that the press and the Eighth Army were showing no signs of backing off with their smear campaign against her, he ordered strict censorship on the *Crusader* – 'It is unfair that Miss Fields should be singled out for an attack in a newspaper published for the troops, and the said publication is also reprimanded for its critical attitude towards the Italian political situation,' the dispatch read. For the time being, the dust was allowed to settle.

Following the unprecedented success of *Holy Matrimony*, Gracie was once more cast opposite Monty Woolley for the film initially titled *Molly, Bless Her*, which had been adapted from Frances Marion's novel of that name more than a decade before as a vehicle for that unlikeliest of superstars, Marie Dressler, and had been kept on hold since her death in 1934. The director, Lewis Seiler, told Gracie, 'Play the part as Dressler would have done, and all will be fine.' Her response: 'Don't tell me how to do my job, love, and I won't tell you how to do yours!' The supporting cast was a good one, headed by a young Roddy McDowall, Reginald Gardiner and Doris Lloyd.

Unable to find work after years on the stage, a singer (Gracie) secures a position as housekeeper to a grumpy prospective Member of Parliament (Woolley) by telling him that she has had plenty of experience. She is sprung by the (she thinks) polished butler (Gardiner), himself a former ham actor, but keeps him quiet by taking him to the local pub and getting him plastered. She then discovers that all the servants in the house are crooked, fires them and installs several unemployed theatrical pals ... and the slapstick begins.

Much of Gracie's screen time is spent trying to prevent her employer from guessing her 'secret'. She comes into her own by promoting a better understanding between him and his estranged son (McDowall), the product of a disastrous marriage which has blighted his political aspirations. When the boy's thought-to-be-dead mother (Lloyd) suddenly arrives from South Africa, to blackmail her ex-husband, the housekeeper and her 'servant henchmen' play tricks on her which soon send her packing. In the process, the old sourpuss politician is transformed into a genial, fun-loving old stick, and all ends well.

Whilst awaiting the release of the film, Gracie was offered the lead in Frank Capra's *The Flying Yorkshireman* based on the novel of that name by Eric Knight. Her co-star was to have been Barry Fitzgerald, but the project was suddenly dropped – according to RKO Pictures, because of a lack of manpower for the special effects. All the company's technical experts were in active service.

In June 1944, following the Allied invasion of Normandy, Gracie returned to England, telling hardly anyone where she was going or why. In London she barged unannounced into Basil Dean's office, and *ordered* him to get her across to France so that she could entertain the troops around Falaise and Caen. The head of ENSA refused to have anything to do with sending her to face such obvious danger. After a brief argument, Gracie stormed out of the room, slamming the door behind her. It took her several weeks to organize everything herself, but in July she did cross the Channel, incognito. Norman Taylor, a 25-year-old private with the intelligence section of the 53rd Welsh Division, told me of Gracie's secret mission.

Our ground troops were trying to take Carpiquet airport, near Caen – the RAF needed it for an advance base, but the German Tiger tanks were hulled down and proving impossible to move. Then from our slit-trenches we saw five hundred Halifax and Lancaster bombers, at a thousand feet, and the next morning, Carpiquet was taken. Within a few days, Gracie arrived on the scene. The Germans were still there, less than two miles away, and the situation was extremely dangerous. She gave a concert, all the same, and offered us that much more to live and fight for. No other living entertainer had Gracie's guts.

Gracie returned to America, once more the unsung heroine. Her *Victory Show* radio series was coming to the end of its run after attracting a cult following across the United States. After her first half-hour broadcast, she had left the studio and been mobbed by a small group of young GIs home on leave. Sensing that the usual autographs may not have been enough, she had invited them back to the house for tea and scones. Word had got around, and Gracie's 'English Teas', home-made by Jenny Stansfield – at midnight! – had become something of an institution. Most of the time, she was only expected to cater for around twenty, but on one occasion Gracie took 150 soldiers back to Amalfi Drive, and Jenny had to unpack her best china which she had kept hidden in boxes since arriving in America, too afraid of risking it on Gracie's friends!

A new Tuesday evening radio spot, sponsored by the makers of Ipana and Mum, was also dropped at the time of the Capra film after an attack by a provincial newspaper. It was all very well it said, referring to another advertising campaign, promoting cigarettes with 'Pass! Shoot! Goal!', but using a sacred song to sell a deodorant was not on. 'Advertising Mum with "The Lord's Prayer", that tells you something about our culture, doesn't it?' screamed the *Denver Rocky*.

Gracie was not in the least perturbed. 'I didn't want to do the blessed thing in the first place,' she said. 'And I'm certainly not interested in putting all that muck under my arms!' She then announced that, in view of the controversy surrounding her last overseas tour, she was now her own boss and intent on doing what she felt was best for herself and the thousands of Englishmen and Americans who were fighting and laying down their lives in order to deliver humanity from tyranny and oppression.

On 27 January 1945 she issued a statement: 'This next tour will be the longest camp-tour on record. I don't expect to be back until January 1946. We'll start toward England by way of Hawaii, the Philippines, Australia, New Zealand, India, and all way-stations where American or British troops are quartered. There'll be two charity concerts a week in the larger places – and one ordinary show to defray expenses – plus the hospitals and camps. On tiny islands and outposts the entertainment will be strictly for the regular soldiers.'

When several leading Hollywood stars and promoters – the so-called 'Lazy Sunbathers' – scoffed at the idea, Elizabeth Wilson of

Liberty was compelled to write,

> Many stars of the entertainment world were born in poverty just as Gracie was – but somewhere in the process of stardom they lost their touch with human beings. Physical contact with ordinary people, people whose dimes and quarters have made their success possible, fills many of them with horror. This lady is a movie-queen with a *difference*!

The retitled *Molly and Me* was premièred in March 1945. It proved hugely successful in Britain, but in America, though the average box-office figures showed a 96 per cent attendance during its early weeks, in the long run it did not fare as well as Gracie's other films. Her reviews were rarely less than excellent, but many critics disliked the way in which Monty Woolley handled his role. *Box Office Digest* was scathing: 'His belief that mumbling is a touch of class playing is strongly dismissed. Picture customers like to hear what they pay for, strange as that may seem.' Some make-or-break critics suggested that *Molly and Me* would be better suited as a secondary feature rather than a top attraction, and even now it is rarely seen.

It is hard to ascertain whether the distinguished film critic James Agate was being entirely tactful of even complimentary when he wrote, 'Miss Fields is about as nice a woman over forty as I have ever seen ... I recommend her highly to anyone who has ceased to believe it possible to grow decently into middle age.'

8

Take Me to Your Heart Again

Before *Molly and Me* went out on general release, Gracie was invited to work with Constance Bennett on the American actress's own production of *Paris Underground*, directed by Gregory Ratoff. This harrowing story of two women Résistance workers in Occupied France was based on Etta Shiber's best-selling book and boasted a fine supporting cast of actors who were virtually unknown outside their respective countries.

The plot could not have been more topical, opening as it does only hours before the Nazis move into Paris. Kitty de Mornay (Constance Bennett) is a flighty American unhappily married to a Frenchman (Georges Rigaud) and Emmyline Quayle (Gracie) is her sedate, tea-obsessed English antique-shop owner companion. When the pair attempt to leave for the Free Zone, they miss the last train out of Paris because Ritty delays the proceedings, thinking herself immune from the enemy because her husband works for the Foreign Office. Emmy tells her, 'Everybody with any sense is in a panic. Perhaps that's why you're so calm – and there's enough confusion here without you running around.'

Caught up in the traffic jam caused by the mass exodus to the South, the friends turn off on a country road and spend the night at an inn, which they discover is hiding a frightened young shot-down RAF pilot (Leslie Vincent). Abandoning any idea of leaving Occupied France, they conceal him in the back of their car, and are on their way back to Paris when they get a puncture. Emmy is changing the tyre when they are rescued by a group of Germans led by the handsome Captain Kurt von Weber (Kurt Kreuger), with whom Kitty is compelled by fear to flirt with when he escorts them

114

home. She explains away Emmy's nervousness, saying 'Like most spinsters, she's shy when there are men around!'

Aided by André, Kitty's estranged husband, the women join the Résistance, enabling Vincent and some three hundred airmen to get out of the country. During the course of the film they are transformed from *gentille* ladies into tough, shrewd underground bosses – before they are rumbled by the Gestapo, arrested, beaten and interned. However, the liberation scene where they are rescued by the Americans prior to being decorated by the French government, was hammered by *Variety*:

> The two women are in the hands of the Nazis, their underground activities broken up, and they're probably about to be shot or tortured to death. Suddenly, in the very next shot the US Army liberators, like the Texas Rangers in an old Western, come to the rescue. There's no effort made to bridge the gap ...

Another leading publication dismissed the film, released in August 1945 when he war was almost over, for having 'as many thrills as a scenic railway', but these were just two mediocre reviews amongst dozens of dazzling ones. *Motion Picture Review* said of Gracie, 'She compliments Miss Bennett's characterization as Yorkshire pudding compliments roast beef, and does it just as tastily. Her low-key playing exhibits exceptional versatility.' The film was a tremendous hit, in spite of strong competition from Twentieth Century-Fox's *State Fair* and Paramount's *Lost Weekend*.

Even so, Gracie considered even the highest accolade but minor consolation following her 'shindigs' with Constance Bennett, whom she had loathed since their first meeting at one of the Vanderbilt parties some years before. Irene Bevan said, 'Constance Bennett was a highly sophisticated American woman who upstaged Grace all the time. To her, Grace must have looked as if she'd come to do the washing, and Bennett treated her that way. Grace couldn't stand up to those sort of people. She would be floored by the very look of them. Grace wasn't there to pose, but to *become* something.' Many years later, Bennett's treatment of her still rankled, and Gracie told her friend Anne Taylor, 'That woman was a devil. She tried to make me face the opposite way, so the camera didn't get my best profile. There was never any compromise – she *always* had to be the centre of attention!'

Because of Constance Bennett's status of producer, Gracie's complaints almost always fell on deaf ears – even the reporter from *Modern Screen*, invited to sit in on some of the rehearsals, could could not resist the quip, 'Connie's the boss-lady on this one!' Bennett told him that in her search for the ideal Kurt von Weber she had interviewed fifty-three 'Aryan studs' within the privacy of her dressing-room before finding one who was authentically German – but unfortunately for her not entirely straight, hence the hoped-for flirtation which had to be reserved strictly for the screen. For Kurt's Nazi cronies, she had vetted another two hundred. Her wardrobe was commissioned from Adrian, one of Hollywood's top costumiers ... Gracie went around telling everyone that her own clothes had been bought from the 'pop-shop'.

Bennett was horrified, too, in January 1945 when the director threw an afternoon party for Gracie's birthday – Gracie asked why there was only one candle, instead of forty-seven. But it was when the American made one or two rather uncomplimentary remarks about 'Miss Fields' dress-sense, or rather lack of it', that Gracie felt compelled to retort, telling Bob Thomas of the *Los Angeles Times*, 'I often wonder how the escort of that so-called glamour girl feels when he sees her eyelashes start slipping and her make-up drip? *Real* glamour consists as much of intelligence and personality as good looks. Like Harry Lauder once old me, "Lassie, it's not wha' ye have, it's how ye use it!"' Constance Bennett is said to have never spoken to Gracie again away from the set.

After the ordeal of *Paris Underground*, Gracie told friends that this would be her last Hollywood film – it turned out to be the very last film she made anywhere. The medium had never interested her much in the first place, and until recently she had never been offered the kind of role that would utilize her talents to their full potential. Critics have since professed that she would have made the perfect St Joan and that it would have been well within her scope to have played Mistress Quickly, Mother Courage, or one of several Ibsen heroines. Now, she said, it was too late. She had had enough. Her only future involvement with the cinema would be singing Harry Seymour's 'My Boy' in a War Bond short for Twentieth Century-Fox – and when she coaxed Monty Banks into playing the part of the Mayor in *A Bell For Adano*, a substantial success in 1949 in Britain and the United States. She would even refuse Monty's request to sing its theme, Don Pelosi's 'It Happened in Adano', which became a minor hit for Donald Peers.

During the filming of *Paris Underground* – released in Britain as *Madame Pimpernel* – now that it was safe to do so, Gracie's family went back to England. Gracie then set about finding a secretary to look after her affairs whilst she and Monty were away on their forthcoming tour, Gracie's longest camp-tour on record. Mary Barratt had left her to work separately for ENSA at the beginning of the war. The parting was but brief. Mary had met and married the set-designer Leon 'Ding' Davey, and would return to the fold immediately after the war.

Neva Hecker was a thirty-two-year-old American who, like Mary Barratt, corresponded with Gracie for a number of years before actually meeting her. She had first become aware of her after *not* hearing her sing 'Walter, Walter' in *We're Going to Be Rich*; her initial letter began on a hardly flattering note – Neva had considered the song so dreadfully raucous that she had fled to sit it out in the cinema toilet! Afterwards, however, she had returned to her seat and had been so overwhelmed by the rest of the film – weeping upon hearing 'The Sweetest Song in the World' – that she had gone to see the film again, sixty-six times on the trot!

For a long time, Gracie assumed that Neva must have been an usherette, yet the more they corresponded, the more she came to like her. When she discovered that the young woman was working as a secretary in one of Hollywood's top hotels, she marched into the foyer, demanded to see her, and hired her on the spot. One of Neva's first tasks was to parcel up all the clothes which her employer would not be taking with her on her tour. These were dispatched to Brighton to be shared out amongst Gracie's family.

In May 1945 there was a heated exchange of letters between Basil Dean and Gracie when she suddenly changed the order of her tour, and one final row with Harry Parr-Davies, who still did not want to do war work – claiming that he had seen enough of uniforms whilst doing his military service to last him a lifetime. For Gracie, this was tantamount to cowardice and she had begged Dean to get her Hal Stead, a young Australian who had occasionally played for her in England and France. The head of ENSA's rejection of Stead – owing to 'problems within his private life' – only increased the bad blood between them. Monty Banks urged her to file an official complaint against Dean, but Gracie would not do this. She wrote to her sisters,

[Harry] didn't mind going to Australia, but he wanted a nice remuneration in American dollars which of course we couldn't afford, so we'll just pick a new Australian lad. I think Basil Dean has been very mean, but maybe it isn't his fault altogether ... being such a disliked man he must have very many enemies who are trying to shake his position, so I guess he has to be wary of everything he does. He was trying to switch the tour around, starting off from England ... but to get our priorities on the airplane we had to promise ten weeks in the Pacific under USO. And seeing as it's over in Europe, we should really entertain the kids who are still in the thick of it. It doesn't make any difference to me, though, so long as my work is pleasing to whoever sees and hears me.

By and large Gracie was uninterested in these petty squabbles – she simply wanted to 'get on with me knitting' and eventually, she was assigned a young pianist named Eric Fox. For her, the next few months were unquestionably the most arduous of her whole life, though in retrospect she said she would not have missed them for the world. 'That was a fantastic period of her life and no one in England appreciated what it must have been like,' Irene Bevan stressed. 'I don't remember Vera Lynn, Anne Shelton or any other big British star did anything quite so dangerous. *Only* Grace did this kind of tour. She wanted to see the world, and to show everyone how patriotic she was after all the horrible things they'd said about her. Some of those places at that time were *horrendous*. Credit needs to be given for that tour more than *anything* Grace did in her latter years.'

At times impervious to the heat, the insects which seemed to single her out from other victims, the mostly inedible food, and countless hair-raising flights in appalling conditions, Gracie never lost her reserve for one moment. She took most of the dresses she had worn during her American tours, though the heat and humidity of the locations she visited made wearing them impractical and she resorted to the previously spurned khaki. Even so, she cut a welcome figure in her drill trousers, regulation Army shirt, and an Australian bush-hat which became so heavy with the badges of all the units she visited that she had to stop wearing it long before the end of the tour. 'When I try to remember some of the places I ended up in, I feel like a bloody atlas!' she later cracked.

Gracie was at Piva, Bougainville (one of the Solomon Islands) on VJ Day, 15 August 1945, when the Japanese surrendered, effectively bringing the war to a close. She had been advised not to visit the place, but as usual she followed the dictates of her conscience and pleased herself – the men had to put up with whatever Fate sent winging their way, and so would she. She was well on her way towards becoming Britain's greatest authority on the human condition, if she was not this already.

She and Monty were given the hut especially constructed for the Duke of Gloucester, the coolest spot on an island which was renowned for is dreadful humidity and daily torrential thunderstorms. The natives had re-netted the thatched roof to keep out the snakes, and they provided the party with crates of Coca-Cola and beer and even rigged up a shower – providing they could see the show, of course.

Suffering from jungle ulcers and a cold caught during a windswept open-air concert in Sydney, Gracie gave five brief 'turns' for hospital patients, followed by a major concert after a thanksgiving service ... standing on a beer-crate, she closed with 'The Lord's Prayer' for the benefit of General Sir Thomas Blamey (later Field-Marshal) and over 25,000 men. Next to this event, even her Freedom of Rochdale paled to insignificance. 'This will remain the most precious moment of my life, now,' she recorded. But there would be many more, in worse conditions. The next day she waved the Americans off as they embarked for Tokyo, on what would be the first leg of their long journey home.

On Saturday 19 August, Gracie's party arrived at Jacquinot Bay in New Britain, the largest island in the Bismarck Archipelago – the flight, in blinding torrential rain, was the most dreadful she had ever experienced, with visibility down to fifty yards, and the pilot narrowly missed crashing the plane. However, this, and the fact that most of the natives who waited on her every need came from a tribe of head-hunters, did not bother her quite so much as the 'lav' being half a mile from her hut!

The next day, suffering from a septic mosquito bite which, she said, had fostered a pet caterpillar all week, Gracie arrived on the New Guinea mainland to be told that 70,000 Japanese were still occupying the island, though their general had recently surrendered to the Americans. She and Monty were once more housed in the Duke of Gloucester's quarters, and even given the services of a batman. On account of the danger, however, restrictions had to be imposed on their show, and they were closely guarded day and night.

While they were there Monty had a rather bizarre mishap. He had cracked his false tooth before leaving Santa Monica, but had to leave before his dentist had made the replacement, so Neva Hecker had posted it out to Australia, where to his dismay Monty discovered that it was the wrong tooth. Now, as he was cleaning his teeth one night, the first, cracked false tooth slipped out of his hand and was washed down the plug-hole. The next morning, Gracie asked a young soldier if he could help her find it – it was located, but only after the entire drainage system to the hut had been taken to pieces. With her wicked sense of humour, Gracie gave the young man a kiss, and sang him the chorus from 'Ring Down the Curtain', (which mentions false teeth). The next morning, as Gracie was leaving the island, the soldier rushed up to her and gave her a necklace which he had made from polished shells – he had risked his life collecting them from the beach. The necklace was sent to Neva Hecker for safe-keeping, and Gracie asked the soldier to stay in touch. There was a tragic epilogue to this little adventure, however: a few days later she learned that he had been killed by a sniper.

On 25 August, the company reached Morotai, where they planned to rest a few days as guests of General Blamey and his wife who worked for the Red Cross. She wrote home, 'Of course, Old Lady Fields said, "Let's do a hospital at least so we'll feel we've done our good deed for the day!"' The scene was pitiful. These soldiers had taken the brunt of the fighting, and many had lost eyes and limbs. She concluded, 'It makes me feel sick when the poor kids ask me to autograph their plaster of Paris, but I just couldn't refuse.'

Afterwards, Gracie and Monty accompanied the Blameys on a boat trip to the next island, where she was allowed to swim – wearing a swimsuit she had made for herself out of an old turban. The natives here flung sticks of dynamite into the sea, collected all the multi-coloured fish that had been killed or stunned, and that evening cooked hundreds of them for supper while the Australian Army Band played crude rugby songs, and Monty did a side-splitting impersonation of Toscanini conducting. And when General Blamey asked Gracie to sing 'People Will Say We're in Love', from his favourite musical, *Oklahoma*, she obliged by singing her way through the entire score.

The next day, Gracie's party reached Balikpapan, the outpost on the south-east coast of Borneo, one of the last bastions to be taken during the war, and still occupied by the Japanese. This was the most heartbreaking location Gracie had seen so far. The sea had been mined by the Dutch, the beach by the Japanese who had also dug oil-trenches, and the Australians had had to bomb it in order to land safely and prevent the enemy from escaping. 'All the oil tanks blown to bits and all the tiny villages – you can hardly tell where they were. There's absolutely nothing for miles, only burned out and shattered shacks,' Gracie wrote home.

A bulldozer was brought in to clear a space in the jungle, and when darkness fell suddenly halfway through her show, Gracie asked each of the 24,000 troops to strike a match, on the count of three, so that she could see their faces. Another show in Borneo was on Labuan Island to the north and took place in the open air during a fierce tropical rainstorm; not one man left his place until she had finished. She sang twenty songs, though she was suffering from fatigue, a heat rash, an eye infection and an upset stomach. She wrote to Neva Hecker, 'It's awful to go to the lav. I was afraid to sit down!'

During the seven-hour plane journey back to Morotai the next day, she wrote in her journal,

I've been awake all night chasing a bloody big mosquito with my nearly blind eyes. Unfortunately, I couldn't find him, so one of my knees has the map of Ireland. Bugger and oh, don't it itch! They say the malaria mosquito doesn't make a noise, but this one did – he was dive-bombing, trying to get up my nose all night, so at 4 a.m. I got up and took the blasted net off. It had got inside and couldn't get out. So I suffocated myself under the sheet, just leaving enough room for my nostrils to breathe. And did I sweat! But he didn't get me nose!

On 5 September, Gracie and Monty reached Leyte Gulf in the Philippines, where General Miller of the American Wildcat Division supplied them with a comfortable bungalow right next to the river's edge. In the middle of the night Gracie got up to catch a breath of fresh air, and opened the door on a three-foot-long lizard. Mistaking it for a crocodile, she had the household in an uproar. In Leyte she was forced to share billing with an American troupe which included a contortionist, a squeeze-box player who played off-key, and an

American dancer-comedian named Ladd, who some years before had achieved recognition in Europe as the lover-partner of Mistinguett – and who had made the front pages of newspapers in 1932 when, after finding out that he had been cheating on her with Damia, La Miss had smacked him in the face with a handbag filled with stolen crockery, breaking his jaw in three places!

Ladd hogged the stage for so long that a false call was given over the tannoy for the sailors to return to ship. They came back upon learning that it was a hoax, and when the beer store – closed while everyone was on stage – opened again. By the time Monty had finished his warm-up patter, prior to introducing Gracie's co-star the – Gilbert and Sullivan specialist, Peggy Shea – then Gracie herself, most of the men were drunk and rowdy. She did not even try to quieten them down, but launched into an hour of community and music-hall songs, ending up hoarse but happy. The last thing she wanted, here in the middle of nowhere, was to fail. The next morning when she left in a motor-boat, dozens of sailors, feeling very much the worse for wear, waded thigh-deep in the water after her, tossing cans of beer into the vessel.

At Batangas, south of Manila, on 7 September, Gracie's regular accompanist fell ill and she was forced to sing to a Polish pianist by the name of Buckovsky – who was so incompetent that the audience started yelling, 'Fuck-offsky, Buckovsky!' Gracie told them, 'I'll keep on singing whatever I start, and Paderewski here can play what the hell he wants!' She did, and the pianist walked off, leaving her to finish her spot unaccompanied. Later in the day, after a replacement had been found, she was halfway through her act when a sudden downpour left her standing in six inches of mud. 'We're up to our necks in mud,' she wrote. 'The poor jeep swings and skids all over the place, which I suppose will be good for the liver. Good job I'm not in the family way – I'd sure lose it in these jeeps!'

On 10 September, when the party reached Manila, Gracie wrote home declaring that conditions were even worse than they had been in Balikpapan – the entire place was virtually reduced to rubble. That evening's concert was cancelled due to adverse weather conditions, but there were compensations. For the first time since leaving Australia the couple had a room with a shower – and a 'lav' which flushed.

At Baguio, to the north, a few days later, Gracie and Monty were the guests of General Lyman, whom she described as 'a full-blooded

Hawaiian, very Chinese-looking, nice and kind'. The food, however, was no better than it had been elsewhere on the tour, and when she complained about the 'bully-beef cooked in seventeen different positions', the native cook offered her a local delicacy – roast dog. Gracie decided to stick with the beef. Most of her concerts were indoors, at hospitals, schools, and one at a convent run by Belgian nuns, though the town was almost as badly bombed and unsafe as Manila had been. The next morning her plane failed to turn up, but General Lyman supplied an army wagon and driver to convey the party the 280 bumpy miles back to the capital. From here they flew out to Okinawa in the Ryukyn Islands, where there was now a US base. Grace was so worn out that the ambulance corps supplied her with a canvas stretcher so that she could sleep during the journey. It took so long to get to Okinawa that her first concert could not take place, but she made up for this with half a dozen shows over the next two days until the proceedings – and the stage – were wrecked by a hurricane.

Back in Manila, Gracie and Monty were ensconced in what was left of the elegant Manila Hotel, where the YMCA presented her with a beautiful Filipino dress, and where she presented them with a cheque for $100 – bringing to exactly $15,000 what she had spent of her own money during the our. On the plus side – if indeed there was such a thing amidst the horrors she was seeing every day – she met up with a small contingent of ex-prisoners of war who told her they were from Rochdale. 'Poor devils,' she wrote. 'They looked dreadful, so bony, you just wonder how they could have survived at all, the state they're in. The lousy Japs gave them rice and grass to eat, and even cut down that ration three months ago.' Yet in spite of their lamentable state, they took an active interest, and once Gracie had sung the now-obligatory 'The Lord's Prayer', they requested her to sing 'It Isn't Fair', a serious song which she aped by impersonating Greta Garbo.

> Why is it you came into my life
> And made it complete?
> I want to be alone ...
> If this is love, I repeat,
> As you desire me,
> It isn't fair for you to want me
> If just for today!

A few days later, pleased that the tour was over and proud of the results it had achieved – this time she had visited everyone, mindless of personal discomfort or of the extra expense from her own pocket – Gracie's company made lightning stops in Bombay and Ceylon before flying to Darwin, where they rested for a while before flying on to Sydney.

By Armistice Day, Gracie and Monty were back in Capri, which had been occupied twice during the war – first by the Germans, then by the Americans, but had remained an island paradise, relatively untouched by the war. The couple's other properties in Bologna, Milan and Cesena had been bombed, though Monty's lawyers lost no time at all putting in a huge claim for compensation. As for Il Fortino, now renamed La Canzone del Mare (The Song of the Sea), both occupying powers had treated the estate with great reverence. . A young GI had taken one of Gracie's favourite books as a keepsake, though he had left more than enough money in the gap in the shelf to pay for its replacement. Alan Moorehead of the *Sunday Pictorial* had been amazed when, having 'braved the bullets of the Front Line', he was ferried across to the island on the day the Germans were leaving.

On the lotus-eating millionaires' island off Naples, even four years of war have failed to unsettle the old tradition of eccentricity, luxury and decadence. A troupe of German gunners and radio-operators languished idly in the place for a bit, and came away so undermined in morale that they forgot to blow up the funicular railway and the water supply. The cosmopolitan millionaires, fretting over the devaluation of the lira, still strolled in flannels through the village square, hopelessly lonely, hopelessly out of date.

On Armistice Day, Gracie was asked to appear in two concerts in Naples. The sea was so rough that no one from the island would ferry her across, and when she asked the Americans, they did not have the facility. So the British Navy sent a motor launch, which had seen better days. Gracie was suffering from influenza and had to be carried onto the boat wrapped in oilskins. 'I spent the next hour wondering why I hadn't died a nice, peaceful death in the jungle,' she later said.

Feeling terrible and utterly drained as she was when carried off the launch, Gracie was completely transformed once on the stage, and closed the first half of a glittering semi-religious gala at the San Carlo Opera House with 'Land of Hope and Glory'. Minutes later she was on stage at the Bellini Theatre as part of a three-hour show for ENSA. There were hundreds of Italians and Americans in the audience who applauded until their palms were sore, hardly knowing that she was on the verge of collapse. A few months later, when President Truman invited Gracie to the White House, he told her that he was truly sorry the Americans did not award titles. To make up for this, he presented her with a set of extremely valuable, rare gold coins – she remains the only Briton to have been awarded this most distinguished honour.

The next year, 1946, was one of rest, though early in February Gracie flew to Athens, where she gave two RAF benefit concerts with Edith Piaf and Les Compagnons de le Çhanson. Again, there was talk of retirement, though all his was put behind her during the summer of 1947. Bert Aza had clinched a deal with the British impresario Bowker Andrews, for six radio broadcasts with the BBC, collectively known as *Gracie's Working Party*. The idea was aimed at boosting public morale at a time when Britain was still suffering the after-effects of the war with rationing and a national coal shortage. Gracie was initially offered £1,000 to do six shows – one each week in a different city or town – boasting a full bill of local talent, with her as Mistress of Ceremonies and the main attraction. The orchestra was to be directed by Richard Valery. She demanded a higher fee, mindless of Bowker's warning that public opinion might not always be on her side, and got it – when word got out that every penny would be going straight to the Variety Artistes Benevolent Fund, six more localities demanded her, pro-rata.

Gracie arrived in London – where she was to stay with Mary Barratt, now Mary Davey – with absolutely no publicity or fuss. It has been suggested that she was desperately worried about her reception, but her visits to England during the war had already proved that her fans were on her side. She *was* worried about the press, and when she arrived at Victoria Station after the long journey from Capri, she hailed a taxi and went straight to Mary Davey's flat, where for several days she saw no one, and refused even to answer the telephone.

The first 45-minute concert took place at Rochdale's Champness Hall on Wednesday 23 July – it was broadcast live on the Light

Programme and repeated twice during the week. Gracie's spot was
relatively short – eight songs, including a medley from *Oklahoma!*
and 'Waiato Poi', a song she had picked up in New Zealand – but
ecstatically received. There was also 'The Wickedness of Men', a
brilliant new song from Bill Haines which, despite the guffaws it
raised, ended with some sound advice.

> So, get to know yer onions, girls,
> And mind yer Ps and Qs,
> There's so much
> That an honest working girl has got to lose!
> Instead of saying No, at first
> Say Yes, and then refuse!
> Oh, the artfulness, the sinfulness,
> The wickedness of men!

Immediately after the broadcast, Gracie was driven to the Town
Hall, where as if on cue it began raining and she sang 'Singing in the
Bathub' to several thousand fans who could not have cared less
about the weather. She then explained that this particular visit to
Rochdale was more important than her others because she had
subsequently seen so much of the world. She added, 'When you're
miles away, you think of everybody you love and you ask yourself,
"Shall I ever get back and see them again?" And now, to look down
on your faces is just wonderful!' After hearing her sing 'I Love the
Moon', the correspondent from the *Yorkshire Evening News* wrote:
'She remains the same forthright genius. Truly, she is the very spirit
of the Northcountry and in her journeys abroad she has been one of
our greatest ambassadors. We welcome her return.'

One thousand of the 1,600 tickets for the Rochdale concert had
been doled out that morning, in complimentary pairs, in a record
fifteen minutes. The others were allocated to guests. Many halls on
the tour circuit had submitted official complaints to the Postmaster
General, objecting to free admission shows. The deputation
emphasized, 'It is simply a question of principle, and not any
objection to Miss Fields.' In truth, with so many complimentary
tickets available – a minimum 400 pairs for each venue – it was
inevitable that the touts would make a killing, which of course they
did, selling them for upwards of £10 each. As usual, wherever Gracie
went the gutter-press and the rumour-mongers were never far behind.

Stanley Jackson of the *Sunday People*, who claimed that he was a friend – Gracie later said that he had proved anything but – ran a lengthy 'confession' piece headed GRACIE FIELDS: 'I Went Away Because I Was In Love and I'm Now Paying For It.' The article began ominously: 'She is standing unofficial trial with the whole nation as judge and jury,' and there were several sarcastically backhanded compliments – 'We missed Gracie in this country during the war ... when the bombs were dropping we thought, not without resentment, of Gracie and others enjoying secure, well-fed lives in the States' – which she could have done without, even though the statement was untrue. Jackson knew only too well how Gracie had spent her war, and so did the rest of Britain.

The tour progressed: Middlesbrough, Huddersfield, Glasgow, Coventry, Swansea, Liverpool, Belfast, Sheffield, Burslem, Newcastle and London, with Gracie always including at least one 'regional' song in her act. Because of the Stanley Jackson episode, she refused to give any press interviews. 'I do like to be quiet, love,' she told a young man from the *Sheffield Telegraph* who saw through her disguise as she was leaving her hotel. 'I've been going about like Tom Mix with a scarf over my face and my glasses on. You'd think I'd got perpetual toothache!'

Nothing, however, quite matched up to Gracie's two-week stint at the London Palladium in October 1948 – her first major London stage appearance for almost a decade, barring the previous year's Royal Variety Show. Ella Fitzgerald was included in the same programme and was scheduled to do nine songs in the first half. The famous jazz-singer's manager took exception to this, demanding top billing for his star and suggesting that Gracie be demoted to appearing before the interval. During the ensuing rows between the two stars' agents, Florence Desmond – Gracie's old pal from *Sally in Our Alley* – was engaged to appear in the show along with Tommy Fields, and Gracie was left with the entire second half to herself. The upset affected Ella's performance so much that she received the most deplorable reviews.

Gracie suffered terribly from stagefright but on this occasion her opening song helped her enormously to overcome this. In November 1947 she had been in New York when Edith Piaf had been making her American début at the Playhouse – no feathered, bejewelled Josephine Baker singing songs such as 'Cest si Bon', as the Americans had expected, but a tiny, maladive woman singing songs of death, despair and unrequited love, in a black dress and in a language they could not understand. Piaf had been all for throwing in the towel, until Marlene Dietrich – soon to be her best friend – had advised her to stick it out. Within days, she had become the talk of New York. Her big song at the time had been 'La Vie en Rose', but if Gracie had always had the pick of other artistes' songs in the past, never failing to stamp them with her personality and almost make them her own, she was not allowed to cover this one. Piaf compromised by personally writing an English lyric to the song especially for Gracie – 'You're Too Dangerous, Chérie' (whose lyrics even then sounded out of date). Gracie opened her Palladium show, tremulously, with Frank Eyton's reworking of the song. Lyrically, it had nothing to do with the Piaf original, but it had everything to do with the British people's re-acceptance of Gracie Fields. The audience were in tears, and so was she.   •

> Take me to your heart again,
> Let's make a start again,
> Forgiving and forgetting ...
> I'm yearning for you by night and by day,
> Praying I'll soon hear you saying,
> "I love you!"
> Then, we'll never part again,
> If you will take me to your heart again!

9

A Dream Is a Wish Your Heart Makes

Gracie's two weeks at the Palladium in 1948 broke all existing box-office records, and there was not a single mention in any newspaper about her 'war problem'. It was not a question of whether her admirers had forgiven her or not – she had done nothing wrong to be forgiven for. Leaving London, she took the boat train, then the Golden Arrow into Paris's Gare du Nord, where she was met by Monty and reunited with Marie Dubas and Maurice Chevalier. She had been booked for her very first one-woman show (the most she usually had was the second half, following the interval – this time both halves were hers alone) at the Théâtre des Champs-Elysees: almost two hours, and thirty songs, ten of them sung phonetically in French. The evening was a triumph, and as she closed with a *serious* rendition of 'Reviens, Veux-tu?', Chevalier strode on to the stage and enveloped her in his arms.

In 1949 Claude Langdon booked Gracie for eight shows at London's impressive Empress Hall. If anything, hot on the heels of her Palladium success, these concerts proved to her that her fans loved her more than ever. She was also happier than she had been for some time. Little did she know, however, that tragedy was waiting around the corner.

Monty had begun extensive renovations at La Canzone del Mare which had brought a deluge of complaints from some of the locals, particularly after the blasting away of part of the rock formation to accommodate the restaurant and pool. For several days, the sea around the Marina Piccola had turned a sickly yellow, though once the sediment settled, so did several tempers. Thus content that they would have all the time in the world together, the couple spent the

Christmas at Telscombe with the Stansfields. Jenny's health had improved slightly, and Gracie had sold the house in Santa Monica – the proceeds were currently earning interest in an American bank, though shortly afterwards Gracie shared the money equally amongst her sisters, brother and their families – much to the disappointment of her closest friends, who maintained that she had already done more than enough for her family, and who are said to have been appalled by their demands on her generosity.

Gracie's family had recently suffered a bereavement with the sudden death of Douglas Wakefield. Her favourite brother-in-law was only in his early forties and for years had been a chronic asthmatic. A wealthy man, he left Edith and their two children over £150,000 in his will. However, as Irene Bevan explained,

> A family meeting took place at the Victoria Theatre. Duggie had left Edith well-off, and she had the big house at Hendon, but the family decided that as Grace was now making a lot of money, then she too ought to do something for them. So she gave Betty, Edith and Tommy £30,000 each.

Gracie always maintained that she preferred returning to Capri via the longest route because this was the only time she could rehearse new songs. There were three new numbers in her portfolio 'Bon Voyage', 'And You Were There', and another Piaf number, 'Bolero', which according to the French star, Gracie sang so well that she herself had stopped singing it. Occasionally, Gracie and Monty would take a detour and drop in on Irene and Lou Ross, now living in Rapallo, the small winter resort in the Bay of Genoa. 'Monty was after a property on the headland,' Irene said. 'He wanted to open a club or a casino.' This time, however, Gracie was anxious to get home. Having enjoyed a fun-filled but traditionally reverent festive season with her family, in spite of Douglas Wakefield's death, she was looking forward to her birthday party on 9 January 1950, and to working on the arrangements for the new songs.

Then, on Saturday 7 January, as the Orient Express was hurtling through the Simplon Tunnel, Monty suffered a heart-attack in their sleeping compartment. Gracie pulled the communication cord and in her limited Italian cried for help, but there was no one on board with medical knowledge. The driver pulled into a siding outside Sempioni, near Milan, where a doctor was waiting with an ambulance. It was too late. Monty had already died in her arms.

Gracie accompanied her husband's body to his native Cesena for the funeral, which took place the day after her fifty-second birthday. Monty had been just a few months younger than her and they should have had many more years together. It had been a happy marriage, slightly marred perhaps by Monty's manic gambling. 'Horses, cards, the wheel, two flies on a wall – Monty would put his shirt on anything. 'Trouble is, it was always my bloody shirt!' she told Denis Pitts. Tommy Fields repeated more or less the same story to the film critic, Barry Norman, though Gracie does not seem to have minded. Her stepdaughter could only praise the chirpy Italian's integrity and sound business sense.

> Monty *was* a great gambler, but he was also clever in that during the war, by whatever means, he was able to save the property in Capri. When you think how wealthy Grace was when she died, and bearing in mind that she earned her big money when she was much younger, *somebody* must have invested it well. Monty was also blessed with good luck. He spent a lot of her money, but he did get her to Hollywood. Although he was not the big cheese, he certainly had some sort of position in those days. If Grace had gone to America without him, if he hadn't been there to introduce her, I don't think she would ever have made any of those films or done much else.

Mary Davey flew out at once to be with her, and a few days later Gracie was joined by Bert and Lillian Aza. Her former secretary Neva Hecker even relocated to Rome, taking up a position with the United Nations Food & Agriculture Organization so that she would be that much closer. Each month she would cross to Capri and help out with the mountain of paperwork. Harold Chorlton, the Mayor of Rochdale, sent a telegram on behalf of her many friends and fans there. She received hundreds of letters of sympathy and for a few weeks seriously considered retirement, thinking that even at fifty-two she was 'ready for t'knackers yard', when in fact, for certain songs her voice was just reaching its peak.

> At that age you can remember the dreams you had at twenty but when Monty died, I tried to throw them all away. That there would never be any children of my own, I'd accepted. But

now there was no husband either. Every time I stopped working and went back to Capri, it seemed empty of every dream I'd ever had for my home there. I couldn't bear it.

Work, Or course, was Gracie's only means of coping with her grief. Two months after Monty's death she flew to Britain with one intention – to star in Henry Hall's Guest Night. Within a few weeks she had ended up recording several radio programmes for the impresario Harry Alan Towers, a guest spot in the television show *Lucky Dip*, and twenty-six half-hour shows for Radio Luxembourg!

Again, Gracie's repertoire varied between the absurd – Bert Aza's 'The Bargain Hunter' – to the sublime – Puccini's 'Oh, My Beloved Father', in those days rarely if ever performed in English. Many admirers firmly believe that for sincerity and sheer vocal brilliance, Gracie's interpretation by far excels the later recordings made by Joan Hammond and Maria Callas. One usually harsh critic, Elizabeth Frank, wrote, 'There is a new dignity and graciousness about her whole demeanour.' Gracie also sang Edith Piaf's 'Bolero' a lot that year, always in tribute to Monty as it had been one of his favourites, but she never got around to recording it and one has to make do with the tape made with Henry Hall, where she seems to be rushing to keep up with him.

> The skies may fall, my love,
> But I will still be true ...
> I can see, as I recall my life,
> I've waited all my life
> To give you all my love!

In November 1950, Gracie appeared in her fifth Royal Variety Show. Also on the bill were Max Bygraves, Frankie Howerd and Donald Peers, but that year this quite exceptional home-grown talent was overshadowed by the fanfare of publicity afforded to transatlantic guests Dinah Shore and Jack Benny. That year too the readers of the *Daily Express* voted Gracie 'Woman of the Year', an award which coincided with the cementing of a close friendship, the seeds of which had been sown three years before, but one which unlike most of the others would strengthen and endure for the rest of her life. Irene Bevan spoke of Gracie's inability to trust almost everyone she came into contact with.

Grace was volatile in her friendships. She would make a great fuss of people for months, sometimes years. You were God, then you would say or do something which may have been a home truth or a slight criticism, then all of a sudden – OUT! She used to call me her ready-made daughter, but over the years she had many ready-made daughters. This girl Neva, for instance, and Mary Barratt. Grace was a complex, difficult woman who overran everybody. If you were not prepared to be submerged by her, you didn't stay her friend. She never threw tantrums. When Grace was weighing you up, or not quite certain that you were telling the truth, she had a habit of chewing the inside of her mouth. When she did that, you had to watch out. She also had a look which could freeze your marrow, particularly if she thought you were trying to put her down by being deliberately posh. We all knew in those days that there was someone very special in her life, someone who understood all these things about her. What we didn't know was *who* he was.

The 'special' friend was John Taylor, a teenage fan from near Durham who had queued outside her dressing-room in October 1947 when Gracie had taken her *Working Party* to Newcastle. Too tired to chat to him then, she had asked him to write to her – one of the oldest brush-offs in the show-business book – and John had gone home feeling dejected. Not expecting any response, he had sent her a letter, and had been surprised to receive a card upon which she had inscribed, 'If you're in another town where I am at, please let me know and I'll try and see you. Keep in touch.' In this and in all her subsequent letters to John, her written English seems to have been deliberately bad, as it had always been in her wartime epistles to her sisters. 'Proper' letters to business contacts, Gracie said, had to be *done* properly. Those to loved ones were either executed in her near-illegible scrawl, or tapped out with two fingers on her 'tripe-writer'. John continued the story,

At first I wrote to the theatres, then I began writing to her in Capri. Sometimes the replies came from Bert Aza's office, but they were always signed by her. Then in 1950 – by which time I'd joined the Navy – she was appearing in Leeds and she sent me two tickets. After the show she asked, 'Do you collect my stuff? In that case, you'd better collect two of everything –

cuttings, records, the lot – and send one lot to me in Telscombe or Capri. I'll pay you every now and then!' And that's how our close friendship began.

John Taylor was sitting in the audience at the Kings Theatre, Southsea, on 27 April 1951 when Gracie gave a benefits concert for the dependents of those lost on the *Affray*, the British submarine which had sunk off Portsmouth earlier that year. The wreck, 258 feet below sea-level, had been detected by a pioneering underwater camera. Besides singing, Gracie auctioned numerous articles donated by local dignitaries – then threw in her own beautiful hand-embroidered stole, a gift from Monty, for good measure. After the show, Gracie insisted on taking John back to Telscombe to meet her parents. She introduced him as her 'latest' – Jenny fell for the ruse, took one look at him and exclaimed, 'Ee, our Grace! Thee boyfriends are getting younger!'

A few days later, Gracie recorded an edition of *Desert Island Discs* which was broadcast on 13 June – as Roy Plomley's 'Castaway Number 91' she selected seven classical recordings … and Stanley Holloway's 'Sam, Pick Up Thee Musket'.

On 6 May, Gracie topped the bill in the *Festival of Variety* at the BBC's Playhouse Theatre – part of the celebrations for the Festival of Britain and she always claimed, her favourite show of all time because her voice had been at its peak. She turned up for rehearsals in an old coat and headscarf – and was stopped by security. Wilfred Pickles introduced her on to the stage, and she sang several comedy numbers, including 'I Never Cried So Much In All My Life', before turning to the serious stuff. Donald O'Keefe's tremendously emotive 'At the End of the Day' was given its world première, and if Dorothy Squires had the subsequent hit with the song, that night it was Gracie Fields who sent shivers running down five thousand spines in what may justifiably be regarded as her personal credo.

> Nobody knows what a power you have found,
> So do what you can for the others around,
> Carry them high when they seem to be low,
> As on your way you go.

Gracie returned to Capri feeling elated, yet she fell into a deep depression the moment she set foot in her home. Monty had left her only £8,000 in his will, though once his complex estate had been sorted out, this would be upped to £150,000. Meanwhile the extensive building programme at La Canzone del Mare was almost complete. Gracie's favourite nephew, Betty's son, Tony Parry and his family had lived with her for a year being 'apprenticed' by Gracie to run her restaurant, but now he wanted to leave. She told John Taylor, 'I really thought he was going to settle down with us. Well, he's had a bloody good holiday – *and* for nowt!'

Gracie was never short of company. A number of small bungalows had been built in the grounds and around the terraces of La Canzone del Mare, and these were invariably occupied by the family and friends. She also insisted that everyone eat all their meals at the villa. Yet in a crowd of thirty people, she admitted that she frequently felt indescribably lonely – and if someone in this crowd was not to her liking, she could be incredibly bad-mannered. Friends remembered these outbursts of rudeness, including John Taylor, though as one of Gracie's special favourites he himself was never a 'victim'. Irene Bevan told me:

> There was a certain lack of etiquette in Grace's make-up. She would suddenly get up and walk out of a room without saying a single word, let alone goodbye, and you would wonder what you'd done wrong. She also had a dreadful habit of letting people down over eating arrangements. She would know that you were preparing a lunch for two o'clock, and she would arrive at four and say, 'I've had a pie! I can do as I like because I'm a star!' It was one of the perks of being who she was.

It was at this stage that her entire life was transformed for ever – and all because of a couple of broken machines!

Boris Abraham Luigi Alperovici had been born in 1903 in Bessarabia (formerly a part of Romania, integrated into the Soviet Union in 1940), but whilst holidaying in Naples in 1927 he had taken a day-trip to Capri and like Gracie had fallen in love with it. Barring the wartime military occupation, he had remained there ever since.

Like Monty Banks, Boris had gone through a nationality crisis holding a Romanian passport until it had been confiscated, thought of as Russian, but considering himself Italian. Whilst young he had studied architecture in Rome, but he had soon lost interest in the subject by becoming involved with the evolution of the wireless. In 1930 his talents as an inventor had attained fruition when he had been taken on by the Cerio Brothers, a pioneering pair who owned a sound-and-picture laboratory on Capri, just two hundred yards from La Canzone del Mare. Two years later he had helped them construct their first television set – one that picked up a primitive picture of Gracie singing in London!

Boris had begun the war badly, as a stateless prisoner in an internment camp. Freed by the Americans soon after Italy's pact with Germany, he had enlisted as a sergeant with the Eighth Army on account of his engineering skills and his phenomenal ability to speak eight languages fluently. Boris had been present at *both* of Gracie's Armistice Day concerts in Naples, but whereas he had wept on hearing her sing 'Land of Hope and Glory', he had disliked every one of her comedy numbers and even branded them openly as sacrilegious for such an occasion.

Boris had also raised the petition complaining about Gracie's and Monty's swimming pool and restaurant – he had taken several official colour photographs of the sea which he had submitted as evidence of the pollution created by their building activities to the authorities – and for this reason he may have been actually frightened of meeting Gracie formally, in case they crossed swords. But whilst it would appear virtually certain that on an island as small as Capri they must have at least seen each other, John Taylor did not think so. John surprised Gracie during the summer of 1951 by turning up at her villa – his ship had just docked in Naples, and he had been given twenty-four hours' leave. He was thrilled to see his idol on home ground for the first time, and she was just as delighted to receive him and make him more than welcome.

During the visit, Gracie indicated the man working silently in her sitting-room. Her record player had broken down, and she had sent out for help. With his extensive knowledge of the island's complicated electricity system, Boris had been everyone's obvious choice, and he had fixed the machine without uttering so much as one word to her. Gracie had readily assumed that he was unable to speak English, and had declined to attempt any conversation with him, she said, because she could only sing and curse in Italian! 'They'd never met until that day,' John Taylor told me. 'Firstly, in those days Gracie was always travelling and didn't spend a lot of time there. Secondly, there are 365 different walkways on Capri.

You can wander around for days and never see a soul.'

In a rare interview many years later, Boris told Scarth Flett of the *Sunday Express*, 'Of course, I knew Gracie Fields was an English film star, and she had this dreadful red hair. Artificial. It was all bright like a fire engine, but when I met her and saw her blue eyes, I thought, "That makes her all right!"'

Several months later, he dropped in to mend her tape recorder, and this time she realized that he spoke good English, and she invited him to stay for tea. He soon began visiting the villa on a more regular basis, initially, as one of the large group around the dinner table. Then he began calling unexpectedly when Gracie was alone, and it did not take her very long to realize that she had fallen in love with him.

In November 1951, Gracie appeared at the London Palladium in *Cavalcade of Variety*, organized by the Water Rats and sponsored by the *News of the World*. She shared the bill with Bud Flanagan, Jewell and Warriss, Wee Georgie Wood and Vera Lynn, the Forces Sweetheart, of whom she remarked to a close friend, 'That girl's probably the best singer in Britain, but I do wish she wouldn't stand there like a slab of cold mutton!'

There was also a series of on-stage radio broadcasts from the BBC's studios in Manchester, where several of her more obscure comedy songs were revived, including 'The Saucy Little Bird on Nelly's Hat', 'Johnny Callaghan' and 'Keep It in the Family Circle', the oddity which had appeared in 1934 on the flipside of 'Play to Me Gypsy'. *Only* Gracie could have got away with recounting the adventures of a Stilton cheese which becomes lost when its owner takes it for a day-trip to the waxworks!

> Down in the Horror Chamber
> I gave Burke and Hare a fright,
> They swear they won't stay with it
> Alone, without a light!
> It strangled both the Princes in the Tower,
> And Charlie Peace is certain to resign!
> So, before it goes too fruity
> As to wake the Sleeping Beauty,
> Won't you keep it,
> Just for auld lang syne?

All the while she was in England, Gracie confessed that she could not stop thinking about Boris, and when she confided in Bert and Lillian Aza that she was thinking of marrying a Russian, they joked that if she did she would be the cause of yet another international incident. They were of course only happy for her, though a little concerned that she may have been moving a little too quickly, on the rebound from Monty's death.

By the time she returned to Capri, Gracie had learned her one and only Russian phrase from Esther Rifkin, her Muscovite blouse-maker. 'Ia tebia liubliu' – 'I love you' – she repeated to Boris the first time they went out together. This was the evening she proposed to him because, she said, he was shy with women and *someone* had to make the first move. In her memoirs she wrote that though she had loved Monty deeply, she had not been *in love* with him, adding, 'And now, just when I thought everything was over for me, I knew I was in love properly and wholeheartedly.'

Boris was initially reticent in accepting her proposal, though it was a leap year, allowing Gracie the privilege of asking. He loved her as much as she adored him, but he was concerned about inheriting the 'Mr Fields' tag, and, more seriously, that he might be accused of marrying her for her wealth. With or without Monty's bequest she was quite easily a millionaire. Gracie soon convinced him otherwise, and at her Christmas Eve party he finally told her what she wanted to hear. She silenced the traditionally noisy gathering with a whistle, and announced that they were engaged. She then sat at the piano and sang a song which began, 'I'm an old goat, but I'm so in love with him ...' Feeling slightly odd that *she* had done the proposing, she later made up the story – 'I tampered with the radio just to have him come up to the villa to repair it. After several of these sessions he saw nothing wrong with the set. He asked me to marry him.'

Ten minutes later, the first reporter came banging on the door. The happy news spread like wildfire, and for the first time in its history the tiny island post office had to open on Christmas Day to cope with the deluge of calls and telegrams. In the midst of this mêlée Gracie asked him to print his full name on a scrap of paper – until that moment she had known him only as 'Mr Boris', and though the press *were* told the facts, for some time he was referred to as 'Abraham Boris Alperovic, Capri's Repairman'. She was also amused when John Taylor pointed out that if she rearranged the letters of her fiancé's surname, it spelled: I LOVE CAPRI!

Gracie and Boris could not cope with the intrusion into their privacy by so many reporters and photographers, and as soon as they could, they escaped to Rome for a brief sojourn. Here they posed for photographs outside the Colosseum – Gracie cracking jokes as usual, and Boris looking shy and embarrassed. His mood changed, however, on New Year's Eve, when Gracie crossed the Bay of Naples to be piped aboard the aircraft carrier, *Franklyn D Roosevelt*, to sing for the US Navy. Not only did he refuse to accompany her, he also snarled at the reporter from the *Daily Mirror* who asked him *why* he was staying at home: 'I don't like the role of Prince Consort. Why can't you people leave us alone, instead of making a sensation of our love-story?' When the reporter gave him a piece of his mind and told him not to be so rude, he apologized and calmed down a little, then concluded, 'OK, so I will simply have to be a good husband. If the publicity of this engagement is so hard on me, you can be sure I would never go through with a divorce!' Many times over the next twenty-seven years Gracie would remember these words, and often suffer unnecessarily for not standing up to Boris's snobbishness.

There was considerable speculation that Gracie might attempt to assuage her fiancé by embracing the Catholic faith, shared by so many of those closest to her, before her wedding, and consulted Monsignor Luigi Lembo, Capri's parish priest, who advised her to take lessons in the Roman Catholic doctrine before making a firm commitment. On 2 January 1952, prior to seeking the dispensation required for a non-Catholic to marry a Catholic, she signed a declaration form so that the banns might be read. At the same time, hundreds of Capricians signed a petition demanding that the authorities grant her honorary citizenship of the island – their declaration read 'Signora Fields has given to us innumerable proofs of philanthropic generosity over many years.' Gracie was tickled that the petition was delivered on the day Capri had its first snowfall in fifty years. 'It was like being in Blackpool for the day,' she said. In fact she was only briefly an Italian citizen, and never became a Catholic.

On 6 January, Gracie embarked on a brief tour of West Germany, performing mostly for Allied Occupation troops stationed in Berlin and Hamburg. She protested when the organizers charged soldiers to get into the theatres – this was against the 'moral code of the music-hall' if programmes were for transmission and British policy would never have permitted such a thing. When her complaint was ignored, Gracie merely cut out several theatres and put on a number of complimentary shows at the Army barracks.

Lillian Aza, who never camouflaged her dislike for Boris once she had met him, and who was convinced that Gracie was rushing into something she would only regret, flew out to Germany and begged her to bide her time at least. But although Gracie 'swore blind' to her agent's wife that she would wait 'a good twelve months' before marrying Boris, she had already finalized her plans, so convinced was she that, at long last, she had found the greatest love of her life.

Then, on 6 February, King George VI died, and Britain entered a period of mourning. Patriotic to the last, out of respect for the royal family, Gracie postponed her wedding until 17 February – then, according to Irene Bevan and Mary Davey, she developed cold feet, and in her own words 'buggered off' to Rome early the next morning, though she soon returned when Boris went after her, and the wedding went ahead on 18 February. The paparazzi merely jumped to the conclusion that the couple had had a violent quarrel, and in the ensuing mix-up several members of Gracie's family and a number of close friends were not told of the ceremony at Capri's tiny San Stefano church until it was over. Mary Davey arrived several days later and cried so much when she saw the couple that Gracie joined in for sympathy!

Gracie's 'excuse' for not getting to the altar on time was not only believed, it was at least *semi*-legitimate. Having spent most of her life in the spotlight, her dream had been to listen to the words of Monsignor Lembo's service rather than have it spoiled by the clicking of shutters. The priest was none too pleased by the change in her plans, however, because she had omitted to tell him – he later complained to the press that Gracie had only given him five minutes' notice to prepare for the ceremony and was snapped shouldering his way almost grudgingly through the crowd, on his way to light the altar candles.

Claiming that it was in respect for the recently bereaved royal family – but more likely because it was her habit to throw on the first clothes she could find in her wardrobe – Gracie wore for her wedding a fetching mauve woollen costume, and covered her head with what she called her 'gay Lancashire scarf'. Only after the quiet formality of the seven-minute service, did Gracie assume her public self. Stepping out into the watery sunshine, she chatted and waved to the hundreds of wellwishers who had gathered in the piazza. Finally, the happy couple drove off ... in a station-wagon.

Gracie later claimed that it was only *after* their marriage that she and Boris had started to get to know one another, and some would say that their initial 'teething problems' and public arguments, albeit minor, were never resolved. Boris did not always appreciate his wife's offbeat sense of humour. As Irene Bevan explained, 'Although he spoke English quite well, he didn't understand the nuances of the English language. Grace would say something to him which he would pick up with an entirely different connotation.' On top of this, Gracie often reprimanded him by calling him 'gawp' or 'piecan' – her trademark terms of disrespect, often affectionate – and she had the amusing, but to him, annoying habit of signing important letters and cheques with the pseudonym 'Fanny Adams', an expression which was lost on a man who hitherto had lived an almost cloistered life.

Many people disliked Gracie's new husband, not least of all most of her entourage, some of whom accused him of being a gold-digger. One source who still lives on the island, and who asked to remain anonymous, told me:

> The Cerios knew that Gracie was absolutely loaded, and once he told them that he'd been to her villa, they encouraged him to get all he could out of her. Boris is thought to have been mixed up in a few shady deals, and he was strapped for cash. Then something weird happened – he fell in love with the woman, as opposed to who she was and what she possessed – and in spite of their ups and downs, it was a successful marriage. She enabled him to live in the lap of luxury for the rest of his life, and he pampered her rotten. They complemented each other.

Irene Bevan, delighted that Gracie had found contentment so soon after Monty Banks's death, said,

> The family and Lillian were absolutely horrified about him. Lillian had no time for him. She found him artificial when he used to put on his act – you couldn't put on an act with Lillian. But Grace couldn't live alone. She had to have a man about the house. I found Boris great fun. With his accent and mannerisms he could charm the birds off the trees. Perhaps his greatest

problem was that he couldn't understand Grace's way of life. After all, he'd lived for twenty-odd years on that island, then he suddenly gets into a milieu of which he has no knowledge whatsoever – where he sees her standing on a stage, with everybody screaming at her. He didn't know what had hit him. But of one thing I *am* certain. They *did* love each other.

Also, Boris had a very caring side to his nature, as Gracie soon found out. She was distressed to awaken, the morning after her wedding, and find his side of the bed empty. Thinking the worst – that Boris had 'done a bunk' having thought that he had made a huge mistake – Gracie searched the villa and grounds, and panicked when her husband was nowhere to be found. She eventually discovered him, in grubby overalls, on his hands and knees, scrambling about in the bottom of the empty swimming pool! It transpired that he and Monty Banks had known each other quite well, and that – in spite of Boris's public objection to the pool, and his raising of the petition – Monty had commissioned him to install a complicated underwater lighting system in the pool, only to die before that part of the project could be started on. Now, as a wedding present, Boris had kept his side of the bargain by getting up at five-thirty in the morning to install the lighting, not just for Gracie but as a lasting memorial to Monty Banks.

Gracie recalled that she had spent her honeymoon on Capri, with her two alsatians dogs keeping unwelcome visitors a bay, simply because she could not possibly have found a more romantic spot. There was more to it than this, however, as she revealed in June 1952 when she signed a contract to do a series of concerts for British and Allied troops stationed in Korea. Boris, still officially listed as stateless because he had no passport, was not allowed to most countries. As with Monty Banks, Gracie refused to travel anywhere without Boris. In any case, on top of this she was advised by her doctor that she was too weak, on account of her being susceptible to chest infections, to withstand the mandatory inoculations. So she gave out a press statement that the tour would have to be cancelled not because Boris would not be permitted to accompany her, but because she had signed a contract to make a film in England, a country he was allowed to visit on the strength of his army papers.

For the man she loved, this incredibly honest woman was prepared to tell a lie. And in spite of the faults on both sides, it *was* love, pure and simple, an emotion which had evaded Gracie since her John Flanagan days. At fifty-four, she found herself feeling and behaving like a young girl again, only this time there was no Jenny Stansfield around to say, 'Grace, don't act daft!' Her old friend Mary Whipp spent a holiday in Capri with the couple soon after their wedding:

> We went to see *The Spiral Staircase* at the tiny cinema in the Piazza. Ethel Barrymore had a character part in it, and Gracie confided to me that several people thought there was a resemblance between them. At the end of the film I turned towards her to say, 'Gracie, Ethel Barrymore has nothing on you!' I was stopped in my tracks – she and Boris were sitting with their arms intertwined and their hands clasped together. I longed to place my own hands around theirs but stopped mid-stream. Would I or would I not have embarrassed her?

Soon afterwards, Gracie experienced another drama, one which she ostensibly brought upon herself because of her unfailing generosity. For decades Capri had been a magnet for the glitterati and members of the world's social set. Lord and Lady Kitchen were neighbours. Maria Callas, Aristotle Onassis, Greta Garbo, Noël Coward, and several of the Kennedy clan had spent holidays there, returning time and time again. During the summer of 1951, Gracie had entertained Egypt's King Farouk Fuad and his teenage bride, Narriman Sadek, on the occasion of their honeymoon. Knowing nothing whatsoever of middle-Eastern politics, or of Farouk's gluttony and sexual excesses, she had described Farouk as 'a nice fat lad', and upon seeing the couple off on their yacht had told him, 'Next time you're passing, love, you must call in for a cuppa!'

Shortly after the coup in July 1952 when General Neguib seized power in Egypt. Farouk arrived in Capri amidst a fanfare of publicity, bringing with him most of his personal possessions, a wealth of state treasures, several million pounds' worth of goods which he had stolen or shoplifted during his reign – crates of toothpaste, keyrings, jewels and even the gold state sword and personal effects filched from the coffin of Shah Pahleri of Iran as it had passed through Cairo – all neatly packed inside his three yachts.

With Farouk were Princess Narriman, his three daughters from his first marriage, and a small army of retainers and bodyguards who treated the Capricians like dirt, though for the time being Farouk himself was extremely polite. A few days later he made his abdication speech, in favour of his infant son Ahmed Fuad II, from the rooftop garden of the Eden Paradiso Hotel, in a mixture of broken English and Italian which impressed Gracie so much that she asked the entire party to move into her complex. When Farouk told her how much he loved swimming, she supplied him with a suite of sitting and changing rooms near the pool. Then she organized a dinner-dance in his honour and announced to the world's press, extremely unwisely, 'I want to see the lad's nerves settled before he gives his press-conference. As far as I'm concerned, Farouk is still a king, and although I'm not going to make him think I've put this club at his disposal just for publicity, I want to help him because he's such a nice man.'

Soon, however, Gracie began to tire of her royal visitors. If Farouk told her persistently that he was *thinking* of buying a property on Capri, he made no effort to search for one, and the photograph which appeared in newspapers at the end of August said it all: Gracie, in evening gown, standing in her club with her back turned on an unkempt, bespectacled Farouk, who is strolling towards her – hands in pockets and whistling, looking like a menacing, 22-stone mugger. By now, the ex-King was taking advantage of Gracie's hospitality by hogging her restaurant and pool. His burly bodyguards, correct in thinking that there might at any moment be an assassination attempt, began barring La Canzone del Mare's other guests from its facilities. Gracie, having seen the light and not one to mince words, summoned Farouk and told him, 'You're still a nice fat lad, but enough is enough. You're going to have to sling your hook!' The ex-King left, without any apparent ill-feeling, for Rome, and before doing so presented Gracie with a diamond and jade brooch and earrings, and a pair of wall-plaques which she later gave to John Taylor's wife, Anne. Two years later, Narriman Sadek returned to Egypt, where she obtained a Moslem divorce. Farouk died in 1965, aged forty-five, after one final gluttonous binge.

Boris's first trip – allowed to travel to Britain on the strength of his Eighth Army papers – outside Italy in over twenty-five years took place in September 1952, when he flew with Gracie to London for her midnight concert with Vera Lynn and Mary Martin in aid of the Lynmouth Flood Disaster. He only agreed to leave the island, however, once he had found someone to look after La Canzone del

Mare – he did not trust the manager Gracie had hired. Irena Bounos was a 45-year-old native of Turin who had known Boris as a child, and who had been employed as a nanny by the Cerios. She agreed to look after the property for one month only – and stayed with the couple for twenty-seven years. John Taylor said, 'Irena was very stern, very loyal and honest, and deep down inside she was in love with Boris, though she never let on.'

The concert at the Coliseum, one of Gracie's favourite venues, raised over £10,000 for the dependants of the flood victims, and Boris was floored by his wife's reception – marred for him only by what he considered was an ill-placed joke when, as her pianist scraped his chair after 'Ave Maria', Gracie quipped, 'Ooh, that was me stomach rumbling!' Boris had never regarded Gracie as anything but a *grande dame* when she was not clowning around, though he had attributed the fever of her Armistice Day concerts as much to the general elation that the war had been over to anything she had done on the platform. Now, he was able to see how much her public *loved* her. And as an expression of her *joie de vivre* she was unable to stop herself, at fifty-four, from turning a couple of cartwheels across the stage!

10

How Changed Is the Old Place Now

In November 1952 Gracie appeared in her seventh Royal Variety Show, where she shared top-billing with Beniamino Gigli. After their respective spots they returned to the stage and duetted on 'Come Back to Sorrento' – Gracie smiling radiantly afterwards as the world's greatest tenor presented her with a basket of roses several times bigger than himself, and he, in her words, 'With a face as glum as a wet weekend in Lytham!' Incredibly, although the performance was taped, the recording did not see the light of day until the end of 1994.

During this trip to England, Boris met his in-laws for the first time – apprehensively, for when Gracie had telephoned Brighton to announce her engagement, Jenny had quipped, 'That's our Grace for you, always marrying t'enemy!' In fact, Gracie's parents got on well with Boris, though they did not see much of him. Jenny Stansfield died in October 1953, aged seventy-four, and Fred died three years later. Both are buried in the cemetery at Peacehaven.

Another loss which affected Gracie badly was that of her lifelong friend and manager, Bert Aza. For many years prone to chest ailments, Bert died on New Year's Day 1953, aged seventy, after a particularly thick fog that enveloped Maida Vale, where he lived. Gracie was in England for the festive season, and stayed at Peacehaven until after the funeral. The Aza business was taken over by Bert's son, Morris, though Lillian Aza stayed at the helm as far as her veterans – Gracie and Stanley Holloway – were concerned.

John Taylor remembers his first 'brush' with the woman who was to guide Gracie through her 'dotage' years, as Gracie called them.

Lillian was shrewd, caring, tough and very protective towards Gracie. We didn't get on at first because she didn't like me doing things for Gracie. I was even put on trial when Gracie sent me a cheque for something or other, and a week later Lillian sent a cheque for exactly the same amount. When I rang Lillian and told her this she said, 'Thank you, John. You'll be doing some more work.' We became good friends. Then, the next time I went to Capri, Gracie said, 'Sorry we had to do that, love, but you've passed the test.'

A lesser drama occurred in 1953 when Gloria Magnus, one of the Alperovicis' closest friends on Capri, came close to being deported. A vivacious 45-year-old Cockney, Gloria had arrived on the island in 1949 with her husband, shocking the community by making several outrageous statements to the local press. Her outbursts had amused Gracie, who had invited Gloria to stay at La Canzone del Mare, where she had met and fallen in love with Pietro Cerrota, a fisherman friend of Gracie's whose brother was the new parish priest. Divorcing her husband and using his settlement for collateral she and Cerrota had then opened a restaurant at the Marina Piccola which proved an instant success.

Gloria may have been regarded as a loose woman by most of the inhabitants of Capri, and she did have a tendency to curse like a sailor on shore leave, but her generosity was second to none. She usually received her guests wearing a toque – an idea said to have been inspired by the equally controversial French actress Alice Sapritch, and she had so many cats running around her small estate that the locals nicknamed her The Mad Cat-Woman of Capri. However, as, like Gracie, she was an invaluable source of island revenue, few people had any genuine right to complain about her. Gloria knew dozens of show-business personalities, from Victor Silvester who had taught her how to dance, to Noël Coward, who had based his song, 'A Bar at the Piccolo Marina', on her. Even Boris held her in great esteem. As Capri's 'second institution', it usually meant that if the holidaymakers could not find Gracie, they were invariably pointed in Gloria's direction. So, when some of the locals took legal action to have her deported from the island – she was branded 'an alien' because she was unmarried and did not have a work permit – Gracie came to her defence, protesting to the authorities that in any case Gloria did most of her trade during the winter, when the Canzone del Mare was closed. Gloria and Cerrota won their case, and the woman whom one journalist described as 'coming free with every course' stayed put.

John Taylor, who spent his first holiday on Capri with Gracie and Boris in 1954, knew Gloria Magnus well and recounted an hilarious episode which occurred some years later when Gracie asked Anne, his wife, to accompany her to the house of a friend whose wife had just died. 'On the way there they met Gloria, who was an incessant talker. She just would not shut up. Afterwards, Anne and Gracie came walking up the drive, arm in arm and splitting their sides with laughter. Gloria had gone with them to the funeral house. She had leaned over the coffin to look at the body, and she'd said, "Doesn't she look *well*?"'

When Gracie flew into Britain in May 1954 to appear in a television show, Boris was able to accompany her without the customary filling in of forms and red-tape as he had finally been granted an Italian passport. The couple returned to Capri on the very first civil flight to the island, an Aquila Airlines seaplane which took just six hours from Southampton, a considerable saving on time compared with the overland journey, which since the death of Monty Banks had never failed to give her the shivers. It was a bumpy ride, and when Gracie arrived looking a little green, almost the entire population of Capri rushed out to greet her.

Gracie and Boris returned to England in November 1954 for a series of sell-out concerts. She was due to sing on the television at exactly the same time as the Queen and Prince Philip, newly returned from an official tour of Australasia, were due to appear on the balcony at Buckingham Palace – an appearance which was inexplicably delayed for thirty minutes. The 'mystery' was unravelled a few days later when the royal couple and Gracie arrived in Rochdale within hours of each other. Gracie's reception was noticeably bigger and more tumultuous than theirs, something which did not go unobserved by the press, and as a Freewoman of the town she was naturally entitled to be presented to her sovereign. The Queen told her, most sincerely, that she had *purposely* delayed her appearance on the balcony because she had wanted to watch Gracie's television show. Gracie is alleged to have told the Queen about her recent concert for the inmates of Wormwood Scrubs, when every song had ended with a wild applause save one, which had received a glacial silence ... 'Bless This House'!

As usual, Gracie eschewed the plush hotel offered her by the Corporation, insisting that she would feel more at home staying with Auntie Margaret and her undertaker husband. The visit began during heavy rain, but in spite of the weather Gracie was unable to resist belting out 'Wish Me Luck As You Wave Me Goodbye', even if she *had* only just arrived! But when the crowd cried out for an encore, she remonstrated, 'I'm not twenty-one any more, so don't wear me out. I've got to give 'em their money's worth when I go on tonight!'

Her friend Mary Whipp remembered this and Gracie's other visits home with great tenderness.

> I always joined the huge crowds to greet her. It was a magical sensation – electricity, chemistry – which passed literally from person to person. Once I looked around me, recognizing Edna Wood, the leading lady from the local Curtain Theatre, just leaning and looking. Near the war memorial was Mr Senior, the Jewish tailor. If it rained, which it often did, a perfect stranger would invite you to share his/her umbrella. Gracie would say from the Town Hall balcony, 'It's raining. You're all going to miss the last bus. I'm just going to sing you one verse, then off you go!' People quite cheerfully missed their last bus. What did it matter if they had to walk the four miles to Littleborough, or the seven to Middleton? Not one iota!

Gracie took Boris to see Chip Sarah's old place in Molesworh Street, where a plaque had been erected commemorating her birth. The next stop was another chip shop, on Drake Street, where she got out of the Cadillac and ordered 'cod and two-pennorth ... and shocked Boris to the core by insisting upon eating them in the traditional way – out of the newspaper. Afterwards she dropped in on her old mate Bertha Schofield and her daughter Ada, and later in the afternoon she sang several songs, including 'Christopher Robin', for the young patients at the Children's Orthopaedic Hospital.

Many of Gracie's fans had queued overnight, waiting for the box office to open at the Theatre Royal, and the licensee of a local pub grew so concerned when he recognized several of his elderly patrons standing out in the cold that he handed out complimentary tots of rum. Most of them kept warm by stamping their feet and having Gracie sing-songs. When the doors opened, however, this general bonhomie subsided – there was a sudden rush forwards, several scuffles ensued, and the police had to be brought in to restore order.

This concert of Gracie's is regarded by every authority as the finest and most emotive she ever gave in Rochdale. She sang for over an hour, beginning with a medley from *The King And I*, and, by way of 'The Rochdale Hounds' and 'The Aspidistra' moved on to her religious repertoire, and a new, portentous work which she had 'picked up' in Capri earlier that year. Few would doubt that 'Twenty' was one of her most beautiful songs.

> Soon, too soon do the years,
> Bring the heart many tears,
> As we sit and dream of the days way back when.
> Youth can live but a day,
> Then it goes on its way,
> Only in our dreams are we twenty again ...

There is of course some confusion as to Gracie's *true* thoughts regarding her hometown – how much of her 'common touch' was genuine, after almost a quarter-century in sunnier climes, and how much of it was exaggerated, or even put on for the benefit of her public. John Taylor called each visit 'An obligation, a reluctant pilgrimage which she ultimately enjoyed'. Irene Bevan said:

She was a Freewoman of the town and she had all these honours and awards. I was with her once when she picked up one of them, and one of the councillors told her, quite seriously, 'The Lady Mayoress has one leg shorter than t'other, but I'd be pleased if tha doesn't joke about it!' Grace *always* fitted in. But the proof of the pudding is in the eating. By the time Grace married Boris, she'd become a very sophisticated woman of the world who knew the difference between caviar and black pudding. And can you imagine how she must have felt, going back to Rochdale after spending all those years on Capri? I don't think anybody in their right mind would have expected her to come back to live in Rochdale, just as the people of Rochdale couldn't understand why she'd gone to Italy in the first place. It's a nice little town, now, but when she left in the Twenties it was a *grim* place. She wouldn't have gone back to live there, as much as she loved it and its people.

La Canzone del Mare, Gracie's beautiful home in Capri. *Top*: the Pink Apartment. *Bottom*: the restaurant. (*John Taylor*)

Entertaining Ford workers on the final assembly line in front of the
B-24 bomber, constructed in one hour and named in Gracie's honour,
April 1941. (*Morris Aza*)

Gracie arrives in Bombay on a
lightning visit, October 1941.
(*Morris Aza*)

New Guinea, 20 August 1945,
with a young soldier who saved
Monty's dentures! A few days later
the young man was tragically
killed. (*Morris Aza*)

Jacquinot Bay, August 1945. Gracie and Monty befriend one of the local natives from a tribe of headhunters. (*Morris Aza*)

Arriving at Hassau airfield, Greece, for an RAF benefits tour, February 1946. (*Morris Aza*)

Scoring another hit with her audience at a concert in the 1950s.
(*John Taylor*)

On stage with Maurice Chevalier,
Paris, October 1948. (*John Taylor*)

With Frankie Howerd in dapper
smoking jacket and cravat, 1950s.
(*John Taylor*)

Gracie with her third husband, Boris Alperovici (standing), being interviewed by Godfrey Wynn, Capri, 1966. (*John Taylor*)

With her beloved friends John and Anne Taylor in Capri. (*John Taylor*)

With her Italian housekeeper Irena Bounos. (*John Taylor*)

Gracie arrives in West Yorkshire for her première at Batley Variety Club, December 1968. (*John Taylor*)

At a cocktail party at the Midland Hotel in Rochdale with her former companion, Mary Davey, and her pianist, Teddy Holmes. (*John Taylor*)

The Royal Variety Show, November 1978. Gracie greets HM The Queen Mother, while Danny La Rue, Frankie Howerd and Lord Delfont look on. (*John Taylor*)

September 1978. Celebrating after her last concert in Rochdale with Ben Warris, Larry Grayson and Sandy Powell. (*John Taylor*)

'The old lady shows her medal!' At Buckingham Palace after her investiture as Dame Commander of the Order of the British Empire, February 1979. (*John Taylor*)

Kenneth Allsop, who covered Gracie's Rochdale visit for the magazine *Picture Post*, fervently admired the way she had always been able to comfortably hold on to her roots, in spite of an opulent lifestyle, and echoed one or two doubts which cynics may have nurtured.

There is a universe of difference between the stars who professionally act out the tedious business of keeping the common touch and those rare ones who have never lost it ... With only a few performances in Britain since the war, had the old dominance lost its sure hold? Had the sparkle dimmed, had that remarkable voice – leather lungs with a silver lining – lost its power? Were we going to be witnesses of that sad speciality of the theatre, the return of a has-been who won't go? When she had left, the questions were seen to have been absurd. Within the theatre, Gracie has the secret of eternal maturity.

At the end of the performance, when Gracie smiled up a Boris in the gallery, the audience began chanting his name so loudly that he had to join her on the stage. Silencing them with a loud whistle, she cracked, 'He's reet shy, tha knows!' After the show, the couple were guests of honour at a supper organized by the Mayor, and on the stroke of midnight she appeared on the Town Hall balcony to face a crowd the same size as the one which had clamoured for her in 1938 when she had become a Freewoman – the only difference with this one was that *it* had remained loyal all throughout her wartime ordeal.

Only weeks after this memorable concert, the Theatre Royal was gutted by fire. Although six fire engines arrived on the scene within minutes of the alarm being raised, they were unable to save the building. Gracie, who was visiting Oldham, came straight away. She muttered a prayer in the burnt-out dress-circle, gazing sadly at the stage which held for her so many indelible, happy memories. For Gracie it was not just the end of an era, it was a personal bereavement.

Ever since their marriage, Boris had been gently urging Gracie to retire, though she always changed the conversation whenever this subject was broached. What Boris might not have known – though he seems to have been steadily coming to terms with the fact – was that like all other chanteuses réalistes, Gracie's *true* marriage was to her public. Also, she was still only in her mid-fifties, possessed of a voice which was unquestionably clear and magnificent, with most of her natural talent still untapped.

On 19 March 1955 Gracie was in New York preparing for a show when she became ill with severe internal pains. She refused to see a doctor, telling Boris that it was no more than constipation and even sending him out to buy a bottle of castor oil because, she said, her mother had sworn by it as a cure for all ills. The next morning, however, she was worse and within minutes of being examined by a hotel doctor was in an ambulance en route for the hospital, where an emergency operation was carried out for gall-stones. Boris, distressed because he was virtually alone in a big, foreign city, panicked and in doing so made a nuisance of himself with the nursing staff, though he genuinely believed that he was acting in Gracie's interest. He refused to leave her side for one moment, terrified that she was going to die, and almost had to be restrained when she was wheeled off to the operating theatre. He returned to their rented apartment whilst the operation was taking place, shoved as many of her personal effects into a plastic bag as he could carry, and arranged them around her hospital room so that she would feel comfortable whilst recovering. As fast as the nurses removed them, insisting that everything had to be sterilized, Boris put them back again. On top of this, he personally prepared most of her food, and washed all her clothes.

Gracie recovered much more quickly than she had after her last serious illness, though she was forced to pull out of that year's 'extra' Royal Variety Show, scheduled to take place at the Blackpool Opera House on 13 April. Then, advised by her doctor in New York that she would benefit from the sea air, in the middle of May she sailed to England on the aptly named American liner, *Constitution*. During the journey she and Boris got on well and mingled with the other passengers, but as soon as the ship docked they were barely on speaking terms because Gracie had called Lillian Aza and arranged an extensive tour of Northern England, beginning with a gala concert in Blackpool on Christmas Day, against Boris's better judgement. During an interview with Anne Sharpeley of the London *Evening Standard*, when he interjected that she was ruining her health by working far too hard for a woman of her years, she turned to him and snapped, 'Don't be so gormless!' – then told her astonished interviewer, 'I'm running so fast, old age will *never* catch up with me!'

On Christmas Eve that year, 1955, the *Daily Express* asked Gracie to name a dozen Rochdalians whom she would invite to an imaginary Christmas party in the town – the idea is thought to have come from Marlene Dietrich's earlier interview, wherein *she* had detailed the twelve imaginary mourners at her funeral! Mary Whipp told me:

> I was feeling very glum as I had a huge stye on one eye. However, I went into the nearest milliner's and bought a silly little pill-box hat, and as I walk across the Broadway, I saw a huge placard: GRACIE'S ROCHDALE CHRISTMAS PARTY. My heart dropped into my shoes. The list read, 'Mrs Bertha Schofield and her daughter Ada, Alderman Charles Bryning and his daughter, Florence, Chief Constable S J Harvey and his wife, Mr and Mrs Norman Scott, Cousin Margaret Fielding and her husband, John, Miss Mary Whipp and 'Uncle' Tom Wolfenden. All are close friends and three are over eighty.' I won't go on, but ... *did it make my Christmas!*

Early in 1956, Norman Wisdom asked Gracie to appear in a film with him, playing his mother. Gracie turned him down, but she did accept the central role in J M Barrie's straight play, *The Old Lady Shows Her Medals*, saying, 'At least they won't have me looking like mutton dressed as lamb!' The play, which was screened live on American television in May 1956, told of a lonely Scots charlady who is so desperate to have a son of her own that she becomes 'probationary mother' to a young orphaned soldier (Robert Brown). Gracie dressed down considerably, in old clothes and a shawl, and the part earned her the prestigious Silvana Award a few months later. She said at the presentation, 'It's taken me years to make people realize that I can do straight stuff. I'm glad they've seen the other side of me.' Her success brought her innumerable offers of work, including a stage-play with Tallulah Bankhead. Gracie turned them all down – it would have meant moving back to the United States.

Gracie re-created *The Old Lady Shows Her Medals* for British television on 4 November 1956 – it became the first drama to be broadcast over the new Emley Moor Transmitter for viewers in the Yorkshire and Lancashire regions. There was a slight hitch when, during rehearsals, Gracie decided that the ITV backdrop was 'not quite right' – Boris was dispatched to Capri to pick up the original which had been used in the American production! One of Gracie's co-stars was Doris Speed, the actress who a few years later would immortalize the acid-tongued landlady, Annie Walker, in *Coronation Street*.

Gracie was planning on taking things easy for a while when she was visited by Henry Thody, of *Illustrated*, in August 1956. She explained that for six months of every year she was resigned to looking after Boris, whilst he was looking after her complex – the other six months, he looked after her whilst she was working. She joked, 'You could say that I'm six months a charlady and six months a star-lady!' By 22 September, however, she was in Malta, entertaining the troops and raising considerable funds for the Malta Playing Fields Association. Russ Conway had accompanied her on her last visit to the island in 1946, but this time he had to turn her down. He told the press how sorry he was, and enthused, 'Gracie taught me my stagecraft. She is one of the two greatest British entertainers of this century – the other is Dot Squires.' When a reporter met her at the airport in Valetta and informed her that the boys were looking forward to seeing her, she replied, 'Not half as glad as I'll be to see them, sunshine!'

In October 1956, Rochdale celebrated its centenary as a borough, and such an auspicious occasion would not have been complete without an appearance by the town's most famous daughter. Gracie was interviewed by *Lancashire Life*, and asked to define what Rochdale *really* meant to her.

Rochdale means 'first'. I first opened my eyes here, first laughed, first cried, heard the birds sing for the first time. I was even spanked for the first time in Rochdale, and in Rochdale I wore my first pair of clogs ... My first job as a winder was in Pouches old cotton mill ... My work since then has meant travelling the world over, to great places and small, but 'home' to me always means Rochdale and its gradely folk.

Nine years before, when Gracie had visited Rochdale with her *Working Party*, there had been another 'first' – the première of her own arrangement of the American vaudeville classic, 'Perfect Day'. Not unexpectedly, this song was used to close her concert for the centenary.

Do you think what the end of a perfect day
Can mean to a tired heart?
For memory has painted this perfect day
With colours that never fade.
And you find at the end of a perfect day,
The soul of a friend you've made.

Gracie told John Taylor of her unexpected meeting with the authoress of this beautiful poem, first recorded by Essie Ackland in the Thirties: 'I was in the Santa Monica house when I answered a knock on the door. This old lady said, "I'm Carrie Jacobs Bond." So I said, "Come in love and I'll make you a cup of tea." Then I dashed into the other room and asked Neva Hecker who she was. Neva explained that she had written "I Love You Truly" and "Perfect Day", then I clicked. The old lady and I remained friends until she died a few years later.'

Gracie was booked to appear on the Royal Variety Show on 5 November 1956, later hailed by the press as one firework that 'did not go off'. That very morning, newsflashes proclaimed that British and French troops had landed in Port Said, Egypt, in what was to form the zenith of the Suez Crisis, and that Russia was threatening rocket attacks unless they agreed to a ceasefire. Buckingham Palace issued a statement: 'Her Majesty regrets that in view of the mounting international crisis, she is unable to attend at the Palladium tonight and therefore wishes to send the cast the sincerest apologies.' This message was relayed by Val Parnell only minutes after the dress-rehearsal, three hours before the audience were due to arrive.

Topping the bill that year was the outrageous American pianist, Liberace, in the midst of a crisis himself after what must surely have been the most waspish but retrospectively funny attack ever on the sexuality of an entertainer. Even the usually tolerant Gracie had said of him, 'He's a lass-lad who needs his clothes feeling.' Refusing to travel by air, Liberace had taken a train from Hollywood to New York, then the ship to Southampton, a total of nine days in which, he said, he had attempted to cool off. Now, faced with a new dilemma, he flung himself into Gracie's arms and wept uncontrollably, watched by a bemused Vivien Leigh and Laurence Olivier. More hilarity was provided by the comic, Jimmy Wheeler, who barged into the master dressing-room brandishing his violin and announced at the top of his voice, 'I've been rehearsing this fucking piece for a fortnight, so somebody's going to hear it!' This brought a smile to Liberace's face, and he, Gracie and the Crazy Gang – who had perfected an irreverent send-up of *A Midsummer Night's Dream* for the show – commandeered the Palladium kitchen and made tea. Then, when everyone seemed suitably calmed down, the entire cast went off to honky-tonk pianist Winifred Atwell's London home and partied until three in the morning. 'Everyone cried in their beer and got over their disappointment,' Liberace wrote in his memoirs.

A few days later, Gracie organized a caravanning holiday so that Boris might see some of the English countryside. Then, hours before they were due to set off, Gracie received a visit from Val Parnell and Bernard Delfont, who 'persuaded' her to do two weeks at the Prince of Wales Theatre. She laughingly told the press, 'I'm like the girl from Oklahoma – I can't say No!'

On 19 November, Gracie told Geoffrey Lake of the *Daily Mail* that she was tying up all her business interests in the United States and Capri, and returning to England for good. She said, 'I love Capri very much, but can you imagine me *not* coming back here for good? I've just been waiting for Boris to get the "feeling". In the past she had often lamented about there being no coal on the island, and that a cosy fire represented the England she loved. 'When she was in Capri, she missed England, and vice-versa,' John Taylor said. 'Sometimes she was never settled.'

This time, however, Gracie really did come close to putting down roots, though she was emphatic about one thing when speaking to Edward Goring, of the same newspaper, less than twenty-four hours later. When Goring asked her if she wanted to live in Rochdale again, she politely but firmly made her point, which only went into print *after* he had edited her English: 'We shall live in London. I want to see what is going on. I love my Rochdale and its folks, but I would not live up North. I am in the theatre. I am not in the factory any more. You are trying to put me in clogs and shawl again!' Gracie denied saying the latter phrase and was so infuriated with Goring that she declared, 'Let me meet him again and I'll wrap me bloody clogs round his neck!'

Lillian Aza had been trying to persuade Gracie to move back to England for years, thinking she badly needed to spend more time amongst her own people, the only ones who really mattered. Closer to Gracie than almost anyone, including Boris, and wise to the 'machinations' within the Canzone del Mare, her manager knew precisely where to pin the blame, and was reported as saying, 'He [Boris] is just a snob, and the way Gracie sees it, she has to stay where she is because she can't go mucking up another marriage.'

Irene Bevan, however, vociferously denied that Lillian would have used such a term.

It's such tripe! She might have said, she 'doesn't want to make further difficulties' for herself, but not that. Lillian *did* say that Grace was terrified of Boris, and that she would have come back to England had it not been for him wanting to stay on the island. Then again, *had* she returned, she would probably have died much sooner than she did on account of the climate and her chest problems.

Only weeks after triumphing at the Prince of Wales, Gracie cut her first long-playing record for the new Conquest label, though she did not always get on with the technicians who, being paid by the hour, found her professionalism irksome – the fact that eight of the fourteen tracks were recorded in single takes, and in one session. She was also uncharacteristically catty towards the producer, Norman Newell, snarling when he offered to take her to lunch, 'Every bugger wants to take me out to lunch now that I can afford to pay for it myself. When I needed it, I wasn't even offered a *sandwich!*'

The *Our Gracie* album was an innovation. Gracie was approaching sixty and her voice was more powerful than ever before, yet in tender moments she was heartrendingly moving. Her top notes were still absolutely flawless. The album was of course a showcase of her greatest hits by public demand: 'The Woodpecker Song' and 'Sally' had to be there, as had comic ditties such as ''Fonso, My Hot Spanish Knight' and 'Ee, By Gum!'. Other songs which had not been especially written for Gracie – 'London Pride', 'Nature Boy' and 'How Are Things in Glocca Morra?' – were performed with such conviction that they practically became her property. Arguably, the most portentous song on the album was J J Niles's 'Go Way From My Window', which had begun life as 'I'm Looking Out the Window', and which was Boris's favourite Gracie Fields song. Marlene Dietrich told me, 'Peggy Lee introduced it, then I changed some of the words and the arrangement, and gave it to Gracie. She sang it so well that I declined to record it myself for two years. It was a revelation for us both.'

> I'll give you back your letters,
> I'll give you back your ring,
> But I'll ne'er forget my own true love,
> As long as songbirds sing ...
> Go 'way from my window.
> Don't bother me no more ...

On 18 November 1957, Gracie appeared in her eighth Royal Variety Show. Top of the bill was Tommy Steele, an up-and-coming young entertainer who admired her so much that he insisted upon being photographed with her. Although she was not impressed by the age of rock 'n' roll, when success began being measured largely in revolutions per minute, Gracie made the almost fatal mistake of attempting to 'demote' herself to pop-star status by performing several up-tempo numbers, which at first brought a reasonable response from the audience. But when instead of closing with a tender ballad, 'When You Are Loved' that she had planned, but had not had enough time to rehearse properly, she be-bopped in her elegant black gown to a song called 'Born To Be Your Baby', she was virtually ignored.

The next morning, Gracie and Boris met the journalist John Lambert for breakfast at the Dorchester – and seemingly mindless of his presence, the couple let rip. Much of what was said, particularly Gracie's cursing, was edited out of Lambert's interview when it appeared in the *Daily Express* on 20 November, under the heading, 'I WONDER IF I'M FINISHED?' ASKS GRACIE FIELDS.

> *Boris*: Darling, it was terrible! When you came on the audience loved you, as always. But when you sang that song and tried to rock and roll, it was ridiculous! The audience looked embarrassed, then bored. You're not a young woman, my dear. You should leave that sort of thing to young girls ...
> *Gracie*: I know that I'm an old woman now – old in years, anyway, if not in the way I feel. And me voice may be going a bit ... and it seems that it's not what the variety stage needs these days. I don't pretend to understand what

young Mr Steele has got – I can't even understand the words he's singing. His is the only sort of act that'll fill variety halls these days. They're all alike these kids. They wear jeans, they imitate Elvis Presley, and they last five minutes!

Boris: Darling, these things are forgivable in youth. It's right, even amusing, to see a bright-looking boy jumping and bawling. But *not* an artiste of your stature.

Gracie: I can't keep on singing the same old songs, day in, day out. The Royal Variety Show's all right for people like Judy Garland and Mario Lanza. They haven't been in one before, so they can use the stuff that made 'em famous. When I was first in the show, *every* act was a headliner – now, the bill's so crowded with bloody recording stars and there's no room for anybody else! My great trouble, my love, is trying to find new songs that the youngsters of today are going to like!

What Gracie probably did not realize was that she had made just one grossly overblown mistake in a career spanning over thirty years at the top, and that many impresarios and certainly the *general* public did not base their judgement on a single performance. Even so, although Gracie was literally bombarded with offers of work as soon as she arrived back in Capri, she turned down amongst other things a lengthy tour of the United States and Canada, and a five-season American television series which would have netted her in excess of $1 million. The woman who only months before had begun 'winding up operations' in Capri, now declared, 'That'd mean me living in Hollywood nine months out of every year. I *need* to get to Capri! That keeps me going!'

Gracie had also turned down the starring role in a West End play, *The Time of the Cuckoo*, which had been filmed as *Summer Madness* with Katharine Hepburn. She told the *Daily Mail*, 'My English fans would never accept me playing an American. And besides, I don't want to get stuck in England.' There was a slight compensation, however, when she had recorded the film's lilting, melodious theme, 'Summertime in Venice', on the flipside of 'Twenty'.

> I dream all the Winter long
> Of mandolins that played our song ...
> I almost feel your lips on mine,
> And though we have to be an ocean apart,
> Let Venice and you and summertime be in my heart!

Gracie even tried to cancel contracts which he had signed for four television shows at the end of the year. One was top of the bill on that stalwart Fifties-Sixties institution, *Sunday Night at the London Palladium*, which not surprisingly filled her with terror, though she was told that she would be sued should she not turn up for rehearsals. She snarled at Edward Goring, who once more was in the wrong place at the wrong time, 'To hear some people talk, you'd think the television would close down if I didn't keep appearing on the blessed thing!'

Fortunately, there was tremendous support not just from her fans, but from Gracie's peers – Bud Flanagan wrote a open letter to the *Daily Express* assuring her that she was still needed, and concluded 'Don't be so daft!' Gracie came to her senses, and the Palladium Show was a resounding success. And she did get around to singing and recording some quite remarkable new songs that year: Jester Hairston's 'Mary's Boy Child', Victor Young's film-theme 'Around the World', and Tony Osborne's lush arrangement of 'Scarlet Ribbons' to mention but three.

In 1959 the writer Grahame Greene, a resident of Capri, introduced Gracie to a young, worldly and tough-looking priest named Mario Borelli. For some years, visitors to the Canzone del Mare who had stopped off at Naples had complained to her of how they had been pestered and even mugged by some of the teenage ruffians hanging around the harbour and tourist areas. In a city which was an unemployment blackspot, in those days there were an atonishing 50,000 homeless children under the age of sixteen. Known locally as the *scugnizzi* – translated literally as 'spinning tops' on account of the way they operated – they were little more than an exceedingly rough army of thugs, thieves and rent-boys. Father Borelli, adopting Gracie's own maxim, 'If you can't beat em, join 'em!', became their undisputed champion. Swapping his dog-collar and cassock for denims and a patched-up blouson, he went out amongst the *scugnizzi* and became one in all but name – hanging around street corners and sleeping rough until he acquired a disused church which he turned into a rehabilitation centre known, and often feared, by the locals, as the 'House of Urchins'.

When Father Borelli invited Gracie to sing to the *scugnizzi* in the middle of their crumbling refuge, she thought it a ridiculous notion. Not only was she not Italian, she said, she was more than old enough to be everybody's grandmother! Unable to resist any challenge, however, she decided to give the project a go. As few of the boys had heard of her, let alone listened to any of her recordings, in her 'Lancashire-Italian' she sang a traditional Neapolitan song, 'Tiritomba', a hit that year for the young German tenor, Fritz Wünderlich. Gracie encouraged them to sing along with the chorus, and there was much stamping of feet and cries of '*Canta!*' – Sing! Then, after several more ditties she delivered a lengthy speech telling them about her own childhood, and of how there were other ways of getting by without resorting to crime.

Some years later, Mario Borelli left the priesthood to marry, though he and Gracie kept up the *scugnizzi* concerts, and did a lot of other work for the underprivileged of Naples. Many of these youngsters were well beyond redemption, though the pair did get through to a few. Borelli became a close friend and as such was amongst those participating in Gracie's *This Is Your Life* in 1960 – an important event at which every single member of her family was conspicuous by their absence. There had been no rows, no angry words, just a serious heart-to-heart with Boris who persuaded Gracie to cut down on her expenditure, so far as her family were concerned. 'We came to the conclusion that Gracie's relatives had had enough,' Boris told John Taylor. 'Her generosity to her sisters continued, of course. They had never asked for anything in the first place. But as for the others – Tommy, and the nieces and nephews – Gracie said that from now on, they would have to fend for themselves. After all, she was no longer earning huge fees. Unfortunately, for the time being, everyone took the huff, though soon afterwards Edith and Betty realized that Gracie had acted sensibly.'

This lack of family support for one of the most important occasions of her career only delighted Gracie, who later told the Taylors, 'Sadly, I wasn't able to choose my family, though thank God I *was* able to choose all my friends!'

11

When I Grow Too Old to Dream

In 1960, Gracie recorded one of her most unusual songs – again, it was a cover-version of an Edith Piaf song, and one for which both artistes attracted some adverse criticism simply because it was so very different. Piaf and Gracie had surprisingly much in common. In spite of numerous husbands and lovers, both had without exception put love of their public before that for any one man. Both had suffered hardship, and had profited from their experiences by containing them within their work. Both were very religious, but reluctant to worship in the conventional way because they quite rightly believed their faith to be a personal matter, to be kept away from the prying eyes of fans and the media. Both said their prayers every night, always on their knees. Both nurtured an unshakeable belief in the precognitive dream – the fact that all will turn out well in the end, so long as one wishes it so.

Many of Gracie's and Piaf's songs were linked with a recurrent religious theme. In Gracie's case it was 'Bless This House', 'The Lord's Prayer' and 'Ave Maria'. In Piaf's, 'Mon Dieu', 'Exodus' and 'Soeur Anne'. 'Jérusalem' went one step further in that its theme was Jesus himself. Robert Chabrier's beautiful poem was given an almost word-for-word translation from the French by Bernie Wayne, under the title 'In Jerusalem'. The music was a Hebrew *chesed* by Joseph Moutet, who insisted that the original Yiddish orchestrations be adhered to.

For its impeccable technique and sheer vocal brilliance, 'In Jerusalem' represents Gracie at her most definitive and as such the recording can perhaps be regarded as the finest of all her later recordings.

In His eyes there is shining the sight of love,
In His heart there is burning the light of love,
In His hands is the power and might of love,
And so He walks alone,
On the way that He must go ...
In His eyes is forgiveness for all the world,
From His heart pours salvation for all the world,
From His hands comes creation for all the world,
And for all time to come,
We pray His will be done!

For a number of years, and even more so since marrying Boris, Gracie had talked about retirement, though few believed that she really wanted to. She could not even relax properly on holiday. In 1961 she and Boris went on a cruise to Hong Kong. She wrote to the Taylors twice – first to complain how very expensive everything was, secondly to inform them that the travel company had refunded her money – in exchange for two concerts on the ship! Boris later said that one of his fondest memories of Gracie was when she had sang 'How Are Things in Glocca Morra?', unaccompanied, as the ship had been passing through the Suez Canal. He told John Taylor, 'The tranquillity, and the lovely breeze coursing along the Canal, with Gracie's magnificent voice – it's a moment I will treasure for the rest of my life.'

During the next two years, Gracie took things easy – to such an extent that when she told a reporter visiting Capri, 'Yes, I've finally put down me knitting!' she was believed. Always prone to stooping slightly when she was on stage she now began doing so on account of her increasing bouts of rheumatism. John Taylor said, 'At the end of her last show in 1960, as she walked off her shoulders seemed to slump. Also, her voice was going down a little bit and she was starting to go deaf in one ear.' Compensation for fans came by way of an album, 'Hey There!', which for once did not have any comedy songs. There was a superb cover-version of the Johnny Mathis hit, 'A Certain Smile', and one of 'Love Is a Many-Splendoured Thing'.

On Christmas Day 1961, Gracie made her second appearance on Radio 4's *Desert Island Discs*. As 'Castaway Number 576', her choice was lighter and more varied than the first time, and included Maurice Chevalier's 'I Remember It Well,' Harry Secombe's 'Little Drummer Boy', and her own version of 'The Holy City'. During this visit to England Gracie was wildly enthusiastic about the teenage pop-star, Helen Shapiro – and she had 'revised her opinion' about Tommy Steele, telling Tony Barrow from Decca, 'Now there's a true artist. He can handle an audience and he knows how to move on stage – unlike some of today's young singers. God help 'em without a microphone!'

In 1963, Gracie received a Cavalier award for her contribution over many years to Capri's tourist industry. There was also very nearly a parting of the ways with her friend and former secretary Neva Hecker, who asked Gracie to loan her the money to purchase a small summer-house in Austia, near Rome. 'Gracie was all for doing it,' John Taylor said. 'Boris, however, didn't like giving money away, so he pulled this act by fainting on the floor and faking a heart attack. He was so convincing that even Gracie thought he was genuinely ill, and she asked Neva to leave. Neva never got her money, and it took her a long time to visit again – when she did, Boris didn't make her very welcome, though Gracie was as friendly as she'd always been to her. And of course, the day after his "attack" Boris was perfectly all right.'

In the autumn of 1964, the impresario Harold Fielding talked Gracie into doing eleven concerts in England. Her conditions for doing the tour were that the dates should be spread across a four-week period, and there should be no more twice-nightly shows. She told him, 'I'm not a spring chicken any more, so I don't want rushing about!' Fielding later applauded her great simplicity and easygoing manner, compared with some of the tetchy Continental and American stars he had handled. She is said to have 'hit him for six' by telling him that she did not even need a mirror in her dressing-room when she was fixing her hair and make-up!

First stop on the road was Fielding's own theatre, the Prince Charles, in London, not for a show, but for a press-conference which saw her looking somewhat ill at ease, even though she soon engaged her media audience in a singalong of numbers from *Hello Dolly!* Most of the journalists present considered her too old to be embarking on a tour. Their subsequent reports were generally uncomplimentary, and a few were downright rude, declaring that if she continued, she would only fall flat on her face. When asked what it felt like to be making a comeback at the age of sixty-six, she put one young man in his place by snapping, 'It isn't a comeback, my love. I've never been away!'

On 4 September, an estimated 12,000 people turned up to watch Gracie fulfil a lifelong ambition – switching on the Blackpool illuminations, before taking a trip along the prom in a decorated tram. Reginald 'Mr Blackpool' Dixon, the organist from the Tower Ballroom who was himself a Northern institution, played her on to the platform with a medley of her songs. She was wearing a simple black dress, and flanked by Boris and the Mayor. Naturally the crowd chanted for her to sing, and she had planned only the usual chorus from 'Sally' – after several years away from the stage, she said, she dared not risk damaging her vocal chords by singing outside. When the chanting grew too vociferous, however, she placated them with her own English 'adaptation' of 'Volare'.

> For a beautiful home by the sea
> You all helped to build it for me,
> Without you, where would I be?
> Most certainly not in Capri!

Two evenings later, Gracie walked on to the stage of the 3,000-seater Blackpool Opera House for the first of her two concerts. Tempting fate by wearing a sea-green outfit under her fur coat, she took off the latter, folded it carefully, placed it on top of the piano and announced, 'You've all seen it. I'll put it down now. It's Boris. he told me to be nice and posh!' She then sang non-stop for ninety minutes – not just old hits and film songs, but her own arragements of 'Summertime in Venice' and Kurt Weill's haunting 'September Song'. There were so many flowers, before and after the shows, that several vanloads of them were dispatched to local hospitals.

As in her 'Mad Hatter' days with Irene Bevan and the Flanagan clique, Gracie was in her element whilst working in Blackpool. Boris, however, who after his years on the road with her should have been used to her foibles by now, was not amused by her typical 'returning to roots' element which was as essential to her psyche as hobnobbing with the elite was to his. He balked at the very idea of her being presented with a huge stick of Blackpool rock – manufactured especially, with 'Our Gracie' running all the way through it – which she smashed into pieces and shared amongst her friends. Even more, he was aghast when late one night she sent the waiter from the Imperial Hotel to get fish and chips for herself and Bernard Braden – then 'rebuked' him for serving them on plates instead of leaving them in the newspaper!

Boris had fought against Gracie doing the tour in the first place, and now he opted to return to Capri. There was no known argument, no harsh words. Gracie's husband simply felt out of place when she was meeting 'her' people, and though she spoke to him every day on the telephone, she did little to disguise the fact that for the time being at least, she was glad to see the back of him.

The tour progressed. In Torquay, one newspaper proclaimed, 'It's Graciemania!' and when a reporter remarked that she was getting a reception that most major pop stars might envy, she cracked, 'Then you'd better start calling me Mother Beatle! And in answer to your next question – yes, I do like The Beatles, though I'd like 'em a whole lot more if they got their hair cut!' Like Piaf, Judy Garland, Marlene Dietrich and Dorothy Squires, she attracted a huge gay following, particularly at the Portsmouth Guildhall, and Bristol's Colston Hall. The latter had an imposing façade with a steep flight of steps, Gracie was about to descend these after her show when she was suddenly confronted by 2,000 screaming fans. Obviously frightened of taking a tumble, after she had quietened them with her errand-boy whistle, she made a deal – in exchange for a song, they would let her through to the waiting car. One journalist reported, 'After "Sally" there came the parting of the Red Sea!'

Gracie ended her tour at the Congress Theatre, in Eastbourne, on 4 October, and at once dashed off to Brighton to spend a week with her family and friends – sparking off rumours that there had indeed been a serious rift between her and Boris, and that this time she would definitely be staying in England.

In fact, it was much worse than this for it has only recently emerged that shortly before leaving Capri, Gracie and Boris had had a blazing row within the grounds of La Canzone del Mare – news of which had been relayed to Lillian Aza probably by Gracie herself, within the hour. Irene Bevan told me, 'Grace at once contacted her solicitor in Brighton, and drew up a will leaving all the English property to her family in England. I don't know what their argument was about, but Lillian said that it was a bad one.' An anonymous Capri source alleged that Boris actually had *assaulted* his wife, implying that Boris was in some sort of shady financial trouble which was putting him under unendurable stress. Whatever the truth of this, it has been confirmed that Boris, with his mysterious mid-European background, almost certainly *had* been involved with criminal activities in his younger years – Lillian Aza and several other visitors to Gracie's complex several times discovered, to their horror, that their rooms had been bugged – and that Boris owed several large debts, which Gracie settled shortly after their wedding, absolutely *no one* connected with the couple would confirm the aforementioned 'violent' aspect of Boris's nature. John Taylor said,

> There were times when Boris could be very hard. He didn't say much, but he would glare. The reports that he hit her are just rubbish, of course. She used to tell me, 'He's a bugger, John. He hits out at me!' – this was her term for saying he'd lost his temper. But all he did when he got angry was to wander off for a few hours. I suppose that in a way it *was* mental cruelty because Gracie never knew where he'd gone, and she would worry. Then he would come back, calmly, and they would make up. What he *never* did was upset her when she was doing her shows. Boris knew exactly where to draw the line.

Fortunately, any real dissension between Gracie and her husband did not last long – she returned to Capri, settled the two of them down over a nice pot of tea to talk things through, and forty-eight hours later she called her lawyer in Brighton and ordered him to cancel the new will.

By 2 November Gracie was back in England to appear in another Royal Variety Show, and at London's Westbury Hotel she was joined by the recently married John and Anne Taylor. Anne, previously an aficionado of Bing Crosby and not a Gracie fan, had been introduced to her husband's idol on Capri. 'Their first conversation was about liver and onions, and how to get rid of unwanted relatives,' John told me. 'They were two Northerners with lots in common, and they got on like a house on fire.' Now, in her suite at the Westbury, Gracie proved what a hardened old trooper she really was. Anne was doing Gracie's hair when she noticed a lump on the crown of her head. 'It was a rodent ulcer,' John said. 'And what do you think happened? Gracie went straight off to Harley Street and had it cut out, then she went on to do the Royal Variety Show that same night. We were amazed!'

Gracie had marvelled at Marlene Dietrich's spine-tingling performance in the previous year's Royal Show, when one of her songs had been Pete Seeger's anti-war anthem, 'Where Have All the

Flowers Gone?' – and when the Beatles had appeared halfway down the bill. Gracie had always wanted to sing the Seeger song, and this formed their brief conversation the next evening when the two stars bumped into each other in the lift at the Westbury. Marlene was in town for a concert at Grosvenor House, and though they had spoken several times on the telephone, this was their first meeting. Truly impressed, Gracie returned to her suite. The maid was tidying up, and she told her, 'I've just been in the lift with Marlene Dietrich, and she looks *beautiful!*' – to which the young woman replied, 'I do her room as well, and she looks just as bad as you do first thing on a morning!'

Early in 1965, Gracie accepted a tour of Australasia, her first in twenty years. Boris was absent again – he was waiting to go into hospital for a hernia operation. There should have been ten concerts in Australia, beginning with a three-day engagement in Sydney, followed by dates in Melbourne, Adelaide and Brisbane. Such was the demand for tickets that most of the theatres asked for, and were given, return shows – twenty-two in all. In Brisbane mindless of the heat, she was on stage for over two hours.

Gracie may not have been too happy, spending her thirteenth wedding anniversary so far away from her husband, but there were compensations. She was reunited with her sister, Betty, now residing in Australia – and engaged temporarily as her dresser. At a school for blind children in Sydney, she realized that her young audience were bored by listening to her regular repertoire – she compromised by squatting on the floor amongst them and giving an impromptu recital of Beatles songs! She got on so well with the lifeguards on Bondi Beach that they asked her to be their mascot for that year's Freshwater Surf Carnival. Gracie declined the car provided by the tour promoter, and rode in the back of the lifeguards' truck. 'I had a good old-fashioned singsong, surrounded by half a ton of muscle!' she cracked. Needless to say, Boris would not have approved! After the event, she sang at the official tea, more often than not an excuse for the competitors to get roaring drunk, though in Gracie's case it *was* only tea. She returned to Melbourne on 2 April for what would be her last concert in Australia and the next day she flew to Capri.

By the end of June, Gracie had played another farewell concert – in front of 8,000 screaming admirers at an outdoor stadium in New York. The event, part of the *Salute to Britain* programe organized by the Metropolitan Opera was taped and subsequently released on an

American album. She is in fine fettle throughout the performance, though one does detect certain weariness by the time she has reached her last song 'There'll Always Be an England'. She told a press-conference, 'Enough is enough, loves. From now on I just want to be with my husband and enjoy the rest of my life.'

Retirement was not on Gracie's agenda, however, when she came to England to appear on a television programme which celebrated ten years of ITV, and stayed to record another for Christmas. She began her 23-song set with the camp classic, 'The Fairy on the Christmas Tree', worked her way through a catalogue of old hits, offered a heartrending 'Can't Help Loving That Man of Mine' – intended as a slap in the face for those critics who had speculated on her marriage problems – and performed 'I Love the Moon' for the first time on air since 1939. She also sang 'Blow the Wind Southerly'. Kathleen Ferrier's famous version had been sung with no accompaniment whatsover, but Gracie whistled the interludes between the verses in such a way that her version cannot fail to bring a lump to the throat. There was also another adaptation of 'Volare' which praised the virtues of being over sixty.

> Though I should be retired,
> I still get inspired,
> Continuing on with the show!
> So when the BBC's calling,
> Without any warning, I go!

In 1966, Gracie took life a bit more easily – for her. Several important visitors spent time with her on Capri, including Hal Roach, the Taylors, Alan J Lerner and Bernard Delfont – who attempted and failed to book her for the Palladium. Then, when Boris suffered a genuine coronary at Peacehaven and had to be hospitalized for several weeks, her admirers truly believed that they had indeed seen the last of her ... until 21 November when she made a suprise visit to the Star and Garter Home for Disabled Soldiers, Sailors and Airmen, at Richmond in Surrey. On Christmas Day she appeared in the BBC's *A Spoonful of Sugar*. She laughed a lot, but lurking behind the mask of the clown were many apprehensions. Gracie was remembering what had happened immediately after that fateful festive season of 1949, and could not ignore the fact that Boris, like Monty, had always been overweight. She therefore devoted almost a whole year caring for him at the Canzone del Mare.

Gracie's 'retirement' was short-lived. On her seventieth birthday she appeared on David Frost's television show, and towards the end of 1968 she was propositioned by Jimmy Corrigan, a North of England entrepreneur who, having made his fortune out of a bingo-hall and amusement-arcade empire, had in 1966 opened the pioneering Batley Variety Club in West Yorkshire. Corrigan prided himself in having attracted, by fat fees, many of the world's greatest entertainers to an area which was virtually monopolized by working men's clubs, without any doubt amongst the toughest audiences in Europe. His 'firsts' had included Ella Fitzgerald, Louis Armstrong, Eartha Kitt, and Jayne Mansfield – but as he told *The Times* after Gracie had signed the contract, 'We've had a great many stars at Batley but no booking has given more pleasure to Gracie's.'

Corrigan's offer – £10,000 for two weeks of cabaret appearances – was an extremely substantial one, but before accepting, Gracie called John Taylor and sought his opinion. She had last appeared in Batley in 1916, when *It's a Bargain* had played the Hippodrome, but remembered little about the town other than that it had been about thirty miles from Rochdale, and convenient at that time for visiting her parents.

Gracie had always admired what she called her friend's 'wisdom and gumption', and John's blunt initial reaction was to say, 'Good God, woman. You're nearly seventy-one, and you'd have to be on stage for an hour and a quarter!' His recompense was an irate telephone call from Lillian Aza, accusing him of usurping her authority, though suffice to say Gracie was apparently more keen on listening to her friend's advice than that of her agent. She called John again and explained that she would accept Jimmy Corrigan's offer, but on her own conditions. First, she would sing for one week, then have a week's rest before completing her contract. Secondly, during her second week she would go on stage one hour before the club's regular cabaret slot at 11:30 pm – this would enable her fans from Rochdale to get home more conveniently after the show.

Again, Boris tried to persuade Gracie not to do it. Having had a close call himself, he was afraid that any lengthy engagement would overtire her. Gracie merely told him to stop fretting. Her 'comeback' accorded her a great deal of press coverage, though when she joked, 'I'm only doing it for the lolly, so my family will have plenty to last 'em when I've popped me clogs!' and said of her fee, 'They paid

Louis Armstrong a lot more than me, but as he had an orchestra and I'm all on me own, I'll let that one pass!' there were some who, harking back to what had happened with Monty Banks in 1940, offered a few gratuitous gripes of their own. A Member of Parliament tabled a question in the House of Commons, enquiring if she would be allowed to take her entire fee out of the country without paying taxes. Gracie's curt response to this remains unprintable, and when one reporter had the audacity to ask her just how much money she would be bequeathing to her loved ones, she snapped, 'Why don't you mind yer own bloody business?' She was more genial towards Douglas Marlborough of the *Daily Mirror*, doubtless because he was one of the few at the time who was willing to treat her with any degree of respect, telling him, 'I'm making a comeback for the love of the theatre, love of work – and for the extra three-halfpence left over for Christmas!'

Gracie and Boris flew into London on 24 November, and after visiting her brother Tommy and his young wife Annette to see the latest addition to their family – their daughter had been born on 21 June – they travelled up to Batley where she at once flung herself into rehearsals. There was a minor drama when a thief broke into Bert Waller's car and stole his sheet music – Gracie's pianist and arranger was forced to sit up most of the night and write it out again in time for the first rehearsal.

Jimmy Corrigan's cleaning staff were astonished to observe how relaxed Gracie was, and not at all perturbed by being watched – even by Shara, the club's alsatian which wandered on to the stage halfway through one of her more arduous numbers. Gracie stopped singing, whistled and yelled, 'Come on, cock!', and the dog lay down at her feet and went to sleep until she had finished.

Her old sparkle had returned! Then she told Rita Marshall of *The Times why* Boris had been so worried about her coming back to England. 'I've not been all that well lately, you know. I was all rheumaticky and thought I'd had it. I thought to myself, this is old age coming on, all of a rush.'

Gracie's première, on 1 December, enabled her to reach quite unprecedented heights. She looked sensational, though a little frail, in a silver lamé dress, and sounded wonderful. As she strode almost defiantly towards the microphone, 1,500 fans who had paid a lot of money to get into the club gave her a standing ovation, and no matter how many times she whistled, the audience would not stop cheering until satisfied that she had been given 'a reet good greeting'. Earlier, whilst the warm-up act had been on, she had peered into the auditorium to see the waiters serving some of the patrons scampi and chips. Now, she cracked, 'I were born over a fish and chip shop, and now I'm singing in one!'

Gracie opened her show with what she called her 'S' songs, but for once 'Sally' did not appear until well into the programme. She then went into a lengthy comedy patter before introducing a medley of new songs – 'Strangers in the Night' and 'Somewhere, My Love' were sung an octave lower than they might have been a few years before. However, when she began 'As Long As He Needs Me' at the top end of the scale – the much younger Shirley Bassey and Dorothy Squires were singing it in the same key in theatres up and down the country – many of those sitting in the auditorium were terrified that she would not hold the momentum until the end of the song. She did, of course. More than this, during the final refrain of the Mary Hopkins song, 'Those Were the Days', she jumped a whole octave ... and in praise of Gracie's never less than perfect diction, one critic remarked that of the dozens of artistes who had already covered the song, she was the only one not to have murdered the line 'For ever and a day', by making it sound like gobbledygook – 'Forever-randa-day'. Gracie also had the room rocking with laughter, with an updated version of Bill Haines's ''Fonso, My Hot Spanish Knight', which had been inspired by Marie Dubas's classic song of 1927, 'Pédro'. Gracie had introduced it back in 1930, when guesting in Marie's show at the Escholiers Theatre in Paris.

> I found him strolling in Madrid-a,
> He say he's got a million quid-da,
> Some day I hope to be his widda ...
> He serenade me with a trumpet,
> I slosh him good upon ze crumpet,
> If he don't like it, he can lump it ...
> Him such a big strong healthy fellow,
> No kick ze bucket none too well-o,
> Ze bull see him and run like hell-o ...
> My tale of woe is never ending,
> His wicked ways he'll not be mending,
> I wish ze bull would catch him bending,
> 'Fonso, my hot Spanish knight!

During her second week at Batley, Gracie changed the order of her programme and included several Christmas songs. One of the shows was recorded by Philips ... after listening to the master tape Gracie declared that her voice was not at its best, and forbade its release. Those who have heard the tape disagree with her.

After Batley, Gracie withdrew from the public glare for more than a year – with the exception of a one-off concert in Paignton, Devon, for a travel agents' convention – though fans were somewhat appeased by Denis Pitts's acclaimed film portrait, *The World of Gracie Fields*, which the BBC broadcast on 28 January 1970.

Shooting began in August 1969. Kenneth MacMillan, the cameraman, had recently completed the award-winning *Civilization* television series for Kenneth Clark. The sound engineer, Mike Turner, would later be praised for his work on the drama series, *Darwin*. The proceedings were initially hampered by an angry and ebullient Boris Alperovici, who accused the television crew of turning Capri into a slum – before announcing that *he* had neither given Gracie leave to make the film, nor agreed to the terms of the contract which she and Lillian Aza had signed! He then went on to insult and attack almost everyone in sight, proving himself anything but the shy, mild-mannered man who had accompanied Gracie all over the world, giving her fans the impression that they were the perfect example of middle-aged married bliss.

August, Boris declared, was the worst month of the year for the 'intellegentsia' of Capri, for it was at this time that the island was invaded by working-class tourists and ferryloads of day-trippers which were detrimental to its image! He told Denis Pitts, 'They bring in money and they buy souvenirs, but they are common people, and this is a sophisticated island!' And if this was not enough, he added, 'The English are the worst of all, for the English have no culture!'

Amongst other things, Boris was referring to an 'incident' that had taken place earlier that day, when Gracie had invited an elderly Yorkshireman to share a pot of tea with her. Taking off his jacket – horror of horrors, he revealed that he was wearing a pair of striped braces over his shirt sleeves, just as Gracie's father had always done – the old chap had asked her for permission to dip his big toe in her pool for luck! Naturally, the request had been granted and Gracie, admitting that her husband was such a snob, told Pitts, 'Boris likes the money they bring in, but he doesn't like the working-class English – my sort of people. He wants to keep them as far from his snooty Italian society friends as he can.'

The next day, Boris apologized ... then told the television crew that the project would have to be called off because Gracie had suddenly been laid low with bronchitis. The crew left, but Pitts stayed put and inadvertently learned from Gracie's doctor, Rosemary Rawnsley, that she was not ill at all – Boris had *ordered* her to stay inside their other house, in Anacapri, until the BBC crew had left the island.

Pitts wrote in the *Sunday People*, a few days after Gracie died, that he had made one or two discreet enquiries amongst friends in Capri – including the carpets tycoon, Cyril Lord; though for once Gloria Magnus did not offer her opinion, which in itself seems remarkable – and all had said the same thing: Gracie was a very unhappy woman who was terrified of her husband. Fortunately, her surviving friends have confirmed that the situation was only temporary, and that Boris quickly came to his senses once the film had been completed, and realized just how important Gracie was to 'her' people.

The World of Gracie Fields, appropriately perhaps after her husband's interference, opened with a lot of noise – Gracie was seen entertaining some of her North of England fans, several of whom remembered her from her days at th'mill. Later she was seen shopping, bathing one of her dogs, recording part of her autobiography for blind admirers, and rehearsing with Bert Waller for a forthcoming tour ... repeating a variation on the familiar old chestnut 'I wouldn't like to continue if I'm going a little mouldy!'

Capri was rather ingloriously described by the narrator as 'a jewel on the bosom of a travel agent's wife', but Nancy Banks-Smith of the *Guardian* complained that there was too much of Capri in the film and not enough of Gracie, and further observed that there was now a noticeable American intonation to her Lancashire twang. Comparing Capri with Blackpool, as Gracie had many times in the past, she analysed its most famous resident as 'A sort of Blackpool Tower tonsils whose voice, which could once have given Melba a run for her money, still has the silver tinsel purity of a shop bell.'

Lillian Aza, filmed being met by Gracie at the island's tiny heliport, was asked what she thought of Boris, and did not beat about the bush: 'He thinks he's protecting her but he's spoiling her life by stopping her doing all the things she wants to do!' This was edited out of the film. Gloria Magnus, who had to have her

'Cockney's twopennorth', according to Gracie, blurted out, 'Gracie Fields, dear, was the only one artiste in the world. She didn't need microphones or anything. When she gave, dear, she gave. *She's* a Capricorn, and so am I. She's the best friend I ever had, and the nicest woman on the island!' She was probably best summed up by the narrator, whose closing statement for the film was: 'Gracie Fields is *still* a very great artiste. A lot of younger ones could *still* learn a great deal from her.'

Gracie was shown at a high camp affair, the Mode del Mare fashion show, held annually in a disused monastery. No less camp was 'Maggie, the Queen of the Rag Trade', one of her new numbers about which she quipped, maybe with underlying seriousness, 'I think Boris'd kill me if I sang that one!'

> I'm a charm that is Latin,
> A sexpot in satin ...
> I can look prude, enticing or rude ...
> But there's no other chassis like mine!
> With a sweet, newly wed look,
> Or a 'Please come to bed!' look,
> I'm Maggie the model, that's me!

When Gracie taped an in-depth interview with Denis Pitts, there was to be a condition: 'Wait till I'm dead, love,' she told him. 'You can then tell the world what bastards men can be. They all envied my wealth and my lifestyle. Only a few people know how desperately unhappy a lot of my life has been. One day people should see the other side of Gracie Fields, like the other side of the moon.'

In 1970, Gracie and Boris travelled to Leeds, where she filmed material for the first of two series of Yorkshire Television's acclaimed religious series, *Stars on Sunday*, on which she was a regular guest. Over five days she recorded twelve songs, including one which she dedicated to John Taylor – during the subsequent series, another would be sung especially for John's wife Anne. Boris, too, was made a fuss of on the occasion of his sixty-seventh birthday when a huge cake was wheeled on to the set.

On one trip to Brighton, Gracie was accompanied by her friends when she went shopping for trousers in a well-known department store, and all were tickled by what happened there. Wrapping the slacks which Gracie had purchased, the assistant asked: 'Has anybody ever told you that you look like Gracie Fields?' – to which Gracie gave one of her impromptu renditions of 'Sally'. 'Oh, you are Gracie Fields!' the young man exclaimed ... then, as Gracie handed him a cheque, asked her if she had any identification.

In October 1970 Gracie returned to Rochdale, where amongst her other duties she was asked to open the Vitool factory, opposite the site of Chip Sarah's shop on Molesworth Street. When asked to 'knock' the nails into the wall-plaque, there was no pretence. Asking for a chair, she belted out 'If I Had a Hammer', climbed up and did the job efficiently.

At around this time, Gracie learned that her brother Tommy's infant daughter, Marisa Grace, was unable to walk properly having been diagnosed to be suffering from congenital dislocation of the hip. She had the child examined by Frank Foster, the osteopath who had treated some of the children at the Peacehaven Orphanage. He referred her to the Royal National Orthopaedic Hospital – the subsequent operation was paid for by Gracie, who later invited Tommy's family to Capri for a holiday.

For almost a year, Gracie was content to stay at home and play the perfect hostess and housewife. To the astonishment of many of her friends, though she was extremely wealthy and able to afford just about every luxury, she liked to keep her hand in with the cooking, cleaning and washing up, which of course suited Boris very well. In the course of that year, Gracie took on a new companion, Hazel Provost. Hazel had only heard her singing for the first time in 1958, and had struck up a correspondence with Gracie; they had met a few years later whilst Gracie had been filming a television special at the Wood Green Empire. Hazel had subsequently visited Capri almost every year since 1965 and Gracie – who often kidded on that Hazel was her daughter – put the young woman on to her payroll in 1972.

There were three sad losses that year, the first on New Year's Day 1972, when Maurice Chevalier died at La Louque, his retreat outside Paris, aged eighty-three. Though not a close friend, Gracie had admired the Frenchman for facing up to his inquisitors, who had wrongfully accused him of collaborating with the Germans during the war. Much more upsetting was the death of Marie Dubas on 21 February, aged seventy-seven. For many years Marie had suffered from Parkinson's Disease, and with incredible fortitude she had continued performing, often sitting down, until 1958. Gracie sent a wreath to her companion Sylvie Galthier and a personal message of sympathy to Marie's son, François Bellair. The photograph of Marie and Gracie, on stage in Paris, still hangs on the wall of the Paris apartment which has become a shrine to Marie's memory.

The third death, that of the impresario Val Parnell, compelled Gracie's return to London at the end of October. She agreed to sing 'The Lord's Prayer' at his memorial service, but she made it quite clear that she did not wish to give any interviews, primarily because so little had happened since her last visit. For some reason, David Taylor of *Punch* slipped through the net.

Gracie was furious, and though she exercised tremendous control, the journalist must have immediately felt unwelcome when she snapped, 'Look sharp, lad – you've got fifteen minutes, and that's it!' Things only went from bad to worse when Taylor told her that he was not a fan, and indeed was not even well acquainted with her work. For fifteen minutes she talked about nothing in particular whilst the magazine's cartoonist, Ffoulkes, sketched her in record time ... an elderly lady, stirring a cup of tea in front of a clogs-and-shawl *Sally in Our Alley* backdrop. When asked if she was feeling sad because her friend had died, she retorted, 'He had a good run. It'll be my turn, soon!' When Taylor wanted to know why she preferred using the public transport system, she levelled impatiently, 'I don't want to sit in a taxi all by myself. I want to look at other people. They *interest* me!' She then turned to Boris, and changed the subject abruptly – for the remainder of the interview Taylor was ignored while she talked about the new cooker she was hoping to buy in London because, she said, in Italy they did not make them with on-top grills.

Gracie's visit to London coincided with the BBC's anniversary exhibition, 'Sights & Sounds of 50 Years', which she toured on the day before it was opened officially by the Queen. She was photographed in the Twenties Room, where visitors were able to push a button and listen to her voice.

The next year, 1973, was another quiet year – both her sisters spent time with her on Capri, she came to London to switch on the Bond Street Christmas illuminations, caught up with Danny La Rue's latest revue, and never stopped telling everyone that she was itching to get back to her knitting. Irene Bevan's view was that:

Grace *was* married to her public, and also married to the effect that she was having on her public. Like Chevalier, she didn't have to rely on being always young. Unlike Dietrich and Garbo, she didn't have to rely on her beauty, and this enabled her to work almost to the day of her death. Because these women rely eighty per cent on their looks, their end is always so terrible. Grace never had that, this death in life which forces them to shut themselves away.

In January 1974, Gracie celebrated her seventy-sixth birthday at Telscombe, and of course she could not stop singing and encouraged everyone to join in every time she opened her mouth. One of her guests was the record producer, Norman Newell, and he asked her opinion about making a 'singalong' album. Gracie was all for it, but Newell was not able to sell his idea to any reputable record company ... eventually, he and the bandleader Geoff Love financed the project from their own pockets, and *Singalong With Gracie* was cut the following month.

That year, when John and Anne Taylor visited Capri, Gracie asked them to bring – in addition to her usual 'shopping order' thirty copies of the album to be distributed amongst friends and important visitors. John told me, 'She always sent us a shopping list when we were due to travel out – records, cassettes, pillow cases, creams, cheese. We went out like pack-horses, and if everything was in Woolworth's carriers, she loved it!'

The new album may only have contained a selection of Gracie's hits, when for years her fans had been begging her to record new material, but it was still an innovation – she surprised even herself with the clear quality of her singing, and her ability still to hit that top C at the age of seventy-six. Even so, she had grave doubts about making an actual comeback. She told Caroline Moorehead of *The Times* that although her voice was in fine fettle, she was afraid of suddenly becoming ill and having to disappoint fans by cancelling a show. She added, without the slightest hint of vehemence, 'I've seen so many people making comebacks, when it's unfair to ask the audience for their money. I want them to remember me in full bloom.'

12

Goodnight, Angel...

In 1975, Gracie came to England to appear as a guest in Arthur Askey's *This is Your Life* and to record *The Golden Years of Gracie Fields* for Ian Miles of Warwick Records. The title was a slight contradiction in terms, for several of the twenty songs had never been performed by Gracie until now, including 'I'll See You Again' and 'On a Clear Day'.

For some time, Gracie had been wanting to cover 'Grande, Grande, Grande', an Italian ballad which had recently been translated into English as 'Never, Never, Never' and recorded by Shirley Bassey. She knew all the original words, and at the last moment decided to cover it in English herself. It and 'Speak Softly, Love', the theme from *The Godfather*, are amongst the most emotionally charged works she ever recorded. Almost every song on *The Golden Years of Gracie Fields* was recorded in a single take – if there were any mistakes, it was never the singer. Several of her classic comedy numbers were polished and given new sparkle by this 77-year-old legend – 'The Punch and Judy Show' was a children's *symphonie-en-miniature* which she had first recorded in 1929, and 'Only a Glass of Champagne' was sung in what she called her 'best Gloria Magnus Cockney'.

Soon after the album's release, Gracie and Boris were visited by Russell Harty, the Yorkshire-born chat-show host, who persuaded her to film a television documentary with fellow expatriate Sir William Walton, who lived on the nearby island of Ischia. She and the Oldham-born composer had never met, and Gracie is even thought to have disliked his music – neither did Harty make himself popular by boasting, 'It's a neat, artistic excercise. She's going to be a pushover!' Although she treated him kindly, fussing over him with endless cups of tea, Gracie very quickly pointed out to Harty that she was boss in her own home, and a force to be reckoned with. Each time he entered the villa he was reminded, vociferously, to wipe his feet and hang his coat on the peg provided, *not* drape it over the back of his chair, *not* to slop his tea, *not* to forget to flush the toilet, and above all *not* to be so 'lippy'!

Harty was also rebuked for expecting Gracie to travel to Ischia. She told him, 'In my day, love, it used to be the gentleman who called on the lady!' The composer is said to have been irate at having to spend forty-five minutes crossing the sea on the hydrofoil, and of having *The Golden Years* album played incessantly during filming, though of course his music was played too. And though it was all smiles when the Waltons met the Alperovicis, when Gracie saw the completed film she fumed at Harty because the Waltons' swimming pool had been shown in all its glory whilst hers had been ignored. When the presenter tried to explain that the cameraman had been asked not to film the pool because Boris had been filling in a crack in its side, she bawled down the telephone at him, 'Then you should have asked us to bloody well fill it for an hour or two, instead of making us look as if we're poverty-stricken!'

The quality and subsequent success of Gracie's new album disproved her theory that her voice was past its best, though soon after its release something happened that raised the fear that she might never work again: whilst posing for a fan to take photographs at the Canzone del Mare, a loose rail gave way and she fell eleven feet on to the concrete below, breaking four ribs and suffering severe bruising. Although she did not know it at the time, this accident would spell the beginning of the end.

Whilst recovering at 'Alcatraz', her temporary new name for the villa, she kept herself busy by adding the finishing touches to the four-part radio series, *The Gracie Fields Story*, which the BBC began broadcasting on 25 January 1976. Produced by Peter Clayton, there were reminiscences by Stanley Holloway, Sandy Powell and Basil Dean. She made the cover of *Radio Times* under the heading 'GRACIE FIELDS: The Late-Victorian Lancashire Lass Who Is Still a Star'.

For the accompanying feature, Gracie was photographed by Tony Evans and interviewed by a cautious D A N Jones, who was warned beforehand that these days Gracie was not always polite. This of course was untrue, though Jones was granted a mere thirty minutes because she was still suffering from fatigue after her fall. With her were Gloria Magnus and David Rawnsley, a sculptor friend who lived with his wife (Gracie's doctor) and children in the villa he had inherited in Anacapri, but who was most at home working alone in his studio – Gracie's garage. A pal of both John Flanagan and Monty Banks, Rawnsley had been employed as art director on several of Monty's films with Gracie.

Gracie told Jones a little about the island's chequered history, sang snatches from 'Grande, Grande, Grande', which she said was on her mind twenty-four hours a day, and pointed to a distant window from which, she said, Boris had watched her all those years ago, before plucking up the courage to speak. She discussed some of her aspirations for the future. One was to appear in the stage version of Paul Callico's *Mrs Harris Goes to Paris*, which she had performed on the radio during the Fifties, and which was subsequently played by Angela Lansbury. Another was to live to see a decent biopic of her early days in Rochdale – but *without* Cilla Black in the title role, as had been suggested. The Liverpudlian star had spent a day with her on Capri, but if Gracie had been 'thrilled to pieces' by her down-to-earth approach and easygoing manner, she did have reservations about being portrayed by her. 'Cilla isn't an actress,' she admonished. 'I'd rather I was done by Maggie Smith.' Other hopefuls for this coveted role included the 'Bobby's Girl' singer, Susan Maugham, and Patricia Routledge – the latter, with John Taylor acting as intermediary, actually got as far as discussing the project with the BBC, until, quite suddenly and inexplicably the idea was shelved.

In July 1976, Gracie came to London to pre-record a programme celebrating forty years of television – she sang the three songs which she had performed on the Baird System in the Thirties only three notes lower than then. Although Lillian Aza had issued a stern statement that there would be no interviews, in spite of over two hundred requests, Gracie did allow James Green of the London *Evening News* into her suite at the Westbury. Earlier that week, Jimmy Corrigan had invited her to name her own fee for a return visit to Batley, but she had turned him down. She told Green, 'I've no intention of starting again at my age. Next February I celebrate my twenty-fifth wedding anniversary, and my only preoccupation is to see that Boris gets a cooked breakfast. It's funny, but I don't even miss show-business.' Then, as if to refute the point – when she had already made appearances on Semprini's *This is Your Life*,

Parkinson, and taped a third series of *Stars on Sunday* – she went to the piano and sang 'Send in the Clowns' so movingly that James Green left with tears in his eyes.

While they were in London Gracie and Boris saw a lot of their friends the Taylors, who were close at hand to help wherever they could, running errands and helping her with letters from friends. John remembered, 'One read, "Dear Gracie: We saw you on TV last night and you looked just like my Aunt Mary!", to which she replied, "The poor bugger!" Another wrote to say he was in the antiques business. She said, "God, he wants me for his shop!"' The hilarity aside, however, Gracie was far from well. John went on, 'She didn't look too good when we saw her off at Gatwick, and soon afterwards she developed this terrible rash around her stomach. The doctor diagnosed shingles, and when we arrived in Capri she was in bed. She got up as soon as she saw us – she'd lost weight, but she stayed up all the time we were there because she didn't want us to be disappointed.'

Gracie received treatment for her shingles at an Oxford clinic, organized by her friends the Iaconos, who ran a restaurant in the town. Giorgio was a Capresi whose parents had a restaurant near the Canzone del Mare, and Gracie had first met him and his future wife, Jenny, there in 1957. In 1977 the couple would take out a ten-year lease on Gracie's restaurant before buying and renovating it. Now, like the Taylors they were effectively the only 'family' needed aside from Boris, and with them helped to make her closing years that much more comfortable. Jenny told me,

> Towards the end, she got tired of bailing people out and paying bills – the ones she set up in hairdressing in Australia, the children's education and medical bills. Over the next few years we grew closer, the more ill she became, and she never stopped talking about her 'scroungers'. Boris cared for her very much, but he couldn't handle a sick, elderly woman because he wasn't well himself. Gracie needed younger people about her, in case one of us had to run and find a doctor. And she loved the fact that I had the same name as her mother – she was always talking about her. I would be cutting her hair and she would say, 'Pick it up off the bloody floor, Jenny, and I'll flog it at Sotheby's!' She was an absolute sweetheart.

Gracie's family inadvertently sparked off another row towards the end of 1976 when she and Boris were invited to lunch with the Queen at Buckingham Palace – on the strength of the Russell Harty documentary. When Harty had asked Boris, 'How do *you* feel about this wife of yours?', he had replied, quite seriously, 'I feel like the Duke of Edinburgh, walking behind the Queen!' The lunch, however, did not take place. Only hours before the couple were due at the Palace, Tommy Fields rang the Westbury Hotel with the news that their sister Betty had died in Australia. Gracie and Boris were naturally deeply upset, though Gracie later lamented about Tommy obliging her to cancel one of the most important events of her life when Betty's death had not been entirely unexpected – she had been ill with cancer for some time. 'Tommy could have waited until we got back from the Palace,' she said to John Taylor.

On 9 January 1978, Gracie celebrated her eightieth birthday on Capri with close friends, and if London's National Film Theatre was seven months late with *its* tribute – a season of her films in chronological order, including rarities such as *Molly and Me* and *This Week of Grace* – Frank Wappatt, a Newcastle-based disc jockey and an acknowledged expert on British music, telephoned her on the actual day and interviewed her on the air for fifteen minutes – thrilling John Taylor, who had orchestrated the interview.

Then, a few days after her birthday, Gracie was reading a fan letter in her house at Anacapri when she stumbled and broke her wrist.

There was another source of pleasure for the Taylors that year, when Anne received the Order of St John of Jerusalem, which delighted Gracie – especially as the presentation fell on the anniversary that she herself had been given that same medal in 1938. In her 29 June letter to the couple congratulating them, she also complained about the various 'boot legs' of her recordings which had begun flooding the market overseas. 'These things happen,' she protested. 'Whatever you are doing, someone else finds a way to do it better and cheaper – and stealing always goes on.' Her appearances on *Stars on Sunday*, described by the *Guardian* as 'touchingly tremulous warbling', had attracted a flood of fan mail and innumerable offers of work, so much so that Gracie was beginning to wonder if it had been a good idea to do the show in the first place. She closed her missive: 'I am getting too old for this theatrical life – I have done it too long.'

A certain melancholy seemed to have fallen upon Gracie at the time. When the Taylors arrived for their annual holiday in Capri at the end of September they saw on their dressing table at the Canzone del Mare, a silver-framed photograph of Gracie, with Bing Crosby. She, Boris and the Taylors had attended Crosby's concert in Brighton the previous October – his last, just three days before his death. The photograph is thought to have been the last one taken, and Gracie had written across the bottom 'My poor friend Bing ... '

That year, 1978, Gracie returned to Rochdale. Her visit was widely regarded as one of the show-business events of the year – doubly important, perhaps, for it was believed that this visit and her ensuing concert would be her last – and it was turned into an occasion, complete with all manner of entertainments. 'It's Graciemania!' proclaimed Francis Lee, the director of these entertainments. Shingles and broken bones had taken their toll however: Gracie looked pitifully thin, admitted that she tired easily, and told how she had been coaxed back to her home town this time by another celebrated Rochdalian, the gargantuan Liberal Member of Parliament, Cyril Smith – the purpose not being to earn money, but to raise it for charity by opening the Gracie Fields Theatre, built and named in her honour at a cost of £800,000 at the Oulder Hill Complex, on the outskirts of the town. Some half-century before, Archie Pitt had craved a similar commercial venture but this one was strictly a local government enterprise.

Tickets for the event went on sale at the end of August – the top-range seats had to be reduced from £10 to £5 following many complaints that Gracie's pensioner.fans were being ripped off. All 670 tickets sold out on the first day, and a further 750 seats had to be squeezed into the auditorium. Even the local dignitaries, used to concessions, had to queue and pay the going rate. Three gigantic cinema screens were set up in an adjacent hall to relay the show to those unable to get in. Many tickets were resold by touts for as much as £100 to American tourists wishing to see a slice of British history in the making ...

Not all of Gracie's fans were elderly or even middle-aged. One teenage girl who had first seen her on *Stars on Sunday*, and whose ticket had been a 'snip' at just £20, told the *Rochdale Observer*, 'If she's a quarter as good as my mum says, then she's special.' The local cinema was showing *Sing As We Go* and *Look Up and Laugh*, and there was a photographic exhibition at the Museum. The *Rochdale Observer* printed a supplement, *Gracie Extra*. When Gracie, still in

Capri, became aware of the build-up to her forthcoming visit, she protested midly over the phone to the *Rochdale Observer*: 'It looks like it's going to be a bit much, but I'm not grumbling. I hope it all turns out – as the lass said to the soldier!'

After spending a few days in Telscombe with Mary and Ding Davey, Gracie and Boris travelled north on 14 September and checked in at the Midway Hotel, in Castleton – this way she hoped she would be sufficiently detached from the events of the next few days, and be able to rest between engagements. The next morning, Friday, she visited Broadfield School, where many of the children did not know who she was ... a problem she soon resolved! She was amused when Stephen Fray of the *Sunday Times* informed her of his 'poll' which had included on-the-spot interviews with some of the town's relatively new 10 per cent Pakistani community. Thus Ramesh Patel asked, 'Is Gracie Fields a new adventure playground?' – and Abdul Qadeer came out with a real corker, 'Gracie? That is something we were taught to say before meals!' Fray, observing how Rochdale had changed more than she had, concluded, 'Its individuality is blunted – hers is undiminished.'

Broadfield School comprised three houses: the Gracie Fields, the Cyril Smith, and the John Bright (the co-founder of the Anti-Corn Law League). With Gracie were the Mayor of Rochdale William Watkin Jenkins, and Cyril Smith – whom she introduced: 'This is my first-born!' Halfway through the proceedings, whilst calico-clad children re-enacted scenes from her life, she got up and demonstrated how she had danced around the maypole as a girl, and mimed to several of her 78 rpm records being played on a wind-up gramophone.

By the time Gracie reached the Town Hall, for lunch, and to open the BBC Local Radio station in the Clock Tower, the visit had taken on the proportions of a royal event. There was the red carpet, the town playing her songs, and flags waving everywhere. During the afternoon she opened the Laing Town Centre Complex. Taking off her mink, she sang 'Now Is the Hour', and unveiled a sculpture of two bronze ewes. When a company executive remarked that these were 'in the family way', she quipped, 'I *wondered* if it was you!'

On the Saturday morning, more than 3,000 fans turned up at Oulder Hill for the unveiling of the theatre plaque ... meant to be in honour of her eightieth birthday, even if it was eight months too late. 'I can't think what I feel like,' she announced. 'I feel a bit daft!'

On the eve of Gracie's performance at the the Gracie Fields Theatre, London's *Evening Standard* announced: 'An Old Pal Waits For Gracie Fields' ... it turned out to be the aspidistra which had been potted way back in 1938, when she had been made a Freewoman of Rochdale. It was now over five feet wide, and the reporter had even counted the 191 leaves. Other pals were there too, including old troopers Sandy Powell and Ben Warriss.

Gracie was welcomed onto the stage by Larry Grayson, and she was so eager to please that she ripped through seventeen songs in less than forty-five minutes, amazing her audience with the vigour of her singing – while a few top notes were diverted in deference to her age, she was never embarrassing and did not once give any impression that she was 'past it'. Her only two mistakes came about through over-excitement. There was so much applause that she missed her cue for 'Sally', and although she had perfected 'Matchstick Men', the song about the Northern painter Lowrie, she threw it out after a couple of bars grumbling, 'I can't get this damned thing through! All these words, they tie your teeth up!' 'Somewhere My Love' and 'I'll See You Again' were performed beautifully, but she purposely bungled the words of 'The Biggest Aspidistra in the The World' to get a laugh. She reminded her pianist, Teddy Holmes, no less than three times that the next one was 'Sing As We Go', then told the audience, 'We're both getting old. Teddy's doing his best, but like me he's going deaf in one ear, and daft in the other!' Then she closed the show with 'He's Got the Whole World in His Hands', and announced, as the stage was assaulted with hundreds of bouquets of flowers, 'Tonight's been one of the most wonderful, fabulous moments of my life. And at eighty it is wonderful having a theatre named after you – so long as I don't have to come back and clean it tomorrow!' The celebrated film critic Jack Tinker posed the question in his column in the *Daily Mail*: 'Was there a living bloom left in Rochdale that didn't end up at her feet?' Gracie, upon receiving a huge bunch of red roses, cracked, 'I'll be able to sell these on the market, on Monday!'

Before leaving England, Gracie attended the Variety Artistes' Luncheon in Manchester, held in aid of the renal unit for Booth Hall Children's Hospital. She was presented with a silver heart for all the work she had done for handicapped youngsters, and Warwick Records presented her with a gold disc for her contribution to the record industry. Cyril Smith was with her, and whilst no one was looking she slipped him a cheque for £500 to boost the fund. There should have been a second *This Is Your Life* – prior to the Rochdale concert, Eamonn Andrews had contacted Boris, who had put him on to John Taylor, whom Andrews asked to participate – John, however, had considered it a bad idea, too much of a shock on top of recent events, and as Lillian Aza agreed with him the idea was dropped.

Only days after arriving back in Capri, Gracie received news that she was to be surprise guest in that year's Royal Variety Show – a special one in that the exclusively British cast would be honouring the Queen Mother. Gracie shared the closely guarded secret with as few people as possible – the Taylors, the Iaconos, and, most strangely, her sister-in-law Annette Stansfield, with whom she did not get on particulary well. In a letter to the Taylors, two weeks before the event (owing to Capri's then primitive postal service, she arrived in England several days before *it* did) Gracie began by complaining about having to respond to so many letters and cards, saying, 'It's nice to be a favourite, but oh hell, who wants to be?' On the subject of the Royal Variety Show, the very last one to be organized by Lord Delfont, she concluded, 'Well, I have committed myself. I hope I can remember the words. I have just got myself a dress – been bothering with fittings, etc., buying magazines, looking through fashion books, just for one frock. Do you know why? Because I am conceited. I want to look the best of the whole lot!'

In fact, there were *four* expensive, beautiful dresses. Giorgio Iacono, who escorted Gracie across to Naples one day earlier than scheduled on account of the forecasters having predicted a storm, told me, 'That was Gracie – at the very last minute saying, "Sod it all! I'll go on in an old frock!" She wasn't the *least* bit vain!' And of course, this little white-haired lady went on to give the briefest but most talked-about performance of her entire career. At the very end, when everyone was gathered on the stage for the finale, she was introduced by David Jacobs. Looking frail but radiant in an ankle-length blue and gold-trimmed kaftan, she walked on to one of the loudest, most exciting and certainly most moving receptions in the Palladium's history. Halfway through the obligatory chorus of 'Sally', she paused to joke: 'I've been singing a man's song all me life!', and there was a loud guffaw from Danny La Rue. Gracie bowed out, typically, with 'God Save the Queen'.

There would be no more.

And, who better than Gracie herself to describe her last two public appearances, as she did in a letter to the Taylors, 'tripe-writing', as she often did, in the third person?

I was thrilled with the overwhelming warmth of Gracie's reception in Rochdale and the success of her performance at the opening of the theatre. Bless her little sloppy clogs, she really is the greatest! Wasn't her Command Performance appearance beaut? How can anyone go on at the end of a three-hour entertainment at which three hundred artists have worked their hearts out, sing half a song and steal the show? But that's what she did!

Gracie's last visit to her homeland, the Royal Variety Show aside, had been a major disappointment. She poured out her feeling in another letter to John and Anne Taylor.

In some ways, London made me sad. The West End is so shabby now, and the changes aren't for the better. The Piccadilly–Leicester Square area is like a rubbish tip ... And all that witless graffiti sprayed on every available wall space – slogans, names of pop stars, footballers, trade union exhortations and other unedifying rubbish. I used to think that, at least, the Blitz scars were a tribute to the folks who suffered, but this kind of thing merely makes me realize what stinkers people can be.

The morning after the Royal Variety Show, Gracie visited Peacehaven, and later in the day was driven to Lillian Aza's house in Hove, where her stepdaughter saw her for the last time. 'It was a very great shock to see how she had changed,' Irene said. 'She was almost skeletal. One of the last things she said to me was, "I never knew what to do with you because you always looked and sounded so posh!" Then I cuddled her, and it was like cuddling a bag of bones.'

That same day, 14 November 1978 – having left 'instructions' with John Taylor to clip the dozens of newspaper reviews of the Royal Variety Show which appeared all over the world – Gracie and Boris left for the United States. Only days before, she had sealed yet another will, as Giorgio Iacono explained.

Every time Gracie left Capri, she would make another will. This time, afraid that something might happen with the plane, they decided to will everything to her relations. She never wanted to. Gracie told me, 'I know they've had far too much already, and that whatever I leave them, they'll waste it like they've always done, but if everybody gets something, then maybe they'll stop fighting amongst themselves.'

Gracie and Boris had planned to return to Capri for the Christmas of 1978, but they were compelled to stay in California when Boris suddenly developed gout. Then at the end of December, the housekeeper Irena Bounos was going through the mail at the Canzone del Mare when she came across a large envelope from Buckingham Palace. Along with opera star Joan Sutherland and round-the-world yachtswoman Naomi James, Gracie had been nominated Dame of the British Empire in the New Year's Honours List.

John Taylor relayed the tidings to Gracie straight away. The letter asked, 'Will you accept the honour, and can you kneel?' She replied, tongue in cheek, 'I can kneel, but I can't get up again ... and if they're going to call me Dame, I hope they don't call Boris Buttons!'

The couple flew into London on 19 February 1979, the day after their twenty-seventh wedding anniversary, by Concorde. The Queen Mother, one of Gracie's most ardent fans, had insisted upon bestowing her personally with the accolade.

The scene outside Buckingham Palace was one of the most touching Gracie had ever seen. Thousands of people crowded around the Victoria Memorial, and the instant her car drove through the gates the crowd surged forwards, bringing it to a halt. Several photographers flung themselves across the bonnet, and when the driver urged her to stay calm until the police had cleared a path for them she said to him, 'Don't talk soft. They want to see me!' Then she climbed out of the vehicle, pulled her new apricot mink about her because it was bitterly cold, and spent the next twenty minutes chatting to fans and posing for snapshots.

Gracie and Boris returned to Capri soon after. Incredibly, though she was now eighty-one, offers of work still poured in. She accepted just two engagements. One was to meet the film critic Barry Norman, who was proposing a television documentary about her life. Prior to this, in the April when the Royal Yacht *Britannia* made a courtesy call on Naples, she and Boris were invited to the reception as dignitaries. They were piped on board by the Band of the Royal Marines, and Gracie, on deck most of the time, sang along to a medley of her songs. On the ferry back to Capri she complained of feeling unwell, and within days had developed severe bronchial pneumonia. 'Several weeks passed and doctor was convinced that she was going to die,' Jenny Iacono said. 'So in July, Giorgio took the risk of getting her over to Naples, knowing that she could have died on the boat, which is almost what *did* happen. She wouldn't allow us to contact her relatives, though.'

In fact, Giorgio had to seek permission to drive his car on to the boat, and leave Gracie and Boris in the back so that the other passengers would not bother her. Weak as she was, she put up a considerable fight. Giorgio explained, 'Gracie wasn't the sort of person you ordered about. She was the boss, even at her age.' Desperately ill, she spent the next six weeks in the International Hospital, where most of the staff spoke English. During this time Boris only left her once – to return to Capri for a change of clothes – and Giorgio crossed the tempermental Bay of Naples every single morning to see her. When she was unable to take solids he pureed fillet steaks and got her to drink the juice, as Monty Banks had done exactly forty years before. Giorgio said, 'She had asked her body for so much more than any normal person, and she told me, "Don't worry about me. Look after you young 'uns. I've done everything in my life, so each new day can only be a bonus for me."'

Gradually, Gracie began to rally, and her physician, Dr Vivo, allowed her to speak on the telephone to close friends only fearing that speaking to members of her family might bring reminders of financial pressures and strained relations among them bring on a relapse. John and Anne Taylor, who were scheduled to spend several weeks at the Canzone del Mare, wanted to cancel their trip but she would not hear of it. Ten days after her discharge from the hospital they arrived, and were visibly shocked by her gaunt appearance.

Yet, the magnificent 'shop's bell' voice was but slightly tarnished as, on the Taylors' fifteenth wedding anniversary, Gracie sat at her piano and gave what would be her last, albeit private, performance – 'I Have to Tell You' from the film *Fanny*, Boris's favourite 'September Song', and for John and Anne, 'I Haven't Said Thanks for That Lovely Weekend'. John said,

Anne noticed that she was wearing thick lipstick – her lips were getting very blue on account of her heart condition. Normally, when we were leaving we would say our goodbyes the night before because we always left on the 8 a.m. boat. This morning she was up very early to give me the several hundred pieces of sheet music she'd promised me, and to give Anne the two wall plaques which King Farouk had given to her. Anne said aftewards, 'She's preparing to die,' and I knew we would never see her again.

On Tuesday 25 September 1979, John spoke to his beloved friend for the last time, over the telephone. She and Boris had arranged to travel to England on the Saturday for the Barry Norman documetary. This was not to be. On the Thursday morning Boris rang him at work.

Gracie was gone ...

Epilogue

Did I Fill the World With Love

The newspaper reports were wrong. Gracie was alone in the Pink Apartment when she suffered her fatal heart attack. Boris was in the kitchen, fixing his breakfast. He had set out Gracie's tray with her usual milky coffee and roll, and when the maid, Maria, entered her bedroom she found Gracie sprawled across her bed breathing laboriously. Maria screamed for Boris, and he in turn called Giorgio Iacono – working in the restaurant below – who summoned the heart specialist who lived in Anacapri. Giorgio then rushed up to the Pink Apartment to find Boris, looking pale and shocked to the core, holding his wife's hand. Fifteen years on, it still choked Gracie's friend to speak of that day.

The doctor tried to give her an injection, but she had already passed away. And in spite of what the newspapers said, it was sudden. Over the last few days, Boris had spent much of his time at the house in Anacapri, checking on the workmen who were changing the central heating. I used to walk Gracie down to the restaurant for lunch every day, and afterwards we would go back – to the apartment, where she would make tea. We used to talk – everyday conversation. She never bragged about who she was, or ever made you feel that you were talking to a very big star. The day before she died, she came down and she was all right. It was a bit drizzly and she only fancied an omelette. Later in the afternoon she went up to the Piazza to pick up her mail and magazines, and to call in on Boris [at the Anacapri house]. They both came down to the restaurant that evening. She didn't feel too good during the night, but she put that down to indigestion. We certainly didn't expect her to die. I loved her so much during those last few years, and she loved me too. She would say, 'With you and John [Taylor] I've found a son at last.' And right until the very last minute of her life she was such fun, always smiling and joking. What she gave out was pure warmth.

Giorgio's wife, Jenny, was equally moved, saying,

I would like to have thought that she could have had better attention during her last few weeks – you know, as the Great Gracie Fields. I knew that she was going to die because she didn't want to eat or get dressed. She very quickly lost the will to live. I thought it superb, however, her being allowed to die the way she did. She never had to suffer the indignity of becoming an old, disabled woman.

At 10 a.m., less than one hour after Gracie's death, a distraught Boris called John Taylor – he had genuinely not known what else to do, and he had been extremely reluctant to call Lillian Aza, let alone Gracie's immediate family. 'He just didn't want to talk to them,' John recalled. 'And when Lillian eventually rang me, I never let on that I'd been the first to know.'

The news was officially announced in Britain on the midday summary, and immediately afterwards Pete Murray played several of Gracie's records on his *Open House* BBC Radio 2 programme. Within minutes, the flag on Rochdale Town Hall, along with every other in the town, had been lowered to half-mast. The MP Cyril Smith, in Margate for the Liberal Party Annual Assembly, learned of Gracie's death five minutes before delivering his speech on party strategy. There were tears in his eyes as he stepped on to the podium, and it took him a while to compose himself before he announced, 'I have just been informed of the death of a close friend of mine – the world's Queen of Song and Rochdale's greatest ambassador, Gracie Fields.'

Other tributes were legion. Harry Secombe rang the BBC to say, 'She was the biggest star Britain ever had.' The comedian Eric Morecambe spoke for the entire nation when he said, 'Many show-business people are liked, but Gracie was *loved*.' The disc jockey Peter Clayton, who had visited Capri in 1975 to be amazed by her fortitude, played a half-hour tribute to her on the radio, and told listeners, 'I felt sure she would have lived to celebrate her centenary – and how sad that she did not experience much in the way of deep human affection, beyond the transient love of her audiences, until quite late in life.' In the United States, there was a two-hour radio portrait of her life, and fans left flowers outside the house on Amalfi Drive, even though Gracie had sold the property years before.

Stephen Dixon of the *Guardian* wrote: 'She always retained the ingenuous air of a Lancashire lass who had won the pools and could not quite believe her luck. Stars didn't come any brighter than Gracie.' The *Daily Telegraph* called her 'This daughter of the people, the last of the truly great stars of music-hall ... a very real, down-to-earth person who never let success make her either forgetful or ashamed of her lowly origins.'

Gracie had insisted that her funeral be no sombre affair, and her wishes were carried out on the morning of Saturday 29 September, beginning with a service in the garden of her home, officiated by Reverend Edward Holland of the Naples Anglican Church, assisted by several of Capri's Catholic clergy. The mahogany coffin was then held up so that Gracie could face the sea for the last time, before being raised onto the shoulders of six of her restaurant staff who were wearing black trousers and white T-shirts embroidered with the Canzone del Mare logo. Surmounting it was the wreath of deep red roses from Boris, who, flanked by Giorgio Iacono and Tommy Fields, led the mourners. Behind them were Irena Bounos, Mary Davey, and Gracie's sister Edith, with her daughter Grace. Edith had almost missed the ceremony because that morning she had been forced to seek hospital treatment after injuring her wrist during a fall in her hotel bathroom. No other members of the family turned up.

Several important people were unable to attend Gracie's funeral, mostly through ill-health. Neva Hecker was in America when Gracie died, but she arrived in Capri a few days later to help Boris and Mary Davey with the paperwork. All their past quarrels had been forgotten. Lillian Aza, recovering from a stroke, was unable to travel. John Taylor had just returned home after spending several weeks with Gracie, only to end up in hospital after injuring his back. Gracie's last letter, received by the Taylors a week after her death ended, 'Thank you very, very much for all that you have been doing for that 'orrible old woman Gracie Fields, ever since I have known you.' *Such* was Gracie's importance that, the following year when

John and Anne attended a reception at Buckingham Palace concerned with Anne's charity work, the Queen Mother invited them to talk to her about their friendship with Gracie for twenty minutes. Indeed, while engaged in writing this book, I had the immense pleasure of receiving a letter from Her Majesty, in which she expressed her admiration for this great entertainer.

Outside the villa, Gracie's coffin was transferred to a blue hearse, whilst the mourners climbed into a succession of cars, taxis, or one of the five Capresi minibuses. The procession then wound its way up the treacherous, mile-long narrow road to the island's tiny, unkempt non-Catholic cemetery. Work had begun on a white marble tomb which would eventually be placed in a corner of the area, but as this was expected to take at least a week to complete, Gracie was placed in the Cerio family vault.

The atmosphere at the Canzone del Mare in the days following Gracie's death was far from convivial. 'Irena Bounos and Mary Davey did not get on at all,' Jenny Iacono said. Giorgio added, 'There were awful problems in proving who were the right beneficiaries.'

According to Irene Bevan, 'Gracie was never keen on jewellery, but she seemed to acquire an awful lot of it. The day after she died, Tommy and a few others were checking up on the place. They opened a cupboard, and out fell about £40,000 worth of jewellery which had been stashed on the top shelf.' At the time of writing, most of this jewellery is still locked away in a safety-deposit box on Capri, the only part of her £4 million-plus estate which has not been dealt with, it is thought because the duties would by far exceed its actual value. Several pieces were given to close friends, as Gracie had wished. The remainder was photographed and catalogued by Boris in 1979.

Gracie's memorial service was held at London's St Martin-in-the-Fields on 15 November – fifty-six years to the day, it was observed since she had cut her first recording. The address was given by Roy Hudd, Michael Parkinson read the lesson, and the soprano Elizabeth Harwood sang 'Ave Maria'. That day there was no outside coverage because of a national television strike, but the photograph circulated to newspapers worldwide said it all – flanked by Tommy and Annette Fields was Boris Alperovici, a sad, lonely old man whose world had fallen apart. 'In losing Gracie, he had lost his anchor,' John Taylor said.

On 20 October there had been a service at St Chad's, Rochdale, where one of the lessons had been read by the actress Violet Carson who had often appeared in *Stars on Sunday* with Gracie. A memorial fund was launched in the town which raised over £10,000 for the Moorland Children's Home. A statue to Gracie, in the Memorial Gardens, seemed like a good idea, but the project is still waiting to be commissioned. A third service, in Peacehaven, was relayed through loud speakers into the village. Veterans from Dunkirk brought a wreath of poppies, which they placed on Jenny and Fred's grave before forming a guard of honour outside the church.

In September 1980, when the Taylors were about to make their annual pilgrimage to Capri, thinking that Boris might not have been in the mood for company, they booked into a hotel. Boris called beforehand, however, and insisted that they stay as usual with him at the Canzone del Mare. They did so then, and every year until he died – always he would beg them to stay a little longer in order to appease his crippling loneliness, always they had to let him down gently because they had to get back to England and their respective work commitments. 'Reports of him sitting at the graveside, moping, were untrue,' John said. 'Boris visited the grave every morning at eight, to wash it and add fresh flowers. To get to the cemetery he had to climb almost four hundred steps. He was simply sitting down to get his breath back.'

Boris survived Gracie by almost four years. In June 1983, his heart problem having become progressively worse, he was taken ill after over-exerting himself during a photographic jaunt on Capri. Friends immediately rushed him to the International Hospital in Naples, but when his condition suddenly deteriorated he signed the discharge papers so that he could be taken back to Capri to die. He passed away, aged seventy-nine, on 3 July 1983, just hours after being settled in at the Pink Apartment. A few days later he was laid next to his beloved Gracie. In spite of his nagging and sometimes surly ways – his only means of trying to keep Gracie under control, and prevent her from working too hard – after John Flanagan he had been unquestionably the great love of her life.

Most of the retainers, sincere or otherwise, are gone . . . Neva Hecker, Mary Davey, Lillian Aza, Bernard Delfont, Larry Grayson, Teddy Holmes, Bert Waller, Gloria Magnus, Edith and Tommy . . . yet many Capresi still refuse to believe that Gracie is dead. When I asked Giorgio Iacono how long it had taken the islanders to get over losing her, he replied tremulously:

> The tourists' boats pause, and the couriers point out, 'There is where Gracie lives ... *lived*.' She was the focal point of the island, and when someone of her stature suddenly disappears, it's so very hard to imagine she's not there any more. They *still* expect her to appear and wave, or to sing them a chorus of 'Sally'. Even the children, now grown up, watch out for her in the Square where she used to buy them all ice-cream. That kind of magic won't go away and allow itself to be forgotten.

One fan impressed Gracie no end – by sending her a 'home cure' for shingles and a poem which she cherished during her twilight years – was Ken Hill, from Rochdale. The poem should serve as her epitaph, for it ends:

> To every person who has seen and heard
> Our Rochdale lass; so kind, and fair of face;
> Now is the hour for you to count your blessings.
> Salute her then! Our own Amazing Grace!

Appendices

1

Discography by John Taylor

The following represents the *entire* Gracie Fields catalogue on shellac, acetate, vinyl, tape and compact disc. Commercial and private recordings are included, but not mixed compilations or 'bootlegs'. The dates refer to release dates. On 78 rpm issues, the prefixes are as follows:

B   HMV 10-in.
MR Regal Zonophone 10-in.
FB   Columbia pre-1950 10-in.
DB   Columbia post-1950 10-in.
F   Decca 10-in.
PB   Philips 10-in.
C   HMV 12-in.

Numbers without prefix are REX label.

(Gracie also recorded the following songs phonetically in French during numerous visits to Paris, almost certainly on the Columbia label. The acetates are in a private collection and are unlikely to be ever released commercially – David Bret.)

1   'Reviens, Veux-Tu?' (Fragson) 1930*
2   'Le Doux Caboulot' (Carco) 1932*
3   'Chantez Pour Moi, Violons' (Réale) 1933**
4   'Le Chaland Qui Passe' (Badet) 1933**
5   'Ne Dit Rien' (Aubret) 1933**
6   'You Know You Belong To Somebody Else' (anon) 1933**

7   'Celle Que Vous Attendez' (Lenoir) 1933**
8   'Ils N'Ont Pas Ça!' (Willemetz-Borel-Clerc) 1939***
9   'Nous Irons a Valparaiso' (anon) 1939**
10   'L'Amour N'Attendra-t-il?' (Poterat) 1939**
11   'La Vie en Rose' (Piaf-Louiguy) 1948****

(*piano Ralph Carcel   ** orchestra Pierre Chagnon
*** orchestra Edmond Mahieux   **** orchestra Henri Christiné)

Gracie also taped two songs in Lisbon with Marie Dubas: 'Cantiga de Primavera', and 'Don Solidon'.

1
78 rpm Recordings

1928

B2733   'Because I Love You'/'My Blue Heaven'
B2739   'So Tired'/'We're All Living at the Cloisters'
B2758   'Our Avenue'/'Under the Moon'
B2782   'Laugh, Clown, Laugh!'/'In the Woodshed She Said She Would'
B2795   'How About Me?'/'Oh, You Have No Idea'
B2839   'Ee, By Gum!'/'My Ohio Home'
B2880   'Ramona'/'Why Does the Hyena Laugh?'
B2914   'If I Didn't Miss You'/'I've Always Wanted to Call You Sweetheart'
B2923   'Like the Big Pots Do'/'I Think of What You Used to Think of Me'

1929

B2965   'Reviens, Veux-Tu?' (sung in French)/'Take a Look at Mine'
B2999   'She's Funny That Way'/'I Lift Up My Finger and I Say Tweet-Tweet'
B3008   'Sonny Boy'/'Mary Ellen's Hot-Pot'
B3032   'Would a Manx Cat Wag Its Tail?'/'That's What Put the Home In "Home Sweet Home"'
B3061   'Scented Soap'/'Nagasaki'
B3092   'When Summer is Gone'/'I've Got a Code in My Doze'
B3104   Toselli's 'Serenade'/'Unlucky Number Thirteen'

B3134	'When You've Gone'/'Cute Little Flat' (with Archie Pitt)
B3147	'Little Pal'/'Why Can't You?'
B3176	'Thoughts of You'/'That's How I Feel About You, Sweetheart'
B3202	'I've Got a Man'/'Oh Maggie, What Have You been Up To?'
B3244	'This Is Heaven'/'Moscow'
B3259	'If I Had a Talking Picture of You'/'I'm a Dreamer, Aren't We All?'

1930

B3291	'Painting the Clouds with Sunshine'/'Nowt About Owt'
B3305	'Stop and Shop at the Co-op Shop'/'Coople o' Ducks'
B3326	'Singing in the Bathtub'/'Punch and Judy Show'
B3383	'Body and Soul'/'You Can't Kill Flies by Scratchin' 'em'
B3415	'Clatter of the Clogs'/'A Little Love, a Little Kiss'
B3463	'Cottage For Sale'/'Crying for the Carolines'
B3494	'Little Pudden Basin'/'Around the Corner'
B3505	'Dream Lover'/'It's Nothing to Do with Me'
B3565	''Fonso My Hot Spanish Knight'/'I Just Can't Figure It Out At All'
B3573	'I'm in the Market for You'/'The Barmaid's Song'
B3592	'Falling in Love Again'/'What Archibald Says, Goes'
B3595	'Three Green Bonnets'/'Fred Fannakapan'
B3600	'Over the Garden Wall'/'I'll Be Good Because of You'
B3688	'Dancing with Tears in My Eyes'/'Lovely Aspidistra in the Old Art Pot'
B3708	'Lancashire Blues'/'What Good Am I Without You?'

1931

B3724	'Sitting on a Five-Barred Gate'/'Go Home and Tell Your Mother'
B3780	'You're Driving Me Crazy'/'The Kiss Waltz'
B3795	'Pass! Shoot! Goal!'/'Clockwork Courtship'
B3824	'River Stay 'way From My Door'/'That Must Have Been Our Walter'
B3879	'Sally'/'Fall In and Follow the Band'
B3908	'I'll Always Be True'/'The Party's Getting Rough'
B3912	'Oh, Sailor Behave'/'The Bargain Hunter'

B3920	'Grannie's Little Old Skin Rug'/'Just a Dancing Sweetheart'
B3968	'The Mockingbird Went Cuckoo'/'Just One More Chance'
B3998	'Obadiah's Mother'/'Oh, Glory!'
B4000	'Life Desire'/'They All Make Love But Me'
B4051	'Down At Our Charity Bazaar'/'Song of the Highway'

1932

B4101	'Home'/'He Forgot to Come Back'
B4109	'The Rochdale Hounds'/'When the Rest of the Crowd Goes Home'
B4168	'We All Went to the Zoo'/'Now That You've Gone'
B4198	'Antonio'/'Can't We Talk It Over?'
B4214	'Waltzing Time In Old Vienna'/'The Fly's Day Out'
B4258	'Looking on the Bright Side'/'He's Dead But He Won't Lie Down'
B4259	''Appy 'Ampstead'/'You're More Than All the World To Me'
B4260	'I Hate You'/'After Tonight We Say Goodbye'
B4277	'John Willie's Farm'/'Underneath the Arches'
B4281	'Why Waste Your Tears?'/'Round the Bend of the Road'
B4316	'The Song of the Bells'/'Let's All Go Posh'
B4317	'Say It Isn't So'/'Mary Ellen's Hot-Pot Party'
B4343	'How Deep Is the Ocean'/'One Little Hair on His Head'
C2378	*Gracie Fields Medley:* 'My Blue Heaven'/'Charmaine'/'Because I Love You'/'Ramona'/'Ee, by Gum'/'Laugh, Clown, Laugh!'
C2487	*Gracie's Christmas Party:* 'My Ohio Home'/'Our Avenue'/'When The Fields are White with Daisies' (sung by Jenny Stansfield)/'Would a Manx Cat Wag Its Tail?'/'Home, Sweet Home' (with Jenny Stansfield)

1933

B4362	'Balloons'/'In Old Siberia'
B4366	'Heaven Will Protect an Honest Girl'/'Puleeze, Mr Hemingway'
B4368	'Play, Fiddle, Play ' ('Chantez Pour Moi, Violons')'/'So

	Long Lads, We're Off'
B4383	'Poor Me, Poor You'/'Fiddler Joe'
B4407	'I'm Playing With Fire'/'A Photograph of Mother's Wedding Group'
B4464	'Whiskers An' All'/'I Can't Remember'
B4469	'Stormy Weather'/'Poor Little Willie'
B4471	'Happy Ending'/'Mary Rose'
B4472	'When Cupid Calls'/'Melody at Dawn'
B4493	'There's a Cabin in the Pines'/'I Had to Go and Find Another Job'
B8064	'It Isn't Fair'/'Laugh at Life'
B8065	'I Took My Harp to a Party'/'Christmas Bells at Eventide'
C2622	*Gracie at Home:* 'Dear Little Shamrock'/'Land Of My Fathers'/'Loch Lomond'/'Love's Old Sweet Song'/'My Mother's Name Was Mary'/'Someone Waiting For Me'
C2625/6/7	*Gracie in the Theatre:* 'There's a Cabin in the Pines'/'Whiskers and All'/'Speech'/'Punch and Judy Show'/'The Rochdale Hounds'/'I can't Remember'/'One May Morn'/'Out in the Cold, Cold Snow'/'Sally'/'Stormy Weather'/Final curtain and speech

1934

B8130	'Play to Me, Gypsy'/'Keep It in the Family Circle'
B8140	'Love, Life, Laughter'/'Chérie'
B8141	'Riding on the Clouds'/'I'm a Failure'
B8185	'Love's Last Word Is Spoken' (Le Chaland Qui Passe)/'Out in the Cold, Cold Snow'
B8192	'Will You Love Me When I'm Mutton?'/'At the Court of Old King Cole'
B8202	'Just a Catchy Little Tune'/'Love, Wonderful Love'
B8209	'Sing As We Go'/'In My Little Bottom Drawer'
B8210	'Little Man, You've Had a Busy Day'/'There's Millions and Millions of Women'
B8232	'Isle of Capri'/'What Do You Buy a Nudist for His Birthday?'
B8233	'The House Is Haunted'/'How Changed Is the Old Place Now'
B8243	'Love In Bloom'/'I Taught Her How to Play Broop-Broop'

B8261   'What Made Little Boy Blue'/'Singing In the Bathtub'
C2705   *Gracie's Film Songs:* 'Sally'/'You're More Than All the
            World To Me'/'Chérie'/'Ave Maria'
C2740   Various Artistes: *Jubilee Songs.* For the 1935 silver
            Jubilee of King George V. Gracie sings 'Sally'

1935
B8286   'If All the World Were Mine'/'Your Dog's Come Home
            Again'
B8289   'You Haven't Altered a Bit'/'Born to Be a Clown'
B8304   'One Night of Love'/'When the Robin Sings His Song'
B8312   'You and the Night and the Music'/''Erbert 'Enery
            'Eppelthwaite'
B8331   'Things Might Have Been So Different'/'I Haven't Been
            the Same Girl Since'
8557   'When I Grow Too Old to Dream'/'Turn 'Erbert's Face
            to the Wall, Mother'
8558   'Lullaby of Broadway'/'I'm Ninety-Nine Today'/'The
            Words Are In My Heart'
8585   'Red Sails in the Sunset'/'South American Joe'
8592   'There's a Lovely Lake in London'/'We've Got to Keep
            Up with the Joneses'
8599   'Love Me Forever'/'When You Grow Up, Little Lady'
8617   'Grandfather's Bagpipes'/'The General's Fast Asleep'
8618   *Gracie Medley:* Old Soldiers Never Die'/'Take Me Back
            to Dear Old Blighty'/'Mademoiselle From
            Armentières'/'Fall In and Follow Me'/'If You Were the
            Only Girl in the World'/'Hello, Hello, Who's Your Lady
            Friend'/'It's a Long Way to Tipperary'/'Let the Great Big
            World Keep Turning'/'There's a Long, Long Trail'
8633   'Winter Draws On'/'Roll Along, Prairie Moon'
8636   'Trees'/'Smiling Thro'
8687   'Danny Boy'/'I'm Only Her Mother'
MR1791   'Sally'/'Fall In and Follow the Band'
MR1792   'One Night of Love'/'You and the Night and the
            Music'
MR1793   'Anna from Anacapresi'/'Love Is Everywhere' (with
            Tommy Fields)
MR1794   'Look Up and Laugh'/'Shall I Be an Old Man's
            Darling?'

MR1814   'He's Dead But He Won't Lie Down'/'Why Does the Hyena Laugh?'

MR1815   'Dream Lover'/'Because I Love You'

1936

8718   'Clogs And Shawl'/'Look to the Right'

8749   'I Give My Heart'/'She Fought Like a Tiger for Her Honour'

8768   'Alone'/'Why Did She Fall for the Leader of the Band?'

8786   'The Glory of Love'/'Poor Little Angeline'

8806   'She Came from Alsace-Lorraine'/'Sweetheart, Let's Grow Old Together'

8818   'Queen of Hearts'/'One of the Little Orphans of the Storm'

8819   'Do You Remember Our First Love Song?'/'Why Did I Have to Meet You?'

8840   'Would You'/'Laughing Irish Eyes'

8868   *Gracie Requests:* 'Because I Love You'/'Looking on the Bright Side'/'My Blue Heaven'/'Sally'/'The Rochdale Hounds'/'Sing As We Go'

8893   'Rose Marie'/'Indian Love Call'

8905   *Gracie's and Sandy's Party* (with Sandy Powell): 'Daisy, Daisy'/'Sing As We Go'/'It's a Sin to Tell a Lie'

8906   'Did I Remember?'/'Ring Down the Curtain'

8921   'Serenade in the Night'/'In a Little Lancashire Town'

8936   'Did Your Mother Come from Ireland'/'A Feather in her Tyrolean Hat'

MR1845   'Serenade'/'Laugh, Clown, Laugh!'

MR1846   'My Blue Heaven'/'In My Little Bottom Drawer'

MR1847   'You Haven't Altered a Bit'/'I Haven't Been the Same Girl Since'

MR1878–80   Songs as HMV C2625/6/7

MR1881   As HMV C2487

MR1882   As HMV C2622

1937

8967   *Showboat Selection:* 'Bill'/'You Are Love'/'Can't Help Loving That Man of Mine'/'Why Do I Love You?'/'Only Make Believe'

8968   'In the Chapel in the Moonlight'/'Have You Forgotten

	So Soon?'
9022	'Gracie and Sandy at the Coronation' (with Sandy Powell)
9095	'Smile When You Say Goodbye'/'I Never Cried So Much in All My Life'
9096	'A Song in Your Heart'/'We're All Good Pals Together'
9097	'My Love For You'/'In a Little Lancashire Town'
9101	*Gracie's Selection*: 'Where is the Sun?'/'September in the Rain'/'When the Harvest Moon is Shining'/'When My Dreamboat Comes Home'
9114	'There's a Small Hotel'/'A Nice Cup of Tea'
9115	'The Desert Song'/'Ah, Sweet Mystery of Life'
9116	'Goodnight, My Love'/'The Coronation Waltz'
9117	'On a Little Dream Ranch'/'Will You Remember?'
9133	'Our Song'/'Where Are You?'
9140	'The Greatest Mistake of My Life'/'It Looks Like Rain in Cherry Blossom Lane'
9159	'Sally'/'Sing As We Go'
9161	'Gypsy Lullaby'/'The Organ, the Monkey and Me'
9166	'Little Old Lady'/'The First Time I Saw You'
9195	'Giannina Mia'/'Sympathy'
MR1917	'Ave Maria'/'Three Green Bonnets'
MR1938	As HMV C2378
MR1949	'Love's Last Word Is Spoken'/'The House is Haunted'
MR1950	'Nagasaki'/'Body and Soul'
MR1983	'Look Up and Laugh'/'Waltz Song Medley'
MR2011	'River Stay 'Way from My Door'/'That Must Have Been Our Walter'
MR2021	'Dancing with Tears in My Eyes'/'The Barmaid's Song'
MR2040	'Happy Ending'/'Heaven Will Protect an Honest Girl'
MR2041	'My Lucky Day'/'Mary Rose'
MR2024	'Melody at Dawn'/'When Cupid Calls'
MR2067	'Fred Fannakapan'/'Mary Ellen's Hot-Pot'
MR2068	'Clatter of the Clogs'/'A Little Love, a Little Kiss'
MR2069	'Isle of Capri'/'Play to Me Gypsy'
MR2086	'Our Avenue'/'Lancashire Blues'
MR2087	'Singing in the Bathtub'/'Love in Bloom'
MR2114	'Sing As We Go'/'How Deep Is the Ocean'
MR2115	'Underneath the Arches'/'We're All Living at the Cloisters'

1938

9221	'Sailing Home'/'Remember Me'
9237	'A Foggy Day in London Town'/'The Family Tree'
9255	'Rosalie'/'London is Saying Goodnight'
9258	'Whistle While You Work'/'Someday My Prince Will Come'
9278	'The Girl in the Alice Blue Gown'/'In Me 'Oroscope'
9302	'Old Father Thames'/'Old Father Thames'
9307	'Walter, Walter'/'The Trek Song'
9308	'Little Drummer Boy'/'The Lambeth Walk'
9325	'The Sweetest Song in the World'/'There Is a Tavern in the Town'
9328	'I Love to Whistle'/'When the Organ Played "Oh Promise Me"'
9350	'Oh, Ma Ma!'/'Somebody's Thinking of Me Tonight'
9354	'Little Lady Make-Believe'/'My Heaven in the Pines'
9361	'Goodnight, Angel'/'Please Be Kind'
9377	'Love Walked In'/'Music, Maestro, Please!'
9429	'Rose Lambeth Walk'/'The Sweetest Song in the World'
9431	'Winter Draws On'/'We've Got to Keep Up With the Joneses'
9478	'She Fought Like a Tiger for Her Honour'/'One of the Little Orphans of the Storm'
9515	'I Give My Heart'/'Turn 'Erbert's Face to the Wall, Mother'
9603	'Danny Boy'/'Grandfather's Bagpipes'
9649	'Little Drummer Boy'/'Smile When You Say Goodbye'
9675	'Rose Marches On'/'Fall In and Follow Me'
9690	'Little Old Lady'/'When I Grow Too Old to Dream'
9765	'Ah, Sweet Mystery of Life'/'Smiling Through'
MR2133	'The Kiss Waltz'/'You're Driving Me Crazy'
MR2134	'I'm a Dreamer, Aren't We All?'/'If I Had a Talking Picture of You'
MR2155	'Cottage for Sale'/'Crying for the Carolines'
MR2236	*By Request*: 'Sing As We Go'/'One Night of Love'/'Look Up and Laugh'/'Sally'/'Can't We Talk It Over'/'Play To Me Gypsy'
MR2156	'Cabin in the Pines'/'Will You Love Me When I'm Mutton?'
MR2237	'The Rochdale Hounds'/'I Took My Harp to a Party'

MR2767	'Ee, By Gum'/'Will You Love Me When I'm Mutton?'
MR2888	'An Old Violin'/'The Dicky-Bird Hop'
MR2889	'The Biggest Aspidistra in the World'/'Now It Can Be Told'
MR2892	'The Holy City'/'Land of Hope and Glory'
MR2893	'Christopher Robin'/'The Donkey Serenade'
MR2917	*Hit Parade and Snow White Medley*: 'Any Broken Hearts to Mend?'/'Heigh-Ho!'/'I'm Wishing'/'A Tisket, A Tasket'/'When Mother Nature Sings Her Lullaby'/'With a Smile and a Song'
MR2924	'Ave Maria'/'O Come All Ye Faithful'
MR2929	'One of Those Old-Fashioned Ladies'/'Alexander's Ragtime Band'
MR2950	'Giddy Up!'/'Swing Your Way to Happiness'

1939

MR2996	'Two Sleepy People'/'The Umbrella Man'(both with Tommy Fields)
MR3000	'Peace Of Mind'/'Mrs Binn's Twins'
MR3001	'The Biggest Aspidistra in the World'/'You've Got to Be Smart to Be in the Army Now'
MR3054	*Gracie Medley*: 'I Promise You'/'Jeepers Creepers'/'Little Sir Echo'/'Little Swiss Whistling Song'/'They Say'/'Sweethearts'
MR3055	'One Day When We Were Young'/'Ramona'
MR3118	'Wish Me Luck'/'Danny Boy'
MR3119	'I've Got the Jitterbugs'/'Grandfather's Bagpipes'/'Annie Laurie'
MR3120	'I Love the Moon'/'Gracie Thanks the Nation'
MR3156	*Gracie With the Troops*: 'The Biggest Aspidistra in the World'/'If You Were the Only Girl in the World'/'Old Lady from Armentières'/'Run, Rabbit, Run'/'Wish Me Luck'/'There'll Always Be an England'
MR3180	'I'm Sending a Letter to Santa Claus'/'The Fairy on the Christmas Tree'
MR3181	*Gracie With The Boys In France 1 & 2*: 'I Never Cried So Much in All My Life'/'An Old Violin'/'Sing As We Go'
MR3182	*Gracie With the Boys In France 3 & 4*: 'I'm Sending a Letter to Santa Claus'/'When I Grow Too Old to

Dream'/'Walter, Walter'/'Wish Me Luck'

MR3189   'I Love the Moon'/'Crash, Bang, I Want to Go Home!'

1940

MR3226   *Gracie Medley*: 'Goodnight, Children Everywhere'/'I Hear a Dream'/'It's a Hap-Hap-Happy Day'/'We're All Together Now'

MR3227   'Over the Rainbow'/'Bella, Bella Bambina'

MR3228   *Gracie With the Royal Air Force*: 'The Bells of St Mary's'/'FDR Jones'/'Please Leave My Butter Alone'/'Romany'/'O Come All Ye Faithful'

MR3229   *Gracie With The Royal Navy*: 'Christopher Robin'/'I Hear a Dream'/'Out in the Cold, Cold Snow'/'They Can't Ration Love'/'Red Sails in the Sunset'

MR3287   *Pinocchio Selection*: 'Give a Little Whistle'/'Hi Diddle Di Dee'/'I've Got No Strings'/'Little Wooden Head'/'Turn On the Old Music Box'/'When You Wish Upon a Star'

MR3288   'The Woodpecker Song'/'The Grandest Song of All'

MR3308   'If I Should Fall in Love Again'/'When Our Dreams Grow Old'

F6331   'There's a Small Hotel'/'A Nice Cup of Tea'

F6388   'Desert Song'/'Ah, Sweet Mystery of Life'

F6403   'Goodnight My Love'/'The Coronation Waltz'

F6426   'Will You Remember?'/'On a Little Dream Ranch'

FB2448   'What's the Good of a Birthday?'/'Little Curly Head in a High Chair'

FB2449   'Begin the Beguine'/'Stop and Shop at the Co-op Shop'

FB2463   *Gracie Medley*: 'Indian Love Call'/'Indian Summer'/'I Never Cried So Much in All My Life'

FB2496   'Roses of Picardy'/'The Last Rose of Summer'

120940*   *Our Gracie With the Boys In France* As MR3181 (*HMV Victor label)

120944*   'The Woodpecker Song'/'Little Curly Head in a High Chair'

120872*   'At the Court of Old King Cole'/'Will You Love Me When I'm Mutton'

120932*   'The Dicky-Bird Hop'/'You've Got to Be Smart to Be in the Army Now'

26377*   'Danny Boy'/'Wish Me Luck'

120937**   'The Holy City'/'O Come All Ye Faithful' (**RCA
              Victor label)
24210**   'Hollywood Party' (with Florence Desmond)

1941
G23868   'Wish Me Luck'/'I've Got the Jitterbugs' (Australian
              Regal label)
F7981   'The Biggest Aspidistra in the World' (Hitler version)
              'He's Dead But He Won't Lie Down'
F8015   'Ave Maria'/'An Old Violin'
18183***   As F7981 (***American Decca label)

1942
F8132   'Rose O'Day'/'O'Brien Has Gone Hawaiian'
F8173   'All for One and One for All'/'Bleeding Heart'
18457***   'The Thingummybob'/'Nighty-Night, Little Sailor Boy'
18458***   'Walter, Walter'/'That Lovely Weekend'
18459***   'Ave Maria'/'An Old Violin'
              (Note: 18457/8/9 and 18183 were issued as a boxed set)

1943
F8356   'In My Arms'/'Wait for Me, Mary'
F8383   'Pedro the Fisherman'/'He Wooed Her and Wooed Her'
F8763   'The Lord's Prayer'/'The Kerry Dance'

1947
F8803   *Annie Get Your Gun Selection*: 'Doin' What Comes
              Naturally'/ 'The Girl That I Marry'/'I Got the Sun in
              the Morning'/'They Say It's Wonderful'/'There's No
              Business Like Show Business'
F8804   *Oklahoma! Selection*: 'I Can't Say No'/'Oh What a
              Beautiful Morning'/'Oklahoma!'/'Out of My
              Dreams'/'The Surrey with the Fringe on Top'/'The
              Surrey with the Fringe on Top'
F8805   'Now Is the Hour'/'Come Back to Sorrento'
F8808   'How Are Things in Glocca Morra?'/'If This Isn't Love'
F8816   'Arrivederci'/'MacNamara's Band'
F8817   'Bless This House'/'The Lord's Prayer'
F8824   'Au Revoir'/'Bella Bella Marie'
F8837   'Serenade of the Bells'/'It Began with a Tango'

F8857   'Core 'Ngrato'/'Waiata Poi'
115*****   'The Lord's Prayer'/'Bless This House' (****American
               London label)
129*****   'Au Revoir'/'Red Sails in the Sunset'

1948
F8985   'White Christmas'/'Christmas Love'
F8993   'Susy'/'Let Us Be Sweethearts'
F8996   'Bluebird of Happiness'/'Buttons and Bows'
F9026   'Count Your Blessings'/'If I Can Help Somebody'
F9027   'Red Sails in the Sunset'/'Underneath the Linden Tree'
F9031   'La Vie en Rose'/'Forever and Ever'
F9066   'Honey Child'/'Papa Won't You Dance With Me?'
300****   'White Christmas'/'Christmas Love'
362****   'Underneath the Linden Tree'/'Forever and Ever'

1949
F9166   'Put Your Shoes On, Lucy'/'The Wickedness of Men'
F9169   'The Last Mile Home'/'She Fought Like a Tiger for Her
               Honour'
F9194   'Church Bells on Sunday Morning'/'Chump Chop and
               Chips'
F9213   'Only a Glass of Champagne'/'Beware of April Rain'
F9219   'The Nun's Chorus'/'Oh My Beloved Father'
F9249   'Christmas Eve in Fairyland'/'I Took My Harp to a
               Party'
F9313   'The Song of the Mountains'/'Shepherd'
483****   'Church Bells on Sunday Morning'/'The Last Mile
               Home'

1950
F9405   'Lock, Stock and Barrel'/'I'd've Baked a Cake'
F9449   *Cinderella Selection*: 'Bibbidi-Bobbidi-
               Boo'/'Cinderella'/'A Dream Is a Wish Your Heart
               Makes'/'So This Is Love'/'The Work Song'
F9501   'Forgive Me, Lord'/'Angels Guard Thee'
F9572   'All My Life'/'And You Were There'
F9629   'Bon Voyage'/'When You Return'
F9700   'Little Old Lady'/'When I Grow Too Old to Dream'
738****   'Forgive Me, Lord'/'Angels Guard Thee'

1951

F9713   'At the End of the Day'/'Somewhere, Somewhere, Someday'

F9828   'At the End of the Day'/'Angels Guard Thee'

1952

PB107   'Don't Let the Stars Get in Your Eyes'/'Thank you, My Dear'

PB116   'The Story of the Sparrows'/'Your Mother and Mine'

PB152   'Golden Years'/'Till They've All Gone Home'

F10028   *Royal Variety Show 1952*: Gracie sings 'Sally'

1956

F10614   'Twenty'/'Summertime in Venice'

F10824   'A Letter to a Soldier'/'The Sweetest Prayer in All the World'

1957

DB3953   'Around the World'/'Far Away'

DB4047   'Mary's Boy Child'/'Scarlet Ribbons'

1959

DB4366   'Little Donkey'/'The Carefree Heart'

2
Acetates and Rejected 78 rpm Recordings
Dates are those of actual sessions

15/11/23	'Deedle-Deedle-Dum'	BB3851-1-2
	'Romany Love'	BB3852-1-2
3/4/28	'Because I Love You'	BB13151-1-2
	'As Long As He Loves Me'	BB13152-1-2
20/9/28	'My Ohio Home'	BB14523-1-2
11/12/28	'I Can't Give You Anything But Love'	BB15244-1-2
14/3/29	'I Kiss Your Hand, Madame'	BB2301-1-2
19/4/29	'She's Funny That Way'	BB16447-1-2-3-4
5/7/29	'Unlucky Number Thirteen'	BB17435-1-2
13/9/29	'I've Got a Feeling I'm Falling'	BB17631-1-2
	'Peace of Mind'	BB17632-1-2

18/10/29	'Sentimental Fool'	BB17725-1-2
14/2/30	'Just You, Just Me'	BB18539-1-2
6/6/30	''Fonso My Hot Spanish Knight'	BB19451-1-2
14/8/30	'Dancing with the Devil'	BB19583-1-2
29/6/31	'Little Bit of Chinese Music'	OB1250-1
13/7/31	'I'm One of God's Children'	OB1279-1
	'When the Circus Comes to Town'	OB1280-1
2/10/31	'Just One More Chance'	OB1188-1
15/3/32	'When We All Went to the Zoo'	OB3037-1
	'Now That You're Gone'	OB3039-1
27/3/32	''Appy 'Ampstead'	OB2267-1
22/9/32	'Free'	OB4214-1
	'Grandfather's Bagpipes'	OB4215-1
22/11/32	'In Old Siberia'	OB4337-1
13/1/33	'Puleeze, Mr Hemingway'	OB6216-1
6/2/33	'Musical Menu Lancashire Lunch'	OB6429-1
25/7/33	'In a Little Second-Hand Store'	OB5038-1
13/2/34	'How Happy the Lover'	OB5894-1
5/3/34	'When the Robin Sings His Song'	OEA1810-1
18/1/38	'The Sweetest Song in the World'	R2568
25/1/38	'My Only Dream'	R2570-1
12/3/38	'Christopher Robin'	OGF9-1
30/739	'Gracie's Thanks to the Nation'	OGF31-1
1/8/39	'In Permamboco'	OGF33-1
25/4/40	'When Irish Eyes Are Smiling'	OGF53-1
15/5/40	'Angels Guard Thee'	OGF59-1

3
45 rpm Recordings

1956	'Twenty'/'Summertime in Venice'	F10614*
1957	'Around the World'/'Far Away'	DB3953**
	'Mary's Boy Child'/'Scarlet Ribbons'	DB4047**
	Souvenirs (EP): 'Love's Last Word Is Spoken'/'Three Green Bonnets'/'Sally'/ 'Ave Maria'	7EG8071***

1958   'The Little Clockmaker'/'Belonging To
               Someone'   DB4200**
               Our Gracie Comedy Songs (EP): 'The Biggest
               Aspidistra in the World'/'Singing in the
               Bathtub'/'The Rochdale Hounds'/'Stop
               and Shop at the Co-op Shop'   7EG8293***
               Gracie Fields (EP): 'Around the World'/
               'Far Away'/'Scarlet Ribbons'/
               'Mary's Boy Child'   SEG7759**

1959   'Little Donkey'/'Carefree Heart'   DB4300**
               'Little Donkey'/'Far Away'   10069****
               At Home With Gracie (EP): 'The Lord's
               Prayer'/'Home'/'The Kerry Dance'/
               'Take Me to Your Heart Again'   SEG8056**
               Gracie's Comedy Songs (EP): 'We've Got to
               Keep Up with the Joneses'/'Photograph of
               Mother's Wedding Group'/'He Forgot to
               Come Back'/'Mrs Binn's Twins'   SEG8207**
               Gracie Fields Favourites No 1 (EP): 'Bless This
               House'/'The Lord's Prayer'/'The Nun's Chorus'/
               'Angels Guard Thee'   DFE6313*

1960   'In Jerusalem'/'Twelfth of Never'   DB4537**
               Gracie Souvenirs (EP): 'Now Is the
               Hour'/'Come Back to Sorrento'/
               'Au Revoir'/'Red Sails in the Sunset'   8BEP640*****
               Gracie Fields Favourites No 2 (EP): 'If I Can
               Help Somebody'/'Forgive Me Lord'/'At the
               End of the Day'/'Count Your Blessings'   DFE6314*

1961   'Do Re Mi'/'My Favourite Things'   DB4622**
               'Sing As We Go'/'Wish Me Luck'   POP2022***
               'Sally'/'The Biggest Aspidistra...'   POP2002***

1962   'Now Is the Hour'/'Small World'   F11561*
               'Twenty'/'Summertime in Venice'   F29583*
               Contrasts (EP): 'A Certain Smile'/'I've Grown
               Accustomed to His Face'/'Loveliest Night of the
               Year'/'Somewhere'   DFE8518*

By Request (EP): 'A Certain Smile'/'Mistakes'/
'If I Should Fall in Love Again'/'Wish Me
Luck'   DFE8531*

(* Decca **Columbia ***HMV ****Paramount *****London)

4
10-in. 33⅓ rpm Recordings

1958   *Presenting Gracie Fields:* 'Oh My Beloved
             Father'/'If I Can Help Somebody'/'Count Your
             Blessings'/'The Nun's Chorus'/'Come Back to
             Sorrento'/'Core 'Ngrato'/'At the End of the
             Day'/'Bluebird of Happiness'   Decca LF1140

1959   *Now Is the Hour:* 'Now Is the Hour'/'Red
             Sails in the Sunset'/'The Song of the
             Mountains'/'Beware of April Rain'/'The Lord's
             Prayer'/'Bless This House'/'Forgive Me,
             Lord'/'Angels Guard Thee'   Decca LF1108

1960   *Gracie Fields Souvenirs:* See LF1108   London LPB254

5
12-in. 33⅓ rpm Recordings

1956   *Our Gracie:* 'Sally'/'London Pride'/'Nature
             Boy'/'Ee, By Gum'/'The Woodpecker
             Song'/'What's the Good of a Birthday?'/'The
             Song of the Mountains'/'The House Is
             Haunted'/'In My Little Bottom Drawer'/'Go
             'Way from My Window'/'Waiata Poi'/'How
             Are Things in Glocca Morra?'/''Fonso My
             Hot Spanish Knight'/   Conquest CL1001
             'A Perfect Day'   Musicassette MC2CC061185

1957 Note: CL1001 was also released as follows:
Marble Arch MRL1183, Hallmark HMR210, TP179,
Liberty LPP3059

1958 *Gracie:* 'Pedro the Fisherman'/'Come Back to
Sorrento'/'The Biggest Aspidistra in the
World'/'The Wickedness of Men'/'Count Your
Blessings'/'Bless This House'/'Red Sails in the
Sunset'/'Only a Glass of Champagne'/'I Took
My Harp to a Party'/'Walter, Walter'/'At the
End of the Day'/'Now Is the Hour'   Decca LK4182

1959 *Gracie:* 'Sing As We Go'/'Young at
Heart'/'You Didn't Want Me When You Had
Me'/'Mrs Binn's Twins'/'The Kerry Dance'/'A
Photograph of Mother's Wedding
Group'/'Home'/'Take Me to Your Heart
Again'/'We've Got to Keep Up with the
Joneses'/'September Song'/'I Belong to
Glasgow'/'The Ugly Duckling'/'He Forgot to
Come Back'/'The Lord's Prayer' Columbia 233SX1198
(Note: LK4182 was also re-released as follows:
Ace of Clubs ACL1042   Liberty LL1677)
Gracie: 'Sing As We Go'/'You Didn't Want Me
When You Had Me'/'Mrs Binn's Twins'/'The
Kerry Dance'/'A Photograph of Mother's
Wedding Group'/'Home'/'Take Me to Your
Heart Again'/'We've Got to Keep Up with the
Joneses'/'September Song'/'The Ugly
Duckling'/'He Forgot to Come Back'/
'The Lord's Prayer'   Music For Pleasure MFP1067

1962 *Sing As We Go:* 'Sing As We
Go'/'Grandfather's Bagpipes'/'I Love to
Whistle'/'Danny Boy'/'I Never Cried So Much
in All My Life'/'There Is a Tavern in the
Town'/'Sally'/'Sing As We Go'/'The Rochdale
Hounds'/'Looking on the Bright Side'/'In Me
'Oroscope'/'Little Old Lady'/'The Sweetest
Song in the World'/'Little Drummer

Boy'/'Smile When You Say Goodbye'   Decca ACL1107
Gracie Fields: 'The Sweetest Prayer in All the
World'/'The Kerry Dance'/'Core 'Ngrato'/'If I
Can Help Somebody'/'Oh My Beloved
Father'/'The Nun's Chorus'/'Bluebird of
Happiness'/'How Are Things in Glocca
Morra?'/'MacNamara's Band'/'I'd've Baked
a Cake'/'Letter to a Soldier'   Decca AC1122
Hey There!: 'A Certain Smile'/'Wish You Were
Here'/'Three Coins in the Fountain'/'As Time
Goes By'/'Somewhere'/'Always You'/'Now Is
the Hour'/'Whatever Will Be Will Be'/'Love Is
a Many Splendoured Thing'/'Small
World'/'Hey There!'/'All at Once'/'I've Grown
Accustomed to His Face'/'Loveliest Night of
the Year'   Decca LK4522
Gracie Fields Special: 'Little Sir Echo'/'I
Promise You'/'Sweethearts'/'Swiss Miss
Song'/'They Say'/'Jeepers Creepers'/'With a
Smile and a Song'/'I'm Wishing'/'Heigh-Ho'/'A
Tisket, A Tasket'/'Any Broken Hearts to
Mend?'/'Charmaine'/'Mother Nature's
Lullaby'/'Because I Love You'/'My Blue
Heaven'/'Sailor Man'/'Red Sails in the
Sunset'/'The Ration Song'/'Christopher
Robin'/'Over the Rainbow'   Private SPECJT2

1964   *Gracie Sings the Favourites*: 'That Lovely
Weekend'/'Walter, Walter,'/'Ave Maria'/'An
Old Violin'/'He's Dead But He Won't Lie
Down'/'The Biggest Aspidistra in the
World'/'Rose O' Day'/'Bleeding Heart'/'The
Thingummybob'/'Nighty-Night, Little
Sailor Boy'   Coral CB30002
(Note: The above was re-released on Point P227)

1965   *It's Me, Back Again!*: 'Getting to Know
You'/'Someone Wonderful'/'Whistle a Happy
Tune'/'Smoke Gets in Your Eyes'/'Your Dog's
Come Home'/'Indian Summer'/'Ciao Ciao

Bambino'/'Moon River'/'Autumn
Leaves'/'Happy Talk'/'Jealousy'/'It's Nice to
Have a Man About the House'/'People'/'Blow
the Wind Southerly'/'You're Breaking
My Heart'   EMI CLP1824
American Farewell Concert: 'Sally'/'Mother
Beatle'/'We've Got to Keep up with the
Joneses'/'What's the Good of a
Birthday?'/'How Are Things in Glocca
Morra?'/'Getting to Know You'/'September
Song'/'Scarlet Ribbons'/'The Woodpecker
Song'/'I Never Cried So Much in All My
Life'/'Now Is the Hour'/'My Hero'/'Smoke
Gets in Your Eyes'/'The Biggest Aspidistra in
the World'/'Blow the Wind Southerly'/'My
Bonnie'/'When Irish Eyes Are Smiling'/'Walter,
Walter'/'Don't Be Angry with Me,
Sergeant'/'Wish Me Luck'/'I Love You'/
'There'll Always Be an England'   AEI AEI2123

1968   *Our Gracie:* 'Sing As We Go'/'I Took My
Harp to a Party'/'Christopher Robin'/'One
Day When We Were Young'/'Will You Love
Me When I'm Mutton?'/'Ave Maria'/
'Sally'/'The Biggest Aspidistra in the World'/
'Three Green Bonnets'/'Falling in Love Again'/
'Wish me Luck'   Music For Pleasure MFP1212
(Note: Also released on Australian MFP8025)
Gracie At Batley Variety Club: 'Sing As We
Go'/'Little Old Lady'/'Isle Of Capri'/'The
Biggest Aspidistra in the World'/'Wish Me
Luck'/'Sally'/'We've Got to Keep Up with the
Joneses'/'Strangers in the Night'/'Somewhere
My Love'/'As Long As He Needs Me'/'Those
Were the Days'/'What's the Good of a
Birthday?'/'How Are Things in Glocca
Morra?'/'What a Wonderful World'/'My Blue
Heaven'/'When I Grow Too Old to
Dream'/'Turn 'Erbert's Face to the Wall,
Mother'/'Walter, Walter'/'The Rochdale

Hounds'/'Charmaine'/'September Song'/'My
Bonnie'/'Around the World'/''Fonso My Hot
Spanish Knight'/'Don't Be Angry with Me
Sergeant'/'Put Your Shoes On, Lucy'/'Now Is
the Hour'/'I Love You'   Private SPECJT1

1970   *The World of Gracie Fields:* 'Sally'/'Come
Back to Sorrento'/'Walter, Walter'/'Heaven
Will Protect an Honest Girl'/'Bless This
House'/'Shall I Be an Old Man's Darling?'/
'At the End of the Day'/'Little Old Lady'/
'The Rochdale Hounds'/'Count Your
Blessings'/'He's Dead But He Won't Lie
Down'/'Oh My Beloved Father'/   Decca SPA82
'Now Is the Hour'   Musicassette KCCP82
Stars on Sunday: 'Three Green
Bonnets'/'Scarlet Ribbons'/'Forgive Me
Lord'/'Round the Bend of the Road'/'The
Story of the Sparrows'/'A Perfect Day'/'An
Old Violin'/'My Way'/'How Are Things in
Glocca Morra?'/'Ave Maria'/'Mysterious
People'/'The Lord's Prayer'   York BKY707

1971   SPA82 was re-released on Decca SPA120

1974   *Singalong with Gracie Fields, Superstar:*
'Sally'/'Getting to Know You'/'Oh What a
Beautiful Morning'/'Red Sails in the
Sunset'/'The Best Things in Life Are
Free'/'Swanee'/'Wonderful
Copenhagen'/'Around the World'/'Little Old
Lady'/'Isle of Capri'/'Somewhere My
Love'/'Tea For Two'/'When I Grow Too Old
to Dream'/   Music For Pleasure MFP50052
'Now Is the Hour'   Musicassette MFPC50052

1975   *Gracie Fields, Stage and Screen:* 'Cabin in the
Pines'/'Punch and Judy Show'/'Whiskers and
All'/'The Rochdale Hounds'/'May Morn'/'Out
in the Cold, Cold Snow'/'I Can't

Remember'/'Fall In and Follow the
Band'/'Sally'/'Stormy Weather'/'My Lucky
Day'/'Happy Ending'/'Heaven Will Protect an
Honest Girl'/'Sing As We Go'/'Love Is
Everywhere'/'Mrs Binn's Twins'/'Danny Boy'/
'Grandfather's Bagpipes'/   World Record Club SH170
'Wish Me Luck'   Musicassette SHC170
The World of Gracie Fields Vol II: 'Sally'/'Sing
As We Go'/'Pedro the Fisherman'/'Out in the
Cold, Cold Snow'/'Red Sails in the
Sunset'/'Turn 'Erbert's Face To The Wall,
Mother'/'In My Little Bottom
Drawer'/'Lancashire Blues'/'I Took My Harp
to a Party'/'The Kerry Dance'/'The Biggest
Aspidistra in the World'/'Bluebird Of   Decca SPA245
Happiness'/'Ave Maria'   Musicassette KSCP245
The Golden Years of Gracie Fields:
'Sally'/'Young at Heart'/'Punch and Judy
Show'/'Speak Softly Love'/'The Biggest
Aspidistra in the World'/'The Woodpecker
Song'/'Christopher Robin'/'On a Clear
Day'/'Only a Glass of Champagne'/'Pedro the
Fisherman'/'I Love the Moon'/'Three Green
Bonnets'/'The Ugly Duckling'/'The Trek
Song'/'What's the Good of a Birthday?'/'Count
Your Blessings'/'Fonso My Hot Spanish
Knight'/'Never, Never, Never'/
'I'll See You Again'/   Warwick WW5007
'Wish Me Luck'   Musicassette WWC5007
Our Gracie: As MFP1212 on Australian   MFPA8025

1976   *The Gracie Fields Story:* 'Sally'/'My Blue
Heaven'/'Because I Love You'/'Isle of
Capri'/'I'm a Dreamer, Aren't We All?'/'Ee, By
Gum'/'One Night of Love'/'Wish Me
Luck'/'Sing As We Go'/'Serenade'/'In My Little
Bottom Drawer'/'Looking on the Bright
Side'/'Mrs Binn's Twins'/'The House is
Haunted'/'Ave Maria'/'Little Old Lady'

'Around the World'/'The Kerry Dance'/'I Took
My Harp to a Party'/'Take Me to Your Heart
Again'/'A Photograph of Mother's Wedding
Group'/'Scarlet Ribbons'/'The Lord's
Prayer'/'Do Re Mi'/'Little Donkey'/'We've Got
to Keep Up with the Joneses'/'Go 'Way From
My Window'/'Song of the Mountains'/'The
Biggest Aspidistra in the World'/'How Are
Things in Glocca Morra?'/'You're Breaking
My Heart'/'Now Is the Hour'   EMI DUO120

1977   *Focus on Gracie Fields:* 'Sally'/'Looking on the
Bright Side'/'Red Sails in the Sunset'/'Little
Old Lady'/'The Biggest Aspidistra in the
World'/'The Wickedness of Men'/'The Last
Mile Home'/'Come Back to Sorrento'/'April
Love'/'Fred Fannakapan'/'I Never Cried So
Much in All My Life'/'The Sweetest Prayer in
All the World'/'At the End of the Day'

'Sing As We Go'/'Like the Big Pots Do'/'The
Loveliest Night of the Year'/'One Night of
Love'/'If I Can Help Somebody'/'Wish Me Luck'/
'Song of the Mountains'/'The Nun's Chorus'/'In Me
'Oroscope'/'Always   Decca FOS37/38
You'/'Now Is the Hour'   Musicassette FOC80073

1978   (Note: *Focus on Gracie Fields* was re-released in a
special edition on EMI EMSP333)
The Amazing Gracie Fields: 'Sally'/'Will You
Love Me When I'm Mutton?'/'Happy
Ending'/'Heaven Will Protect an Honest
Girl'/'Sing As We Go'/'In My Little Bottom
Drawer'/'Grandfather's Bagpipes'/'Danny
Boy'/'Wish Me Luck'/'The Biggest Aspidistra
in the World'/'Ave Maria'/'Sally' –
reprise   Evergreen ML7079EV

1980   *This Is Gracie Fields:* 'Sally'/'My Blue
Heaven'/'Isle of Capri'/'I'm a Dreamer, Aren't

We All?'/'Sing As We Go'/'Ee, By
Gum'/'Serenade'/'In My Little Bottom
Drawer'/'Little Old Lady'/'Wish Me
Luck'/'The Biggest Aspidistra in the
World'/'How Are Things in Glocca
Morra?'/'Scarlet Ribbons'/'I Took My Harp to
a Party'/'Take Me To Your Heart Again'/'The
Lord's Prayer'/'You're Breaking My
Heart'/'Little Donkey'/'Now Is the   EMI THIS8
Hour'/'Around the World'   Musicassette THISC8
Gracie Fields: The Best of her BBC
Broadcasts: 'Sally'/'Roses Of Picardy'/'When I
Grow Too Old to Dream'/'Walter,
Walter'/'Gracie's Thanks to the Nation'/'I
Love the Moon'/'The Rochdale Hounds'/'Stop
and Shop at the Co-op Shop'/'An Old
Violin'/'Sing As We Go'/'Mocking Bird Hill'/'I
Never Cried So Much in All My Life'/'So in
Love'/'The Biggest Aspidistra in the World'/'At
the End of the Day'/'Land of Hope and
Glory'/'Strangers in the Night'/'Somewhere
My Love'/'How Are Things in
Glocca Morra?'/   Regal Zonophone REG380
'Volare'/'Sometimes'   Musicassette REGL380

1983   *Life Is a Song:* 'Life Is a Song'/'The Words
Are in My Heart'/'Broadway Melody'/'Red
Sails in the Sunset'/'Have You Forgotten So
Soon?'/'Desert Song'/'Ah, Sweet Mystery of
Life'/'The Greatest Mistake of My Life'/'It
Looks Like Rain in Cherry Blossom
Lane'/'Bluebird of Happiness'/'He Wooed
Her and He Wooed Her'/'It Began with a
Tango'/'Forever and Ever'/'Come Back to
Sorrento'/'Honey Child'/'You're Too
Dangerous'/'Somewhere, Sometime,
Somehow'/'Papa, Won't You Dance
with Me?'/'Serenade of the Bells'/   Decca RFL36
'Au Revoir'   Musicassette KRFL36

1984   *Sing As We Go:* Re-release of ACL1107 on ACL7914

1985   *Amazing Gracie:* 'My Blue Heaven'/'We're All
Living at the Cloisters'/'Take a Look at
Mine'/'Like the Big Pots
Do'/'Serenade'/'Singing in the
Bathtub'/'Reviens, Veux-Tu?'/'Punch and Judy
Show'/'Gracie's Christmas Party'/'Looking on
the Bright Side'/'They All Make Love But
Me'/'Clatter of the Clogs'/'Life's Desire'/'I
Took My Harp to a Party'/'Just One More
Chance'/'In My Little Bottom Drawer'/'The
Mockingbird Went Cuckoo'/   Saville SUL170
'Sing As We Go'/'Isle of Capri' Musicassette SULC170

1986   *A Musical Review of Gracie Songs:* 'Body and
Soul'/'Dancing With Tears in My
Eyes'/'Falling in Love Again'/'Just One More
Chance'/'River Stay 'Way from My
Door'/'Home'/'How Deep Is the Ocean?'/'I'm
a Dreamer, Aren't We All?'/'Singing in the
Bathtub'/'Around the Corner'/'The Barmaid's
Song'/'Fred Fannakapan'/'Take a Look at
Mine'/'Ee, By Gum'/'We're All Living at
the Cloisters'   Sterling ST141
(Note: SUL170 was re-released on EMI GX412350.
MFP50052 was re-released on EMI Australia AX1063)

1987   *Isle of Capri:* 'There's a Lovely Lake in
London'/'South American Joe'/'The
Mockingbird Went Cuckoo'/'We've Got to
Keep Up with the Joneses'/'Chérie'/'In My
Little Bottom Drawer'/'I'm Ninety-Nine
Today'/'Sally'/'Isle of Capri'/'Sing As We Go'/
'Roll Along, Prairie Moon'/'One of the Little
Orphans of the Storm'/'Just One More
Chance'/'Winter Draws On'/'Red Sails in the
Sunset'/'What Can You Give a Nudist for His
Birthday?'/'Love, Life and Laughter'/'I Took
My Harp to a Party'   President 287

Laughter and Song: 'Charmaine'/'Because I Love You'/'My Blue Heaven'/'The House Is Haunted'/'Dancing with Tears in My Eyes'/'Home'/'I'm Playing with Fire'/'Take a Look at Mine'/'How Deep Is the Ocean?'/'Say It Isn't So'/'You're Driving Me Crazy'/'I Lift Up My Finger and I Say Tweet-Tweet'/'One Little Hair on His Head'/'Fred Fannakapan'/ 'Heaven Will Protect an Honest Girl'/'Little Pudden Basin'/'A Photograph of Mother's Wedding Group'/'Sitting on a Five-Barred Gate'/'He Forgot to Come Back'/ 'Sally'/'Chérie'/'You're More Than All   EMI SH510 the World to Me'   Musicassette TSH510 *This Is Gracie Fields:* re-release of THIS8 on EMI MID166077

1988   *Sally:* 'Sally'/'Sing As We Go'/'Red Sails in the Sunset'/'One of the Little Orphans of the Storm'/'There's a Lovely Lake in London'/'Isle of Capri'/'We've Got to Keep Up with the Joneses'/'In My Little Bottom Drawer'/'Roll Along, Prairie Moon'/'It Looks Like Rain in Cherry Blossom Lane'/'I Never Cried So Much in All My Life'/'The Greatest Mistake of My Life'/'Smile When You Say Goodbye'/'I Haven't Been the Same Girl Since'/'Did Your Mother Come from Ireland?'/'When I Grow Too Old to Dream'/'Turn 'Erbert's Face to the Wall, Mother'/   Counterpart BUR001 'You Haven't   Musicassette CBUR001 Altered a Bit'   Compact Disc CDBUR001

1989   *Queen of Hearts:* 'Queen of Hearts'/'The First Time I Saw You'/'It Looks Like Rain in Cherry Blossom Lane'/'Did Your Mother Come from Ireland?'/'One of the Little Orphans of the Storm'/'A Song in My Heart'/'Gypsy Lullaby'/'In the Chapel in the Moonlight'/'We're All Good Pals

Together'/'When My Dreamboat Comes
Home'/'September in the Rain'/'Little Old
Lady'/'Giannina Mia'/'Clogs and
Shawl'/'Would You'/'My Love for
You'/'Laughing Irish Eyes'/'Where Is the Sun?'/
'When The Harvest Moon Is Shining'/
'A Feather in Her Tyrolean Hat'/
'The Organ, the Monkey and   Conifer CHD144
Me'/'Smile When   Musicassette MCHD144
You Say Goodbye'   Compact Disc CHCD144
That Old Feeling: 'The Sweetest Song in the
World'/'Turn 'Erbert's Face to the Wall,
Mother'/'Home'/'Remember Me'/'Round the
Bend of the Road'/'Will You Remember?'/'When
I Grow Too Old to Dream'/'That Old Feeling'/
'My First Love Song'/'Walter, Walter'/'This Year's
Kisses'/'The Song Is Ended'/'How Deep Is the
Ocean?'/'Goodnight My Love'/'Red Sails in the
Sunset'/'Ah Sweet Mystery of Life'/'Smiling
Through'/'How Are Things in Glocca Morra?'/
'There's a Lovely Lake in London'/'We've Got
to Keep Up with the Joneses'/'I Never Cried
So Much in All My Life'/'The First
Time I Saw   Living Era AJA5062
You'/'Fall In and   Musicassette LCAJ5062
Follow the Band'/'Sally' Compact Disc CDAJ5062

1990 *Sing As We Go:* 'Sally'/'My Blue Heaven'/'I'm
a Dreamer, Aren't We All?'/'Lancashire
Blues'/'Three Green Bonnets'/'He Forgot to
Come Back'/'My Lucky Day'/'I Took My
Harp to a Party'/'The House Is Haunted'/'In
My Little Bottom Drawer'/'Happy
Ending'/'Ave Maria'/'I Can't Remember'/'Sing
As We Go'/'Love Is Everywhere'/'I Never
Cried So Much in All My Life'/'The
Woodpecker Song'/'The Umbrella Man'/'Wish
Me Luck'/'Cabin in the Pines'/'Whiskers and
All'/'Punch and Judy Show'/'Out in the
Cold, Cold Snow'/'The Rochdale EMI SH520

Hounds'/'May Morn'/   Musicassette TCSH520
'Stormy Weather'/'Sally'   Compact Disc CZ308
The Classic Years of Gracie Fields: 'Sally'/'The
Biggest Aspidistra in the World'/'Clatter of the
Clogs'/'I Took My Harp to a Party'/'The
Dicky-Bird Hop'/'Ee, By Gum'/'Singing in the
Bathtub'/'Pass, Shoot, Goal!'/'Ring Down the
Curtain'/'Fall In and Follow the Band'/'Little
Pudden Basin'/'Nowt About Owt'/'She Fought
Like a Tiger for Her Honour'/'You've Got to
Be Smart to Be in the Army Now'/'Will You
Love Me When I'm Mutton?'/'Just One of
Those Old-Fashioned Ladies'/   BBC Records REB690
'Smile When   Musicassette ZCF690
You Say Goodbye'   Compact Disc BBCCD690

5
Cassette Recordings
The following were released on cassette only

1978   *Young at Heart:* 'Young at Heart'/'Pedro the
        Fisherman'/'The Biggest Aspidistra in the
        World'/'The Woodpecker Song'/'I'll See You
        Again'/'Sally'/'Count Your Blessings'/
        'The Trek Song'/'Christopher Robin'/'Never,
        Never, Never'/'Wish Me Luck'/
        'Only a Glass of Champagne'   Warwick CHV063

1987   *Looking on the Bright Side:* 'Because I Love
        You'/'The Kerry Dance'/'One Night of
        Love'/'Looking on the Bright Side'/'Mrs Binn's
        Twins'/'The House Is Haunted'/'Chérie'/'A
        Photograph of Mother's Wedding Group'/'Do
        Re Mi'/'We've Got to Keep Up with the
        Joneses'/'Go 'Way From My Window'/'The
        Song of the Mountains'/'Sally'/'You're More
        Than All the World to Me'   EMI TCFA157073

1990   *The Very Best of Gracie Fields:* 'Sally'/'Wish

Me Luck'/'Sing As We Go'/'The Biggest
Aspidistra in the World'/'I Took My Harp to a
Party'/'Will You Love Me When I'm
Mutton?'/'Christopher Robin'/'My Blue
Heaven'/'Isle of Capri'/'Three Green
Bonnets'/'Ee, By Gum'/'One Night of
Love'/'I'm a Dreamer, Aren't We All'/'In My
Little Bottom Drawer'/'Looking on the Bright
Side'/'The House Is Haunted'/'Ave
Maria'/'Because I Love You'/'Crash, Bang, I
Want to Go Home'/'One Day When We
Were Young'   Prism PLAC29
An Hour With Gracie Fields: 'Take Me To
Your Heart Again'/'Sing As We
Go'/'September Song'/'Mrs Binn's
Twins'/'Around the World'/'You Didn't Want
Me When You Had Me'/'The Kerry
Dance'/'Little Donkey'/'The Ugly
Duckling'/'Mary's Boy Child'/'A Photograph
of Mother's Wedding Group'/'The Biggest
Aspidistra in the World'/'Sally'/'Home'/'Scarlet
Ribbons'/'We've Got to Keep Up with the
Joneses'/'The Lord's Prayer'/'Far Away'/'He
Forgot to Come Back'/'My Favourite
Things'/'The Twelfth of Never'/'Singing in the
Bathtub'/'Stop and Shop at the Co-op
Shop'/'Ave Maria'   Prism HR8186

1992   *A Musical Memory of Our Gracie: Fifty Songs
from the Heart:* 'Sally'/'You're More Than All
The World to Me'/'Chérie'/'Dancing With
Tears in My Eyes'/'Love's Last Word Is
Spoken'/'Just One More Chance'/'Life's
Desire'/'Little Drummer Boy'/'The Isle of
Capri'/'Home'/'Play to Me Gypsy'/'Would
You?'/'Little Old Lady'/'Where Is the
Sun?'/'When the Harvest Moon Is
Shining'/'One Day When We Were
Young'/'Goodnight Children Everywhere'

'An Old Violin'/'In the Chapel in the
Moonlight'/'You're Driving Me Crazy'/'The
Greatest Mistake of My Life'/'When My
Dreamboat Comes Home'/'September in the
Rain'/'It Looks Like Rain in Cherry Blossom
Lane'/'Ave Maria'/'My Blue Heaven'/'Gypsy
Lullaby'/'If I Should Fall in Love Again'/'Did
Your Mother Come from Ireland?'/'Giannina
Mia'/'Ah, Sweet Mystery of Life'/'When I
Grow Too Old to Dream'

'That Lovely Weekend'/'My Love for
You'/'Rosalie'/'With a Smile and a Song'/'I'm
Wishing'/'Now it Can Be Told'/'Sailing
Home'/'Life is a Song'/'Smile When You Say
Goodbye'/'Red Sails in the Sunset'/'Any
Broken Hearts to Mend?'/'When Mother
Nature Sings Her Lullaby'/'Melody at
Dawn'/'Smiling Through'/'This Year's
Kisses'/'The Song Is Ended'/'How Deep Is the
Ocean?'/'Little Curly Head in a High
Chair'/'Goodnight My Love'
(Boxed set with souvenir booklet) Everest EV17/18/19

*Our Gracie's Comic Songs and Old
Favourites:* 'Sing As We Go'/'The Biggest
Aspidistra in the World'/'There Is a Tavern in
the Town'/'Turn 'Erbert's Face to the Wall,
Mother'/'Walter, Walter'/'Heaven Will Protect
an Honest Girl'/'Looking on the Bright
Side'/'The Thingummybob'/'My Ohio
Home'/'Our Avenue'/'When the Fields Are
White with Daisies'/'Would a Manx Cat Wag
Its Tail?'/'Home Sweet Home'/'Let's All Go
Posh'/'I Love to Whistle'/'The Umbrella
Man'/'Wish Me Luck'/'Sally'
            (A companion cassette to Everest EV17/18/19)
                                            Everest EV20

1993   *Gracie Fields, A Musical Portrait:* 'Sally'/'Shall
          I Be an Old Man's Darling?'/'Walter,

Walter'/'Little Old Lady'/'Oh My Beloved
Father'/'Gracie's Thanks to the Nation'/'I Love
the Moon'/'The Biggest Aspidistra in the
World'/'Happy Ending'/'The Rochdale
Hounds' (live)/'Sally' (live)/'Count Your
Blessings' (narrated by Doreen
Goodwin) Mastersound CLP88

7
Compact Disc Recordings

1989   *Gracie Fields:* 'Sally'/'One Night of Love'/'Our
Avenue'/'A Foggy Day in London Town'/'I
Never Cried So Much in All My Life'/'Three
Green Bonnets'/'Lancashire Blues'/'The
Rochdale Hounds'/'Home'/'Love Is Every-
where'/ 'Look Up and Laugh'/'He's Dead
But He Won't Lie Down'/'Whistle While You
Work'/ 'Because I Love You'/'In My Little Bottom
Drawer'/'Out in the Cold, Cold Snow'/
'Ave Maria'/'Sing As We Go'   Stagedoor SDC8084

1990   *Favourites and Rarities:* 'Sing As We
Go'/'Body and Soul'/'Looking on the Bright
Side'/'Sally'/'You're More Than All the World
to Me'/'Love in Bloom'/'Isle of Capri'/
'Painting the Clouds with Sunshine'/'Stormy
Weather'/'Ring Down the Curtain'/'I Give My
Heart'/'Oh, Ma!'/'Where Are You?'/'Turn
'Erbert's Face to the Wall, Mother'/'An Old
Violin'/'The Biggest Aspidistra in the World'/
'Snow White Medley'/'The Holy City'/'Now It
Can Be Told'/'Hit Medley'/'Alexander's
Ragtime Band'/'Love Is Everywhere'/
'Melody at Dawn'   Flapper PASTCD9710

1993   *Sally:* 'Sally'/'Singing in the Bathtub'/'Pass,
Shoot, Goal!'/'Ring Down The Curtain'/'Fall

In and Follow the Band'/'Dicky-Bird Hop'/'I
Took My Harp to a Party'/'Clatter of the
Clogs'/' She Fought Like a Tiger for Her
Honour'/'Nowt About Owt'/'You've Got to
Be Smart to Be in the Army Now'/'Will You
Love Me When I'm Mutton?'/'Smile When
You Say Goodbye'/'One of Those Old-
Fashioned Ladies'/'Let's All Go Posh'/'Little
Pudden Basin'/'Ee, By Gum'/'The Biggest
Aspidistra in the World'   Tring International GRF099

A Vintage Christmas: This compilation album, a
collector's 'rarity' in that *Gracie's Christmas Party*
includes 'Singing in the Bathtub', previously
'removed' from the 1932 78 rpm before being
transferred to vinyl/tape, is now restored.
Also included are *Gracie With the Royal Air Force,*
and 'Christmas Bells at   Flapper PASTCD9768
Eventide'   Musicassette MCPAST7768

Sixteen Classic Favourites: 'A Song in Your
Heart'/'My Love For You'/'Goodnight My
Love'/'Gypsy Lullaby'/'It Looks Like Rain in
Cherry Blossom Lane'/'Giannina Mia'/'The
First Time I Saw You'/'Little Old Lady'/'The
Sweetest Song in the World'/'Turn 'Erbert's
Face to the Wall, Mother'/'Remember
Me'/'Fred Fannakapan'/'My First Love
Song'/'Round the Bend of the Road'/
'That Old Feeling'/'Walter, Walter'   EMI 8140972

1994   *Sing As We Go:* 'Sally'/'Sing As We Go'/'Oh
Sailor Behave'/'In My Little Bottom
Drawer'/'Just One More Chance'/'Laugh at
Life'/'It Isn't Fair'/'I Took My Harp to a
Party'/'The Bargain Hunter'/'The Mockingbird
Went Cuckoo'/'Mary Rose'/'My Lucky
Day'/'Stop and Shop at the Co-op
Shop'/'There's a Lovely Lake in London'/'We
Have to Keep Up with the Joneses'/'Walter,
Walter'/'All for One and One for All'/'The

Bleeding Heart'/'He's Dead But He Won't Lie
Down'/'The Biggest Aspidistra
in the World'/'Gracie and Sandy's
Party' (with   Empress RAJCD833
Sandy Powell)   Musicassette RAJMC833

That Old Feeling: 'Turn 'Erbert's Face to the Wall,
Mother'/'Remember Me'/'Fred Fannakapan'/'Walter,
Walter'/'There's a Lovely Lake in London'/'We've Got
to Keep Up with the Joneses'/'I Never Cried So Much
in All My Life'/'Round the Bend of the Road'/'That
Old Feeling'/'Red Sails in the Sunset'/'Goodnight My
Love'/'Sally'/'The Biggest Aspidstra in the World'/'In
My Little Bottom Drawer'/'Wish Me Luck'/'Sing As
We Go'/'If I Should Fall In Love Again'/'Will You
Love Me When I'm Mutton?'/'I Took My Harp
to a Party'/'Three Green Bonnets'/'Little Old
Lady'   Flapper PASTCD7050

2

Stage Productions

1915 *Yes, I Think So* (London)
Written and produced by Archie Pitt. With Archie Pitt, Mona Frewer.

1916 *It's a Bargain!* (London)
Written and produced by Archie Pitt. With Archie Pitt, the Three Aza Boys, Mona Frewer, Doris Paul, Annie Lipman.

1918 *Mr Tower of London* (London)
Written and produced by Archie Pitt. With Archie Pitt, Edith and Betty Fields, Mona Frewer, Annie Lipman.

1925 *By Request* (London)
Written and produced by Archie Pitt. With Archie Pitt, the Three Aza Boys, Annie Lipman, Mona Frewer, Tommy Fields.

1928 *SOS* (London)
Written and produced by Gerald du Maurier. With Gerald du Maurier, Grace Wilson, Herbert Waring.

1929 *Topsy and Eva* (London)
Gracie stood in for Rosetta Duncan for twelve performances of this adaptation of *Uncle Tom's Cabin*.

1929 *The Show's the Thing* (London)
Written and produced by Archie Pitt. Cast included Archie Pitt, Tommy Fields, Edward Chapman, Harry Milton, Monty Ryan, Dorothy Whiteside, Mary Ludlow.

1931 *Walk This Way!* (London)
Written and produced by Archie Pitt. With Archie Pitt, Irene Pitt, Renée Foster, Douglas Wakefield, Billy Nelson, Morris Harvey, Pat Nelson, Chuck O'Neil, Tommy Fields.

1940 *Cantine De Taburin* (Paris)
Written and produced by Jean Saint-Granier. With Mistinguett, Jean Saint-Granier, Damia, Fernandel, Lucienne Boyer.

1942 *Top Notchers* (New York)
Written and produced by Clifford Fischer and Lee Shubert. With Frédéric Rey, Argentinita, Zero Mostel, The Hartmans, Pilar Lopez, Think-A-Drink Hoffman, Carlos Montaya.

3

Filmography

1931 *Sally In Our Alley*
Directed by Maurice Elvey. Cast includes Ian Hunter, Florence
Desmond, Ben Field, Gib McLaughlin, Fred Groves.
Songs: 'Lancashire Blues'; 'Sally'; 'Fred Fannakapan'; 'Fall In and
Follow the Band'.

1932 *Looking On the Bright Side*
Directed by Basil Dean. Cast includes Wyn Richmond, Julien Rose,
Richard Dolman, Viola Compton, Betty Shale, Toni de Lungo.
Songs: 'Looking on the Bright Side'; 'After Tonight We Say
Goodbye'; 'You're More Than All the World to Me'; 'He's Dead
But He Won't Lie Down'; 'I Hate You'.

1933 *This Week Of Grace*
Directed by Julius Hagen. Cast includes John Stuart, Helen Haye,
Frank Pettingell, Henry Kendall, Douglas Wakefield, Marjorie
Brooks, Vivian Foster.
Songs: 'My Lucky Day'; 'Melody at Dawn'; 'Happy Ending';
'When Cupid Calls'; 'Mary Rose'.

1934 *Sing As We Go*
Directed by Basil Dean. Cast includes John Loder, Dorothy Hyson,
Stanley Holloway, Lawrence Grossmith, Frank Pettingell, Arthur
Sinclair, Morris Harvey, Maire O'Neill. Script: J B Priestley.
Songs: 'Sing As We Go'; 'Just a Catchy Little Tune'; 'Love,
Wonderful Love'; 'In My Little Bottom Drawer'.

1934 *Love, Life and Laughter*
Directed by Maurice Elvey. Cast includes John Loder, Robb
Wilton, Esmé Percy, Veronica Brady, Norah Howard, Allan

Aynesworth, Ivor Barnard.
Songs: 'Out in the Cold, Cold Snow'; 'I'm a Failure'; 'Chérie'; '
Riding the Clouds'; 'How Happy Is the Lover'.

1935 *Look Up and Laugh*
Directed by Basil Dean. Cast includes Tommy Fields, Billy Nelson,
Douglas Wakefield, Robb Wilton, Vivien Leigh, Henry Tate. Script:
J B Priestley.
Songs: 'Look Up and Laugh'; 'Anna from Anacapresi'; 'Love Is
Everywhere'; 'Things Might Have Been So Different'.

1936 *Queen Of Hearts*
Directed by Monty Banks. Cast includes John Loder, Enid Stamp-
Taylor, Fred Duprez, Edith Fields, Tom Payne, Carl Balliol and
Jessica Merton, Jean Lester, Hal Gordon.
Songs: 'Queen of Hearts'; 'One of the Little Orphans of the Storm';
'Why Did I Have to Meet You?'; 'Do You Remember?'

1937 *The Show Goes On*
Directed by Basil Dean. Cast includes Owen Nares, John Stuart,
Horace Hodges, Arthur Sinclair, Cyril Ritchards.
Songs: 'Smile When You Say Goodbye'; 'I Never Cried So Much in
All My Life'; 'A Song in Your Heart'; 'My Love for You'; 'We're
All Good Pals Together'; 'In a Little Lancashire Town'.

1937 *We're Going To Be Rich* (US: *He Was Her Man*)
Directed by Monty Banks. Cast includes Victor McLaglen, Brian
Donlevy, Coral Browne, Gus McNaughton, Hal Gordon, Ted
Smith, Charles Carson, Alex Davies.
Songs: 'The Sweetest Song in the World'; 'There Is a Tavern in the
Town'; 'Walter, Walter'; 'The Trek Song'; 'Ee, By Gum'; 'Will You
Love Me When I'm Mutton?'; 'Please Don't Hang My Harry'
(sung by Coral Browne).

1938 *Keep Smiling*
Directed by Monty Banks. Cast includes Mary Maguire, Asta,
Tommy Fields, Roger Livesey, Eddie Gray, Jack Donaghue,
Edmund Rigby, Peter Coke; Hay Petrie.
Songs: 'The Holy City'; 'Giddy Up!'; 'Swing Your Way to
Happiness'; 'You've Got to be Smart to Be in the Army Now';
'Peace of Mind'; 'The Biggest Aspidistra in the World'.

1939 *Shipyard Sally*
Directed by Monty Banks. Cast includes Oliver Wakefield, Sydney
Howard, Norma Varden, Morton Selten, Tucker Maguire.
Songs: 'I Got the Jitterbugs'; 'Wish Me Luck'; 'In Pernambuco';
'Danny Boy'; 'Annie Laurie'; 'Grandfather's Bagpipes'; 'Land of
Hope and Glory'.

1943 *Stage Door Canteen*
Directed by Frank Borzage. Cast includes Lon McCallister,
Marjory Riordan, Judith Anderson, Tallulah Bankhead, Katharine
Cornell, Lynn Fontanne and Alfred Lunt, Yehudi Menuhin.
Songs: 'The Lord's Prayer'; 'The Machine-Gun Song'.

1943 *Holy Matrimony*
Directed by John Stahl. With Monty Woolley, Laird Cregar, Una
O'Connor.

1945 *War-Bonds Short*
Shot in Hollywood for Twentieth Century-Fox. Gracie sings 'My
Boy', composed by Harry Seymour and Moe Jerome.

1945 *Molly and Me*
Directed by Lewis Seiler. Cast includes Monty Woolley, Roddy
McDowall, Edith Barrett, Reginald Gardiner, Queenie Leonard,
Doris Lloyd, Aminta Dyne.
Songs: 'My Bonnie'; 'Christopher Robin'; 'Let's All Sing Like the
Birdies Sing'.

1945 *The Flying Yorkshireman*
Directed by Frank Capra. This film, for which Gracie and Barry
Fitzgerald were screen-tested and contracted, was abandoned due
to lack of technicians.

1946 *Madame Pimpernel* (US: *Paris Underground*)
Produced by Constance Bennett. Directed by Gregory Ratoff. Cast
includes Constance Bennett, Kurt Kreuger, Charles André, Georges
Rigaud, Leslie Vincent, Vladimir Sokoloff, Andrew McLaglen, Eric
von Morhardt, Adrienne d'Ambricourt.

4

Royal Variety Shows

1 March 1928	London Coliseum
11 May 1931	London Palladium
15 November 1937	London Palladium
3 November 1947	London Palladium
13 November 1950	London Palladium
29 October 1951	Victoria Palace
3 November 1952	London Palladium
13 April 1955	Blackpool Opera House

(Gracie could not appear owing to illness)

5 November 1956	London Palladium

(Cancelled because of Suez Crisis)

18 November 1957	London Palladium
2 November 1964	London Palladium
13 November 1978	London Palladium

5

Stars on Sunday

Recording Dates

28 October 1970
'Three Green Bonnets'; 'Scarlet Ribbons'; Christopher Robin'; 'The Story of the Sparrows'; 'Bless This House'; 'How Are Things in Glocca Morra?'; 'An Old Violin'

29 October 1970
'A Perfect Day'; 'Forgive Me, Lord'; 'Ave Maria'; 'The Lord's Prayer'; 'All Kinds of Everything'; 'My Favourite Things'; 'Danny Boy'; 'Round the Bend of the Road'; 'My Way'

30 October 1972
'Mysterious People'; 'Count Your Blessings'; 'If I Can Help Somebody'; 'At the End of the Day'

20 September 1976
'If I Can Help Somebody'

3 October 1977
'What a Wonderful World'; 'The Holy City'; 'Sometimes'

4 October 1977
'He's Got the Whole World in His Hands'; 'In a Monastery Garden'
Bible readings: Genesis; John (subsequently not televized)

Index